PLANE TRIGONOMETRY

Bernard J. Rice
Jerry D. Strange

UNIVERSITY OF DAYTON

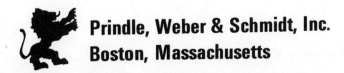

Prindle, Weber & Schmidt, Inc.
Boston, Massachusetts

Library of Congress Cataloging in Publication Data

Rice, Bernard J
    Plane trigonometry.

    1. Trigonometry, Plane.   I.   Strange, Jerry D.,
joint author.   II.   Title.
QA533.R5   516'.24   74-22263
ISBN 0-87150-177-5

Printed in the United States of America.

Third Printing: January, 1976

Cover photograph by Michael E. Katin

PREFACE

Many present day trigonometry books place their primary emphasis on the analytical aspects of trigonometry while almost ignoring triangular trigonometry. Our purpose in writing this book is a result of our belief that trigonometry is best learned, best understood, and best remembered with respect to its right triangle definitions extended to angles in standard position on the rectangular Cartesian coordinate system. This approach might be considered "old fashioned" by some, an opinion with which we not only agree but suggest to be desirable. The initial use of the more classical definitions of the trigonometric ratios combined with a modern flavor in the applications*provides a justifiable alternative to the recent trend of making trigonometry an entirely analytical subject. This is especially true for students in science and engineering.

The modern analytical aspects of trigonometry are far from ignored; most of Chapters 5–8 is devoted to analytic trigonometry and related non-triangular applications. Set notation is used whenever appropriate and heavy emphasis is placed on graphing so that the student can "see" solution sets as well as derive them.

As with most books, there are more topics included that even the most ambitious instructor would reasonably cover in a normal one semester or one quarter course. This book is constructed so that topics can frequently be omitted without losing continuity. For instance, Chapters 2 and 4 include a large variety of practical applications allowing the individual instructor a wide range of personal choice. Chapter 9 on logarithms and Chapter 10 on complex numbers are dependent on earlier chapters, but complex numbers themselves are not used elsewhere in the book.

Chapter 1 is a review of those areas considered to be fundamental to understanding the concepts of trigonometry. Some classes will be able to

---

*The symbol ➤ is used in examples and exercises to indicate practical applications of mathematical concepts.

skim this chapter or skip it completely; others will need to spend more time if they are deficient in these areas. In either case, the chapter is a convenient reference for the student. We have found it useful to spend a day or two reviewing the notation and facts about angles presented in this chapter before proceeding to Chapter 2.

Several different types of courses are possible using this book. For a course which is "triangle oriented," the concentration will be on Chapters 2, 3, and 4 with selected topics from Chapters 5, 6, and 7 to complete the course. Chapter 9 should be covered if the computational advantages of logarithms is desired. For an analytical approach with emphasis on graphing and precalculus trigonometry, the course should begin with detailed emphasis on Sections 2.1–2.5, 3.1, 3.2, and 3.5 before proceeding to Chapters 5–8 and 10. We would recommend that some attention be given to Sections 4.1–4.3 to give the student some idea of how to solve the general triangle.

We wish to publicly thank Mr. Myrl H. Ahrendt and the National Aeronautics and Space Administration for their kind permission to use some of the unique applications of trigonometry to space technology from the book *Space Mathematics: A Resource for Teachers.*

Since its conception, *Plane Trigonometry* has undergone several major revisions and has been critically reviewed at several stages. We wish to single out the following who assisted us with their valuable comments: Professor H. D. Perry of Texas A & M, Professor Glenn Mattingly of Sam Houston State University, Professor Jay Welch of San Jacinto College, and Professor Curtis Rogers of the University of Houston.

We wish also to thank Mrs. Joan Haas who typed the original manuscript and Mr. John Martindale who encouraged us to undertake this task.

BERNARD J. RICE
JERRY D. STRANGE

CONTENTS

1

**SOME
FUNDAMENTAL
CONCEPTS**

1.1   HISTORICAL BACKGROUND

Trigonometry is one of the oldest branches of mathematics. An ancient scroll called the Ahmes Papyrus, written about 1550 B.C., contains problems that are solved by using similar triangles, the heart of the trigonometric idea. There is historical verification that measurements of distance and height were made by the Chinese about 1100 B.C. using what is essentially right triangle trigonometry. The subject eventually became intertwined with the study of astronomy. In fact, it is the Greek astronomer Hipparchus (180–125 B.C.) who is credited with compiling the first trigonometric tables and thus has earned the right to be known as "the father of trigonometry." The trigonometry of Hipparchus and the other astronomers was strictly a tool of measurement, and it is, therefore, difficult to refer to the early uses of the subject as either mathematics or astronomy.

In the 15th century, trigonometry was developed as a discipline within mathematics by Johann Muller, (1436–1476). This development created an interest in trigonometry throughout Europe and had the effect of placing Europe in a position of prominence with respect to astronomy and trigonometry.

In the 18th century, trigonometry was systematically developed in a completely different direction, highlighted by the publication in 1748 of the now famous "Introduction to Infinite Analysis" by Leonhard Euler (1707–1783). From this new viewpoint, trigonometry did not necessarily have to be considered in relation to a right triangle. Rather, the analytic or functional properties became paramount. As this wider outlook of the subject evolved, many new applications arose, especially as a tool for describing physical phenomena that are "periodic."

In this book we proceed more or less as the subject developed historically. First, we consider the trigonometry of a right triangle and only later introduce the analytic generalization that is so valuable in other areas of mathematics and physics.

To read the book profitably, you should have some ability with elementary algebra, particularly manipulative skills. Some of the specific background knowledge you will need is presented in this chapter.

1.2   MEASUREMENT

In the early history of mathematics, as it is today, people were very much concerned with measuring distances of one kind or another. Technically, when measuring distances, we are actually measuring line segments. The actual measurement is called the *length* of the segment. Relatively small line segments are measured *directly* using a device such as a ruler or odometer. A line segment is designated by giving its end points, as in Figure 1.1, where the line segment is called AB. The length of such a line segment is variously denoted by $|AB|$, $\overline{AB}$, or $m(AB)$.

FIGURE 1.1 Line segment AB

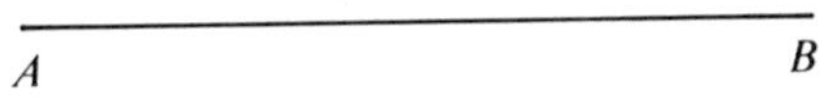

A B

Units of length depend not only on the size of the segment being discussed but also on the system being used. For instance, in the English system, the fundamental unit of length is the foot, and in the metric system, it is the meter. Table 1.1 lists some of the fundamental units derived from these two systems and also the relationship between the two systems.

TABLE 1.1 Table of Length Equivalents

12 inches = 1 foot	1 inch = 2.54 centimeters	1 meter = 100 centimeters
3 feet = 1 yard	1 yard = 0.914 meter	1 kilometer = 1000 meters
5280 feet = 1 mile	1 mile = 1.6 kilometers	

Trigonometry was originally developed as a tool for indirectly measuring the length of a line segment; that is, for determining the length of a line segment without using a physical measuring device. Of course, some measurements must be made but not necessarily of the line segment in question. For instance, the early astronomers could not measure the distance to the moon, but they could use trigonometry and a distance measured along the surface of the earth to compute the distance to the moon.

1.3   ANGLES

When two line segments meet, they form what is called an *angle*. We ordinarily think of an angle as formed by two half-lines OA and OB that extend from some common point O, called the *vertex*. The half-lines are called the *sides* of the angle. (See Figure 1.2.)

We refer to an angle by mentioning a point on each of its sides and the vertex. Thus the angle in Figure 1.2 is called "the angle AOB," and is written $\angle AOB$. If there is only one angle under discussion whose vertex is at O, we sometimes simply say, "the angle at O," or more simply, "angle O." It is also customary to use Greek letters to designate angles. For example, $\angle AOB$ might also be called the angle θ (read "theta").

FIGURE 1.2

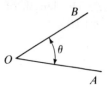

Often, in trigonometry, we must conceive of an angle as being "formed" by rotating one of the sides about its vertex while keeping the other side fixed as shown in Figure 1.3. If we think of OA as being fixed and OB as rotating about the vertex, OA is called the *initial* side and OB the *terminal* position of the generated angle. Other terminal sides such as OB' and OB'' result in different angles. The *size* of the angle depends on the amount of rotation of the terminal side. Thus, $\angle AOB$ is considered smaller than $\angle AOB'$ which, in turn, is smaller than $\angle AOB''$. Two angles are equal (in size) if they are formed by the same amount of rotation of the terminal side.

FIGURE 1.3

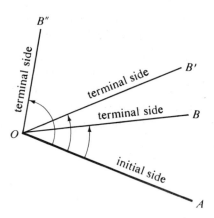

By definition, a *right* angle is one formed by the following geometric construction:

(1) Draw a line through O. (Figure 1.4a.)

(2) Put a compass point at O and draw two small arcs, one to the left of O and one to the right, intersecting the line segment at A and A'. (Figure 1.4b.)

(3) Put the point of the compass at A' and extend it to A. Draw a small arc above and below O. Repeat with the compass point at A. This will yield two points of intersection of the arcs at B and B'. (Figure 1.4c.)

(4) Now draw the half-line *OB*. The angle *A'OB* is a *right* angle. (Figure 1.4d.)

FIGURE 1.4 Construction of a right angle

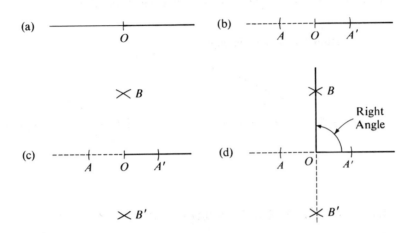

(a)

(b)

(c)

(d)

Right Angle

Two rays are said to be *perpendicular* if the angle formed at their point of intersection is a right angle.

A *straight* angle is one whose sides form a straight line, as in Figure 1.5.

FIGURE 1.5 Straight angle

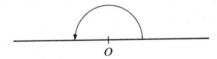

An angle is *acute* if it is less in size than a right angle and is *obtuse* if it is larger than a right angle but smaller than a straight angle (see Figure 1.6). Figure 1.7 shows an angle larger than a straight angle.

FIGURE 1.6

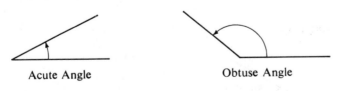

Acute Angle   Obtuse Angle

FIGURE 1.7 Angle larger than a straight angle

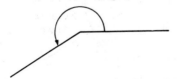

Angles with the same initial and terminal sides are said to be *coterminal.* The two angles shown in Figure 1.8 are coterminal, but they are obviously not equal. Coterminal angles are sometimes considered equal, but there are many important considerations, both practical and theoretical, when we must know how the angle was formed.

FIGURE 1.8 Coterminal angles

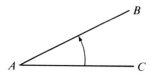
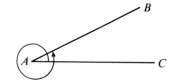

1.4 MEASUREMENT OF ANGLES

The most commonly used unit of angular measurement is the *degree.* We will take as a definition that the measure of an angle formed by one complete revolution of the terminal side about its vertex is 360 degrees, also written 360°. Then, it follows that the degree measure of a straight angle is 180 degrees (180°) and that of a right angle is 90°. The measure of an acute angle is between 0° and 90°, that of an obtuse angle between 90° and 180°. An angle of 0° is said to be determined when the terminal side and the initial side coincide, and the terminal side is not rotated.

To distinguish between an angle and its measurement, we should write $m(A)$ to denote the measurement of the angle A. Popular usage, however, allows us to say "the 30° angle" rather than the more precise "the angle whose measure is 30°." The context should always be sufficient for you to tell in what sense the word "angle" is being used.

Sometimes it is necessary to consider the angle to be "directed," that is, to make a distinction between the direction of rotation of the terminal side in forming the angle. The almost universal convention is to

FIGURE 1.9

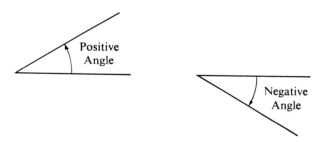

consider those angles obtained by a counterclockwise rotation of the terminal side as *positive* and those obtained by a clockwise rotation as *negative* angles as shown in Figure 1.9.

There is no numerical limit to the measure of an angle since a terminal side may be rotated either clockwise or counterclockwise as much as desired.

EXAMPLE 1.1

Draw the following angles: (a) θ (theta) of measurement 42°, (b) ϕ (phi) of −450°, (c) β (beta) of 1470° and (d) α (alpha) of −675°.

Solution: See Figure 1.10.

FIGURE 1.10

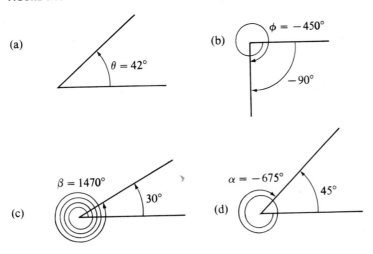

EXAMPLE 1.2

Determine angles whose measurements are between −180° and 180° and which are coterminal with angles whose measure is the same as those of the previous example.

Solution: Using Figure 1.10, we can see that (a) 42° is the desired angle, (b) −90° is coterminal with −450°, (c) 30° is coterminal with 1470° and (d) 45° is coterminal with −675°.

The basic angular unit of the degree is subdivided into 60 parts each of which is called a *minute* and denoted by the symbol ('). The minute is further subdivided into 60 parts each of which is called a *second* and is denoted by the symbol ("). As the next example shows, arithmetic calculations are sometimes a bit more cumbersome with these subdivisions than with the decimal system.

EXAMPLE 1.3

Find the sum and difference of the two angles whose measurements are 45°41′09″ and 32°52′12″.

Solution: The sum of the two angles is found by adding the corresponding units; that is, degrees to degrees, minutes to minutes, and seconds to seconds. Thus,

$$45°41′09″ + 32°52′12″ = (45 + 32)° (41 + 52)′ (09 + 12)″$$
$$= 77°93′21″.$$

Here, we see that 93′ = 1°33′ so we write our answer as 78°33′21″.
To find the difference in the two angles, we must write 45°41′09″ in the following form:

$$45°41′09″ = 45°40′69″ = 44°100′69″.$$

Thus,

$$45°41′09″ - 32°52′12″ = (44 - 32)° (100 - 52)′ (69 - 12)″$$
$$= 12°48′57″.$$

In passing, we note that if the sum of the measures of two angles is 90°, the two angles are said to be *complementary*. If the sum of the measures is 180°, they are *supplementary* (see Figure 1.11).

FIGURE 1.11

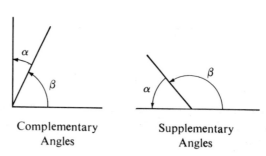

Complementary
Angles

Supplementary
Angles

Another commonly used measure of an angle is the *radian*. Although less familiar to the beginner, in a sense, the radian is a more natural choice for a unit of angular measure than the degree. The radian measure is used almost exclusively in more advanced applications of trigonometry.

DEFINITION 1.1

One *radian* is the measure of an angle whose vertex is at the center of a circle and whose sides intersect an arc on the circle equal in length to the radius of the circle (see Figure 1.12).

FIGURE 1.12   One radian

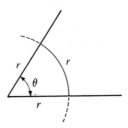

Hence, the radian is a measure of the ratio of arc length to radius. Since the circumference, C, of a circle of radius r is known to be $2\pi r$, it follows that $C/r = 2\pi$. Thus there are 2π radians in an angle of $360°$. In equation form,

$$2\pi \text{ radians} = 360°$$

from which

1 degree = $\pi/180$ radians $\approx$ 0.0175 radians

and

1 radian = $180/\pi$ degrees $\approx$ 57.3 degrees.

The next two examples show you how to use these formulas to convert from degrees to radians and conversely.

EXAMPLE 1.4

Express in radian measure,

(a) 60°   (b) 225°

Solution: (a)   60 degrees $= 60(\pi/180)$ radians $= \pi/3$ radians.

(b)   225 degrees $= 225(\pi/180)$ radians $= 5\pi/4$ radians.

When the radian measure is a convenient multiple of π, you will usually find it beneficial *not* to convert it to a decimal fraction. When such a conversion is necessary, 3.14 is a good decimal approximation to π.

EXAMPLE 1.5

Express $\pi/6$ radians, $3\pi/4$ radians, and 2.6 radians in degrees.

Solution:

$\pi/6$ radians $= (\pi/6)(180/\pi)$ degrees $= 30$ degrees.
$3\pi/4$ radians $= (3\pi/4)(180/\pi)$ degrees $= 135$ degrees.
2.6 radians $= 2.6\,(57.3) = 148.9$ degrees.

Table 1.2 is a conversion table showing frequently occurring angles with both their degree and radian measure. Eventually, you should know the entries in this table without making the conversion calculation.

TABLE 1.2 Table of Degree and Radian Measure for Commonly Occurring Angles

Angle in Degrees	Angle in Radians
0	0
30	$\pi/6$
45	$\pi/4$
60	$\pi/3$
90	$\pi/2$
120	$2\pi/3$
135	$3\pi/4$
150	$5\pi/6$
180	π
270	$3\pi/2$
360	2π

The word "radian" is often understood without being written. Such is not the case with degree measurement; its units must always be included.

EXAMPLE 1.6

Compare the angle of 60 degrees with that of 60 radians.

FIGURE 1.13

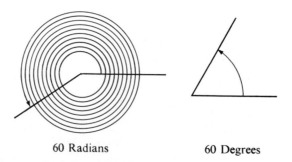

60 Radians   60 Degrees

Solution: Note from the adjoining figure that the angle of 60 radians is obtained by 9 repeated revolutions of the terminal side, (each revolution being approximately 6.28 radians) plus an additional 3.58 radians. Thus, the angle of 60 radians is coterminal with one whose measure is 3.58 radians. The angle is shown in Figure 1.13 along with a 60° angle.

The question of whether to measure an angle in degrees or radians is sometimes a matter of personal preference, but more often than not the unit is dictated by the particular problem under discussion. For instance, the length, s, of the arc intercepted by the central angle, θ, in Figure 1.14, can be found by the formula

(1.1) $\quad s = r\theta$

if the angle θ is measured in radians. This formula follows immediately from the definition of a radian as the ratio of arc length to radius, that is, $\theta = s/r$. *Formula 1.1 is not valid if θ is measured in degrees.*

FIGURE 1.14

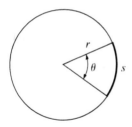

EXAMPLE 1.7

Find the length of arc on a circle of radius 5 inches which subtends a central angle of 38°.

Solution: To use the above formula, the degree measure must first be converted to radian measure. Thus

38 degrees $\times$ $\pi/180$ radians $= 19\pi/90$ radians.

Therefore, $s = 5 \times 19\pi/90$ inches ≈ 3.32 inches.

EXERCISES FOR SECTIONS 1.1–1.4

1. What is the difference in radian measure of two coterminal angles?

2. What is the difference in degree measure of two coterminal angles?

11

In Exercises 3–12, find the sum $A + B$ and the difference $A - B$ of the two given angles.

3. $A = 45°10'$, $B = 30°5'$

4. $A = 72°12'$, $B = 30°38'$

5. $A = 58°35'40''$, $B = 50°34'20''$

6. $A = 42°40'10''$, $B = 65°50'50''$

7. $A = 60°10'15''$, $B = 70°45'$

8. $A = 138°40'20''$, $B = 23°52'30''$

9. $A = 240°45'40''$, $B = 333°25'14''$

10. $A = 320°50'20''$, $B = -30°55'10''$

11. $A = -40°42'57''$, $B = -80°18'13''$

12. $A = -90°0'49''$, $B = 269°57'1''$

In Exercises 13–28, draw the angles, name the initial and terminal sides. Indicate another angle between $-180°$ and $+180°$ coterminal with the given one. Express each of the given angles in radians.

13. 30°   14. −30°   15. 45°   16. 500°

17. −225°   18. −270°   19. 290°   20. 120°

21. 720°   22. 780°   23. 840°   24. 765°

25. 1485°   26. 2000°   27. −25°   28. −205°

In Exercises 29–38 draw the angles, name the initial and terminal sides, indicate another angle between $-\pi$ and $+\pi$ coterminal with the one given. Express each of the given angles in degrees.

29. 1   30. 2π 31. π 32. $\pi/6$

33. -3π 34. −100   35. 100   36. 30

37. 100π 38. -100π

39. A pendulum 10 feet long swings through an arc of 30°. How long is the arc described by its midpoint?

40. A racing car travels a circular course about the judges' stand. If the angle subtended by the line of sight is 120° while the car travels 1 mile, how large is the entire track?

1.5 MEASURING INSTRUMENTS

Figure 1.15 shows a simple form of a *protractor*, the simplest instrument used to measure angles. It is marked in degrees around its rim.

A more accurate device used by engineers and surveyors is called a *transit*. A transit measures an angle by locating two different line of sight objects. See Figure 1.16.

FIGURE 1.15

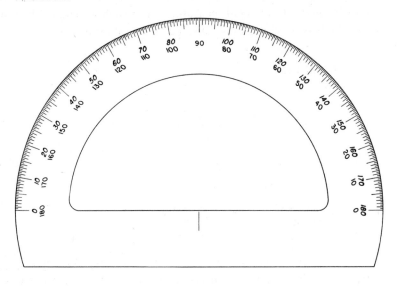

FIGURE 1.16

1.6   SOME FACTS ABOUT TRIANGLES

Much of Chapters 2 and 3 is devoted to a discussion of triangles and how the subject of trigonometry can be used to compute unknown parts of a triangle. Therefore, in this section, some geometrical facts about triangles are summarized.

   A triangle is said to be *equiangular* if the measures of each of its three angles are exactly the same; it is said to be *equilateral* if all three sides have the same length. A theorem of geometry tells us that *a triangle is equiangular if and only if it is equilateral.* A triangle is said to be *isosceles* if two of its angles have equal measure, and in such a triangle, the sides opposite the two equal angles are also equal (see Figure 1.17).

FIGURE 1.17

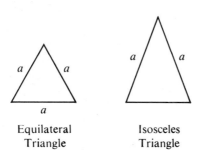

Equilateral
Triangle

Isosceles
Triangle

A *right* triangle is one in which one of the angles is a right angle. An *oblique* triangle is one without a right angle. In any triangle, the sum of the measures of the angles is 180°. Thus, in an equilateral triangle, each of the angles measures 60°. In a right triangle, each of the two remaining angles is acute and the sum of their measures is 90°.

In any triangle, for example, a triangle with vertices A, B, and C, there is a relatively standard method of referencing the sides and the angles. The sides AB and AC are called the sides *adjacent* to the angle at vertex A. The side BC is called the side *opposite* angle A. There are similar statements concerning the sides opposite and adjacent to angle B and those opposite and adjacent to angle C. There is some special terminology used when the triangle is a right triangle. The side opposite the right angle is always called the *hypotenuse.*

Referring to the right triangle in Figure 1.18, we see that side AC is called the adjacent side to angle A, side BC is called the side opposite angle A, and side AB is called the hypotenuse.

FIGURE 1.18

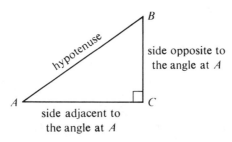

The subject of trigonometry has its origins with some simple geometric ideas of similarity. Generally, we say that any two geometric figures are *similar* if they have the same shape (not necessarily the same size).

To describe similarity between two triangles, you should ordinarily specify a *correspondence* between the vertices, sides, or angles. For example, referring to Figure 1.19,

(1) The vertices A and A', B and B', C and C' are the "corresponding vertices."

(2) The sides AC and $A'C'$, AB and $A'B'$, BC and $B'C'$ are the "corresponding sides."

(3) The angles A and A', B and B', C and C' are "corresponding angles."

FIGURE 1.19   Two similar triangles

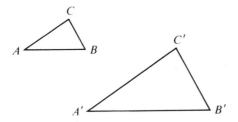

Two important properties of similarity are given in the following two theorems (without proof). These properties may be used to give a more precise definition of similarity.

THEOREM 1.1

Two triangles are similar if and only if the vertices of the triangles can be matched in such a way that corresponding sides are proportional.

Thus, in Figure 1.19, we have, by matching A with A', B with B' and C with C',

$$\frac{|AB|}{|A'B'|} = \frac{|AC|}{|A'C'|} = \frac{|BC|}{|B'C'|}.$$

The next theorem explains how the corresponding angles of similar triangles are related.

THEOREM 1.2

Two triangles are similar if and only if the angles can be matched in such a way that corresponding angles are equal.

COROLLARY

Two right triangles are similar if and only if any two corresponding acute angles have the same measure.

Thus, in Figure 1.20, the right triangle $OP'Q'$, OPQ, and $OP''Q''$ are similar since each has one acute angle (at O) in common. In fact, any triangle similar to OPQ can be superimposed on OPQ in a manner similar to the figure.

FIGURE 1.20

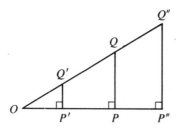

You may already know how to put the principle of similarity to good use. The most important use is to indirectly measure quantities that are almost impossible to measure by more direct means.

EXAMPLE 1.8 ◄

High divers tend to dive from some unusually large heights. A spectator who knows he is 200 yards from the diving site notes that his pencil of length 6 inches is just large enough to cover the diving height when he holds the pencil about 3 feet from his eye. How high is the dive? (See Figure 1.21.)

FIGURE 1.21

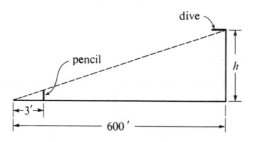

Solution: Because of the relatively large distances involved, we may for the sake of approximation, ignore the fact that the sighting is taken somewhere about 5 feet or so above ground level. Then, since the small triangle and the larger triangle are obviously similar, we have that

$$\frac{3 \text{ feet}}{600 \text{ feet}} = \frac{1/2 \text{ foot}}{h \text{ feet}}$$

from which

$$h = \frac{1}{6}(600) = 100 \text{ feet}.$$

In trigonometry, as in practically every other branch of mathematics, we will have to use the famous theorem relating the lengths of the sides of a right triangle.

THEOREM 1.3 (Pythagorean Theorem)

A triangle is a right triangle if and only if the square of one of its sides is equal to the sum of the squares of the lengths of the other two sides.

FIGURE 1.22

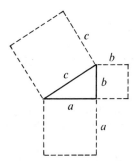

Referring to the triangle in Figure 1.22, the Pythagorean theorem can be written

$$a^2 + b^2 = c^2.$$

With the use of the Pythagorean theorem, a third side of a right triangle may be found if any two of the sides are known.

EXAMPLE 1.9 ➤

The line of sight distance to the top of an antenna attached to the chimney of a house is known to be 50 feet. If the sighting is taken 20 feet from the house, how high is the top of the antenna off the ground?

Solution: A diagram of the situation is shown in Figure 1.23. As you can see, the unknown measurement is the third side of a right triangle in

FIGURE 1.23

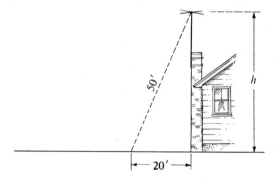

which two of the sides are known. Hence from the Pythagorean theorem,

$h^2 + 20^2 = 50^2$

so $h^2 = 2500 - 400 = 2100$

and $h = \sqrt{2100} \approx 46$ feet.

EXERCISES FOR SECTIONS 1.5–1.6

1.   Using a protractor draw angles of $30°$, $90°$, $140°$, $-60°$, $-130°$.

2.   The edges of the Great Pyramid of Egypt slope at an angle of about $52°$. Using a protractor, draw this angle.

3.   Draw a triangle that has only acute angles. From each vertex, draw a perpendicular to the opposite side (extending the side if necessary). Repeat this with a right triangle. In each of the cases, what can be said about the intersection of the perpendiculars?

4.   Draw a triangle of any shape, and through each vertex, draw a line parallel to the opposite side. How do the angles of the new triangle thus drawn compare in size to the angles of the original triangle?

5.   In the larger triangle in Exercise 3, draw, through the vertex of each angle, a line parallel to the opposite side of that triangle. How do the angles of this third triangle compare with those of the first triangle?

6.   If the sides of a triangle are 2, 4, and 5 inches, what is the perimeter of a similar triangle in which the longest side is 15 inches?

7.   If the angle between the equal sides of an isosceles triangle is $32°$, how large is each of the other angles?

8.   How many degrees are there in each angle of an equilateral triangle?

9.   A baseball diamond is a square 90 feet on a side. What is the distance across the diamond from first to third base?

10.   One side of a rectangle is half as long as the diagonal. The diagonal is 4 feet long. How long is the other side of the rectangle?

11.   At a certain time of day, a tree casts a shadow 100 feet long, and a nearby post 12 feet tall casts a shadow 15 feet long. How tall is the tree?

12. What is the line of sight distance to an airplane known to be directly over the center of the city, which is 3 miles away, if the plane is flying at 5000 feet?

13. What is the length of the diagonal of a cube that is 5 inches on an edge?

14. If a room is 21 feet long, 15 feet wide, and 10 feet high, what is the length of the diagonal of the floor? of an end wall? of a side wall of the room?

15. Show that the triangles with sides having the following measures are right triangles:

a. 6, 8, 10   b. 5, 12, 13   c. 7, 24, 25   d. 9, 40, 41
e. 11, 60, 61   f. 10, 24, 26   g. 28, 21, 35   h. 40, 96, 104

16. A snapshot is 3 inches wide and 4 inches long. It is enlarged so that it is 10 inches wide. How long is the enlarged picture? What is its area? its perimeter?

17. Is every equilateral triangle similar to every other equilateral triangle? Is every isosceles triangle similar to every other isosceles triangle? Give reasons.

18. At the same time that a yardstick held vertically casts a 5 foot shadow, a vertical flagpole casts a 30 foot shadow. How high is the flagpole?

19. Assume that the three triangles in Figure 1.24 are similar. Find the measure of the unknown sides.

FIGURE 1.24

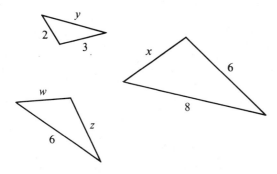

20. If the measure of the hypotenuse of a right triangle is $(m/2) + 1$, and one leg has measure $(m/2) - 1$, find the measure of the other leg. (Figure 1.25.)

FIGURE 1.25

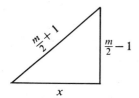

1.7 COORDINATIZATION

We often wish to make an association between points on a line (or in a plane) and numbers, a process called coordinatization. The number (or numbers) assigned to a point is called the *coordinate* (or coordinates) of the point.

To associate points with real numbers, choose any straight line, and choose any point on the line to be the starting point or origin. Take any unit distance and measure to the right of the origin. Then the number 0 is associated with the origin, the number 1 with the point a unit distance to the right of the origin, the number 2 with the point two units to the right of the origin, etc. In this way, the so-called *integral points* are determined. Similarly, points in between are coordinated by other real numbers. The line, illustrated in Figure 1.26, is then called a (real) number line.

FIGURE 1.26   Real number line

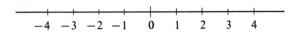

$$-4 \quad -3 \quad -2 \quad -1 \quad 0 \quad 1 \quad 2 \quad 3 \quad 4$$

For purposes of elementary trigonometry, the most important type of coordinatization is the association of each point in the plane with a pair of numbers. In this case, we choose two mutually perpendicular intersecting lines as shown in Figure 1.27. Normally, the horizontal line is called the x-axis, the vertical line is called the y-axis, and their intersection is called the origin. When considered together, the two axes are called the *coordinate axes*. As you can see, the coordinate axes divide the plane into four zones or *quadrants*. The upper right quadrant is called the first quadrant, and the others are numbered consecutively from this one in a counterclockwise direction as in Figure 1.27.

FIGURE 1.27   Cartesian coordinate system

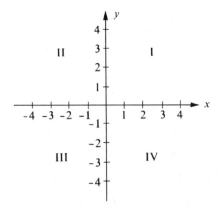

We can now locate the points in a plane by using the origin as a reference point and laying off a suitable scale on each of the coordinate axes. The displacement of a point in the plane to the right or left of the y-axis is called the *x-coordinate*, or *abscissa* of the point, and is denoted by *x*. Values of *x* measured to the right of the *y*-axis are considered to be *positive*, and to the left, *negative*. The displacement of a point in the plane above or below the *x*-axis is called the *y-coordinate*, or *ordinate* of the point, and is denoted by *y*. Values of *y* above the *x*-axis are considered to be *positive*, and below the *x*-axis, *negative*. Considered together, the abscissa and ordinate of a point are called the coordinates of the point. It is conventional to write the coordinates of a point in parentheses, with the abscissa written first and separated from the ordinate by a comma, that is, (x, y). Because of this ordering, the coordinates of a point are referred to as an *ordered pair* of numbers.

By employing the rectangular coordinate system, we can establish a one-to-one correspondence between the points in a plane and ordered pairs of numbers (x, y). That is, each point in the plane can be described by an ordered pair of numbers (x, y), and, conversely, each ordered pair of numbers (x, y) can be represented by a point in the plane.

EXAMPLE 1.10

Locate the points $A(2, 1)$, $B(-1, 5)$, $C(-2, -3)$, and $D(2, -5)$ on the rectangular coordinate plane. The letter preceding each ordered pair of numbers is the name of the point.

Solution: See Figure 1.28.

FIGURE 1.28

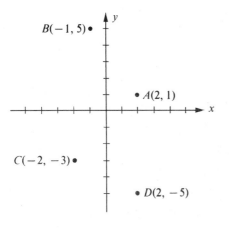

We are sometimes interested in finding the distance between two points in the plane. The following discussion explains how this is done.

FIGURE 1.29

Consider two points, P_1 and P_2 on the x-axis as shown in Figure 1.29. The distance between these two points can be found by counting the number of units between them. In the rectangular plane, distances measured from left to right are considered to be positive, and from right to left, negative. Thus, the distance from P_1 to P_2, which is denoted by $\overline{P_1P_2}$, is counted as 5 units, while the distance from P_2 to P_1, which is denoted by $\overline{P_2P_1}$, is counted as -5 units. The distance $\overline{P_1P_2}$ can also be found algebraically by subtracting P_1 from P_2; that is, $\overline{P_1P_2} = 3 - (-2) = 5$. It should also be observed that if we subtract P_2 from P_1, the distance $\overline{P_2P_1}$ is given by $\overline{P_2P_1} = -2 - 3 = -5$, the minus sign indicating the direction of measurement. In order to avoid negative distances, we shall always subtract the leftmost point in the plane from the rightmost point. In general, the horizontal distance between two points in the plane can be found by the following rule:

RULE 1 The horizontal distance between two points in the plane is the abscissa of the rightmost point in the plane minus the abscissa of the leftmost point.

Similarly, the vertical distance between two points in the plane can be found by Rule 2.

RULE 2 The vertical distance between two points in the plane is the ordinate of the uppermost point in the plane minus the ordinate of the lowermost point.

FIGURE 1.30

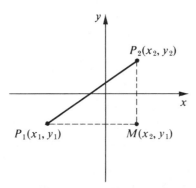

Now consider two points $P_1(x_1, y_1)$ and $P_2(x_2, y_2)$ which determine a slant line segment as shown in Figure 1.30. Draw a line through P_1 parallel to the x-axis and a line through P_2 parallel to the y-axis. These two lines intersect at the point $M(x_2, y_1)$. Hence, by the Pythagorean theorem, the distance $\overline{P_1 P_2}$ is given by

$$(\overline{P_1 P_2})^2 = (\overline{P_1 M})^2 + (\overline{MP_2})^2.$$

We see from the figure that $\overline{P_1 M}$ is the horizontal distance between P_1 and P_2. Therefore, by Rule 1, the distance $\overline{P_1 M}$ is given by

$$\overline{P_1 M} = x_2 - x_1.$$

Likewise, by Rule 2, the vertical distance $\overline{MP_2}$ is given by

$$\overline{MP_2} = y_2 - y_1.$$

Making these substitutions into Equation 1, and denoting $\overline{P_1 P_2}$ by d, we have

$$d^2 = (x_2 - x_1)^2 + (y_2 - y_1)^2.$$

(1.2) $d = \sqrt{(x_2 - x_1)^2 + (y_2 - y_1)^2}.$

where, by convention, the radical gives the nonnegative square root. Equation 1.2 is called the *distance formula* and is used to find the distance between two points in the plane directly from the coordinates of the points. The order in which the two points are labeled is immaterial, since $(x_2 - x_1)^2 = (x_1 - x_2)^2$ and $(y_2 - y_1)^2 = (y_1 - y_2)^2$.

EXAMPLE 1.11

Find the distance between $(7, -2)$ and $(-3, 1)$.

Solution:

$$d = \sqrt{(7 - (-3))^2 + (-2 - 1)^2}$$
$$= \sqrt{10^2 + (-3)^2}$$
$$= \sqrt{109}.$$

EXAMPLE 1.12

Find the distance from the origin to any point (x, y). This distance is called the *radius vector* of the point P.

Solution: From the distance formula

$$d = \sqrt{(x - 0)^2 + (y - 0)^2}$$
$$= \sqrt{x^2 + y^2}.$$

In trigonometry, we also use the rectangular coordinate system to locate angles in *standard position*. An angle is said to be in standard position in the plane if its vertex is at the origin and its initial side is along the positive *x*-axis. When an angle is in standard position, any point on its terminal side will uniquely locate the angle. This is a significant and important property since, with this convention, you can draw an angle in standard position from the coordinates of a point on its terminal side.

EXAMPLE 1.13

Draw an angle in standard position whose terminal side passes through $(-2, -2)$. What is the measure of this angle in degrees? in radians?

FIGURE 1.31

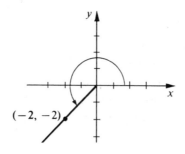

Solution: See Figure 1.31. The measure of this angle is not unique, since there are many angles with the indicated side as the terminal side. Each of these angles differs by 360 degrees. Thus, $\theta = 225° + m \cdot 360°$ where m is any integer.

Also, if θ is measured in radians, we have $\theta = 5\pi/4 + m2\pi$.

Any angle in standard position is coterminal with one whose measure is between 0 and 360°, or, in radians, between 0 and 2π. For example, $-45°$ is coterminal with an angle of 315°, the angle 101π is coterminal with an angle of π.

An angle is called a first quadrant angle if the terminal side is in the first quadrant, a second quadrant angle if the terminal side is in the second quadrant, and so on for the other quadrants.

EXERCISES FOR SECTION 1.7

Plot each of the following ordered pairs.

1. $(3, 2)$

2. $(4, 6)$

3. $(-2, \frac{1}{2})$

4. $(-6, -5)$

5. $(\frac{1}{4}, -\frac{1}{2})$ 6. $(-2.5, 1.7)$

7. In what two quadrants do the points have positive abscissas?

8. In what two quadrants do the points have negative ordinates?

9. In what quadrant are the abscissa and the ordinate both negative?

10. In what quadrants is the ratio y/x negative?

11. What is the ordinate of a point on the x-axis?

Plot each of the following pairs of points, and find the distance between the points.

12. $(1, 2), (5, 4)$ 13. $(0, 4), (-1, 3)$

14. $(-1, 5), (-1, -6)$ 15. $(\frac{1}{2}, \frac{1}{2}), (\frac{1}{2}, -\frac{3}{4})$

16. $(-5, 3), (2, -1)$ 17. $(0.5, 1.6), (6.2, 7.5)$

18. $(-3, 4), (0, 4)$ 19. $(2, -6), (-\sqrt{3}, -3)$

Find the radius vector of the following points.

20. $(1, 2)$ 21. $(-1, -5)$

22. Show that the triangle with vertices $(6, 3), (4, -3)$ and $(2, 1)$ is a right triangle.

23. Show that the triangle with the vertices $(3, 1), (4, 3)$ and $(6, 2)$ is an isosceles triangle.

Draw an angle in standard position whose terminal side passes through the given point.

24. $(5, 4)$ 25. $(1, 4)$ 26. $(-3, 2)$ 27. $(2, -5)$

1.8 THE LANGUAGE OF SETS

During the last decade, it has become customary to use the idea of a *set* to describe many elementary mathematical ideas that are awkward to express in any other way. You probably have used the language of sets in many informal ways. The emphasis here will be to formalize briefly the language and notation.

Basically, a set is a collection of objects, not necessarily mathematical ones, although in a book like this, most of the sets we use will have some connection with mathematics. We might speak of the set of students in a given class, a set of books in a library, the set of transistors in a given television set, the set of pebbles of sand on a beach, the set of all possible circles, etc. We use the idea of set whenever we wish to consider the objects as a whole. Synonymous with the word set are the terms "collection," "class," and "aggregate."

The individual objects of a set are called *elements* of a set and the elements are said to be *members* of the set.

Notationally, capital letters are often used to denote sets and lower case letters for the elements. The symbol $\in$ is used to denote "is a member of" and $\notin$ means "is not a member of." Set descriptions are usually included between braces { } and can take several different forms. For example, if we let A equal the set of people in a given room, and if only Jack, Jim, and Tom are in the room, then we would write: $A = \{$Jack, Jim, Tom$\}$. This is called the *enumeration* or *tabulation* method of describing a set.

The tabulation method becomes inappropriate if the sets have very many elements. Membership is then often denoted by the use of a descriptive statement or rule of membership, called *set builder notation*. For example, the set of all people in a given room can be denoted by

$$A = \{x \mid x \text{ is in the room}\}.$$

The expression on the right-hand side is read "The set of all x such that x is in the room." Then, no matter how many people are in the room, be it 1 or 1000, the basic description remains the same. Note that the vertical line in set builder notation is read "such that."

If the set builder notation is used, the letter x, or whatever other letter is used to denote the elements in the set, is called a *variable* over the set. In the above example, the variable x denotes people in the given room.

The set which has no elements is called the *empty* or *null* set and is denoted by { } or by $\emptyset$. Do not confuse the number 0 with the null set. A set may be the null set without it being immediately apparent—such as the set of women in a given room who are over 40 or the set of Americans who walked on the moon in 1958.

A set is said to be *finite* if you can enumerate all the members of the set; otherwise, the set is called *infinite*. If a set is finite, the notation $N(A)$ is used to denote the number of elements in the set. For example, if $A = \{a, b, c, d\}$, $B = \{0\}$, and $C = \emptyset$, then

$$N(A) = 4, N(B) = 1, \text{ and } N(C) = 0.$$

EXAMPLE 1.14

Use set notation to describe

(a) A, the set of counting numbers between 2 and 5.

(b) B, the set of counting numbers between 2 and 3.

(c) N, the set of counting numbers.

Solution: Using set builder notation, we write

(a) $A = \{x \mid x \text{ is a counting number between 2 and 5}\}$. Since this is a finite set, we can also write it as $A = \{3, 4\}$. Both descriptions are correct.

(b) $B = \emptyset$ since there are no counting numbers between 2 and 3.

(c) $N = \{x \mid x \text{ is a counting number}\}$. This set cannot be enumerated since the set is infinite.

EXAMPLE 1.15

Write the set consisting of those angles, θ, between $0°$ and $90°$ which are multiples of $10°$.

Solution: (a) By enumerating the angles, we have

$\{10°, 20°, 30°, 40°, 50°, 60°, 70°, 80°\}$.

(b) Using set builder notation, the same set can be written $\{\theta | \theta = m \cdot 10°, m$ is a positive integer and $0° < \theta < 90°\}$.

If M is the set of all automobiles and H is the set of sports cars, then we say that every member of H is also a member of M. Technically, we say that H is a *subset* of M and write, symbolically, $H \subseteq M$. More precisely, we say that A is a subset of B, denoted $A \subseteq B$, if every element of A is also an element of B. Note that for every set A, it is true that $A \subseteq A$ and $\emptyset \subseteq A$. If $A \subseteq B$, but $A \neq B$, then A is said to be a *proper* subset of B and we write $A \subset B$.

EXAMPLE 1.16

List all subsets of the set $\{a, b, c\}$. Which are proper? How many subsets does the set $\{a, b, c\}$ have? How many does a set of 10 elements have?

Solution: The subsets are $\{a, b, c\}$, $\{a, b\}$, $\{a, c\}$, $\{b, c\}$, $\{a\}$, $\{b\}$, $\{c\}$, $\emptyset$. All of these except the first are proper subsets. A set of 10 elements has 1024 subsets.

You should note that when listing elements of a set it makes no difference in which order the elements are listed. Thus $\{a, b\}$ and $\{b, a\}$ represent the same set. In most discussions, one has a fixed set of objects on which to focus his attention. If all the sets to be discussed are subsets of this one set, we call this the *universal set*, or simply the universe and denote it by U. Generally, the universal set is established from the discussion but may vary from situation to situation. Changing the universal set may very well result in a change to the "answer" to a given problem.

EXAMPLE 1.17

Determine the subset of even counting numbers if the universal set is

(a) $U_1 = \{2, 3, 4, 5, 6, 7\}$.

(b) $U_2 = \{1, 3, 5, 7\}$.

Solution: Let $E =$ the set of even counting numbers. Then

(a) $E_1 = \{2, 4, 6\}$.

(b) $E_2 = \emptyset$ since there are no even counting numbers in U_2.

Sets are often represented pictorially by drawings called *Venn**
diagrams. These diagrams are used to assist in the understanding of the
relationship of one set to another. For example in Figure 1.32, the universal
set U is represented by all points within the rectangle, the circular region
A as a proper subset of U, and x as an element of the set A.

FIGURE 1.32

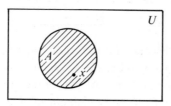

The complement of set A is the set of elements in U which are *not*
in the set A. The complement of A is denoted by $\overline{A}$ or comp A. For instance,
in Example 1.17:

$$\overline{E}_1 = \{3, 5, 7\} \quad \text{and} \quad \overline{E}_2 = \{1, 3, 5, 7\}.$$

There are two fundamental methods of forming new sets from
old ones.

DEFINITION 1.2

(a)   The *union* of two sets A and B, denoted by $A \cup B$, is the set
$\{x \mid x \in A \text{ or } x \in B\}$.

(b)   The *intersection* of two sets A and B, denoted by $A \cap B$, is the
set $\{x \mid x \in A \text{ and } x \in B\}$.

In words, $A \cup B$ is the combined set of elements which are in A or in B or in
both A and B. The intersection is the set of elements common to A and B
(see Figure 1.33).

FIGURE 1.33

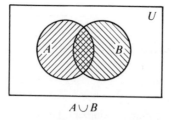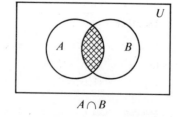

$A \cup B$ $A \cap B$

*John Venn, English logician, 1834–1923.

EXAMPLE 1.18

Let $A = \{a, b, c, d, e\}$ and $B = \{d, e, f\}$. Find $A \cup B$ and $A \cap B$.

Solution: $A \cup B = \{a, b, c, d, e, f\}$ and $A \cap B = \{d, e\}$.

EXAMPLE 1.19

Consider the following sets.

$A = \{\theta | \theta = m \cdot 10°, m$ is a positive integer and $0° < \theta < 90°\}$,

$B = \{\theta | \theta = m \cdot 15°, m$ is a positive integer and $0° < \theta < 90°\}$.

Find $A \cup B$ and $A \cap B$.

Solution:

$A \cup B = \{10°, 20°, 30°, 40°, 50°, 60°, 70°, 80°\} \cup \{15°, 30°, 45°, 60°, 75°\}$
$\qquad = \{10°, 15°, 20°, 30°, 40°, 45°, 50°, 60°, 70°, 75°, 80°\}$,
$A \cap B = \{30°, 60°\}$.

If two sets A and B have no elements in common, we say they are *disjoint*, and we write $A \cap B = \emptyset$.

Unions and intersections of more than two sets may be considered and many interesting relationships can be established. Some of these are included in the exercises for this section.

EXERCISES FOR SECTION 1.8

1. Let A be the set $\{1, 2, 3, 4\}$. Which of the following statements are true, and which are false? Give reasons.

    a. $2 \in A$ b. $5 \in A$ c. $\pi \in A$ d. $\emptyset \in A$

    e. $\emptyset \subset A$ f. $A \subseteq A$ g. $A \subset A$ h. $A \in \{a, \emptyset\}$

    i. $\{2, 3, 4, 1\} = A$

2. Determine all subsets of the set $\{1, 2, 3\}$.

3. Use set builder notation to describe the following sets:

    a. The set of people whose age is equal to their spouse.

    b. The set of air-conditioned cars in the city of New York.

    c. The set of people who own color TV sets in the United States.

4. Which of the following sets are infinite, and which are finite?

    a. The number of men who have walked on the moon.

    b. The number of men who have walked on the earth.

    c. The fractions with denominator 2.

d. The citizens of the world.

e. The points on the head of a penny.

5. Suppose the universal set is given by $U = \{1, 2, 3, 4, 5, 6, 7, 8, 9, 10\}$.
   a. Find the subset of even numbers.
   b. Find the subset of numbers which are bigger than five.
   c. Find the complement of the set $\{2, 3, 4\}$.

6. Repeat Exercise 5 with $U = \{1, 2, 3, 4, 5\}$.

7. Use Venn Diagrams to show how the following could be true.
   a. $A \cap B = \emptyset$ b. $A \cup B = A$ c. $A \cap B = A$

8. Tell why the following are true.
   a. $\emptyset \cap A = \emptyset$ b. $A \cap B \subseteq A$ c. $A \cap A = A$
   d. $A \subseteq A \cup B$ e. $A \cap U = A$

9. Let A = $\{1, 2, 3, 5, 7, 8\}$, B = $\{1, 3, 6, 8\}$, and C = $\{2, 3, 4, 5\}$. Form:
   a. $A \cup B$ b. $A \cup C$ c. $A \cap B$
   d. $(A \cup B) \cup C$ e. $(A \cup B) \cap (A \cup C)$ f. $A \cup (B \cup C)$
   g. $A \cap (B \cup C)$ h. $(A \cap B) \cup C$

10. Use Venn Diagrams to determine when the following are true:
    a. $N(A \cup B) = N(A) + N(B)$ b. $N(A \cap B) = N(A) - N(B)$

1.9   FUNCTIONS

There are basically two kinds of number symbols used in algebraic and trigonometric discussions: *constants* and *variables*. Constants have fixed values throughout a discussion, while variables may take on many different values, called the set of permissible values of the variable, or more technically, the *domain* of the variable. If the domain is not specifically mentioned, we usually allow the variable to take on all permissible real values in the discussion.

Sometimes the values of one variable determine the values of some second variable. For example, the set $\{2, 3, 4\}$ is said to *determine* the set $\{4, 6, 8\}$ by obeying the rule of doubling each of the elements of the first set. The notion of two variables being related to one another is used extensively in mathematics and is basic to our understanding of the physical world.

DEFINITION 1.3

A variable y is said to be a *function* of the variable x if for each value of x there corresponds a unique value of y.

The first variable is called the *independent* variable, the second is called the *dependent* variable, and the defining relation is called a functional relationship.

The domain of the independent variable is called the *domain of the function* while the domain of the dependent variable is called the *range of the function*.

EXAMPLE 1.20

The equation $y = x^2$ essentially defines a function with x as the independent variable and y as the dependent variable. The function has an understood domain of all real numbers and a range of nonnegative numbers.

The functional relationship between two variables is often given by an equation (as in the previous example), but it may also be given by other means, such as a table of values. The definition of a function does not require that the value of y change when the value of x changes, but only that y have a unique value corresponding to each value of x. In light of this, we usually consider an equation such as $y = 5$ as defining a function since, regardless of the value of x chosen from the domain, the corresponding range value is uniquely determined to be 5. On the other hand, $y = \pm\sqrt{x}$ does not satisfy the definition because there are two values of y corresponding to each positive value of x, namely the positive and negative square roots of x.

In some discussions, we will want to indicate that y is a function of x without specifying the particular relationship. This is true particularly when discussing the general properties of trigonometric functions. The notation commonly used to indicate that a functional relationship exists between x and y is $y = f(x)$. This is read "y is the f function of x" or simply "y equals f of x." The letter f is the name of the functional relationship between x and y; it is not a variable. While there is a tendency to use the letter f as the name of the function, any other letter or symbol will serve as well. The letter x represents the domain value of the function and is sometimes called the *argument* of the function.

The function designated by $f(x)$ may or may not have a definite mathematical expression. If a specific expression is available, functional notation offers a convenient way of indicating substitutions into the expression.

EXAMPLE 1.21

Find the value of the function $f(x) = x^2 + 3x$ at $x = 2$.

Solution: We denote the value of $f(x)$ at $x = 2$ by $f(2)$. To find $f(2)$, we substitute 2 for x in $x^2 + 3x$; that is,

$$f(2) = (2)^2 + 3(2) = 10.$$

31

A function determines a set of ordered pairs:

$$\{(x, y) | y = f(x)\}$$

and conversely *some* sets of ordered pairs determine a function. Can you tell which sets of ordered pairs determine a function? The key is that for any given x there must be only one value of y. Thus, if the set of ordered pairs has two pairs with the same first element, the set does not represent a function. In this case the set is said to represent a *relation*.

EXAMPLE 1.22

The set of ordered pairs

$$\{(2, 3), (3, -1), (-1, 0), (0, 2)\}$$

represents a function.

EXAMPLE 1.23

The set of ordered pairs

$$\{(2, 3), (3, -1), (2, 5), (0, 2)\}$$

does not represent a function because the first and third pairs have the same first element. This set represents a relation.

The *graph* of a function is the geometric analogue of the equation defining the function. It consists of the set of *points* corresponding to the set of ordered pairs given by the function. Usually to graph a function we plot a "reasonable" number of the points and connect them with a smooth graph.

EXAMPLE 1.24

Sketch the graph of $y = \sqrt{4 - x}$.

Solution: A table is constructed using some reasonable values of x and

FIGURE 1.34

$y = \sqrt{4 - x}$

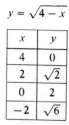

x	y
4	0
2	$\sqrt{2}$
0	2
-2	$\sqrt{6}$

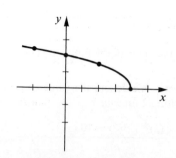

determining the corresponding values of y. Both the table and graph are shown in Figure 1.34.

EXAMPLE 1.25

Sketch the graph of $y = 32x - 16x^2$.

Solution: See Figure 1.35.

FIGURE 1.35

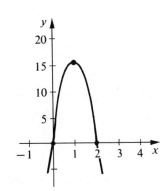

x	y
-1	-48
0	0
1	16
2	0

Just as certain sets of ordered pairs determine functions, so too, some sets of points of the Cartesian coordinate system determine a function. Usually, the sets of points will be in the form of continuous curves as in Figure 1.36. Not all of the graphs of Figure 1.36 determine functions; the first two do represent functions and the other two do not. Again, as in the case of sets of ordered pairs, the key lies with the fact that for any one value of x, there must be only one value of y. Geometrically, this means that if a line is drawn parallel to the y-axis, there should be, at most, one point of intersection with the graph.

FIGURE 1.36

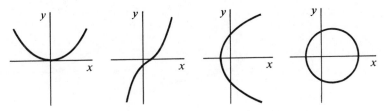

EXERCISES FOR SECTION 1.9

1. Given $f(x) = x^2 - 5x$, find $f(2)$ and $f(-1)$.

2. Given $g(x) = x^2 - 4$, find $g(2)$ and $g(-4)$.

3. Given $f(t) = (t - 2)(t + 3)$, find $f(-4)$ and $f(0)$.

4. Given $\emptyset\,(y) = y(y + 1)$, find $\emptyset(3)$ and $\emptyset(-3)$.

5. Given $h(x) = 2(x^2 - 3)$, find $h(5)$ and $h(1)$.

6. Given $g(z) = (1 - z^2)/(1 + z^2)$, find $g(-1)$ and $g(4)$.

Symbolize the following expressions in functional notation.

7. The area A of a circle as a function of the radius r.

8. The circumference C of a circle as a function of its diameter d.

9. The perimeter P of a square as a function of its side length s.

Give the domain and range of each of the following functions.

10. $f(x) = x^2 - 5x$ 11. $f(t) = (t - 2)(t + 2)$

12. $f(x) = x^3$ 13. $f(x) = \sqrt{x - 25}$

14. $f(x) = \sqrt{x}$ 15. $f(x) = 1/x$

Graph each of the following functions:

16. $y = x^3$ 17. $f(x) = -x^2$ 18. $z = t^2 + 4$

19. $i = r - r^2$ 20. $y(x) = \sqrt{x}$ 21. $\emptyset = w^2/2$

22. $p = z^2 - z - 6$ 23. $v = 10 + 2t$ 24. $y = \sqrt{16 - 4x^2}$

Which of the following sets of ordered pairs determine a function?

25. $\{(1, 1), (2, 1)\}$ 26. $\{(1, 1), (1, 2)\}$

27. $\{(x, y)|y = 3\}$ 28. $\{(x, y)|x = 1\}$

29. $\{(x, y)|y = x\}$ 30. $\{(x, y)|y^2 = x\}$

Which of the following graphs represent a function?

31. 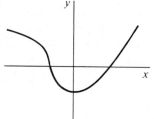   32.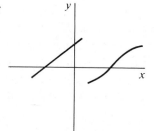

33. 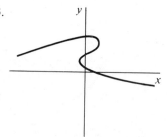   34.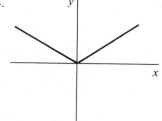

2

RIGHT
TRIANGLE
TRIGONOMETRY

2.1   DEFINITIONS OF THE TRIGONOMETRIC FUNCTIONS

Trigonometry was invented as a means of indirectly measuring the parts of a right triangle; in fact, the word *trigonometry* means "three angle measure". Today, trigonometry has many applications that have nothing to do with triangles, but the basic concepts are still best understood relative to the right triangle. For this reason, we begin our discussion of trigonometry with the right triangle. In Figure 2.1, the capital letters A, B, and C designate the vertices and the corresponding angles at these vertices while the lower case letters a, b, and c designate the lengths of the sides opposite these angles. This convention is somewhat standard and will be used throughout this book.

FIGURE 2.1

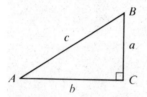

Consider a right triangle ABC as shown in Figure 2.1. For reasons that you will understand shortly, we are interested in the ratios of the lengths of the sides of the triangle. By inspection you can see that the three sides a, b, and c can be used to form six ratios, namely,

$$\frac{a}{c}, \frac{b}{c}, \frac{a}{b}, \frac{b}{a}, \frac{c}{b}, \frac{c}{a}.$$

For similar right triangles these six ratios are independent of the lengths a, b, and c. That this is true may be seen from the following argument. In Figure 2.2, two similar right triangles ABC and $A_1B_1C_1$ are drawn, one obviously larger than the other.

FIGURE 2.2

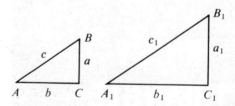

From Section 1.6, or from your knowledge of the geometry of similar triangles, we know that the corresponding sides of the two triangles are proportional. Thus, since triangles ABC and $A_1B_1C_1$ are similar, we can write

$$\frac{a}{a_1} = \frac{c}{c_1} \text{ and } \frac{b}{b_1} = \frac{c}{c_1} \text{ and } \frac{a}{a_1} = \frac{b}{b_1},$$

or, rearranging terms

$$\frac{a}{c} = \frac{a_1}{c_1} \text{ and } \frac{b}{c} = \frac{b_1}{c_1} \text{ and } \frac{a}{b} = \frac{a_1}{b_1}.$$

Each proportion says that the ratio of two given sides in the smaller triangle is equal to the ratio of the corresponding sides in the larger triangle. Recognizing that these are the first three ratios of the six ratios mentioned above and, that the other three could be handled in a like manner, we conclude that the six ratios are independent of the lengths of the sides of the triangle.

While the six ratios are independent of the length of the sides, they are dependent upon the angles. For instance, if in Figure 2.1 angle A increases, the ratio a/c increases and the ratio b/c decreases. Thus, the six ratios are functions of the angle A and have come to be called the *trigonometric functions*. To facilitate discussion of the trigonometric functions, each is given a name as indicated in the following definition.

DEFINITION 2.1

With reference to Figure 2.1, the six trigonometric functions of angle A are as follows.

$$\text{sine } A = \frac{a}{c} \quad \text{(abbreviated } \sin A)$$

$$\text{cosine } A = \frac{b}{c} \quad \text{(abbreviated } \cos A)$$

$$\text{tangent } A = \frac{a}{b} \quad \text{(abbreviated } \tan A)$$

$$\text{cotangent } A = \frac{b}{a} \quad \text{(abbreviated } \cot A)$$

$$\text{secant } A = \frac{c}{b} \quad \text{(abbreviated } \sec A)$$

$$\text{cosecant } A = \frac{c}{a} \quad \text{(abbreviated } \csc A)$$

The sides of a right triangle are often referenced to one of the two acute angles. For example, the side of length a is called the *side opposite* angle A, the side of length b is called the *side adjacent* to angle A, and the side of length c is called the hypotenuse. Using this terminology, the six trigonometric functions in Definition 2.1 become

$$\sin A = \frac{a}{c} = \frac{\text{opposite side}}{\text{hypotenuse}} \qquad \cos A = \frac{b}{c} = \frac{\text{adjacent side}}{\text{hypotenuse}}$$

(2.1) $$\tan A = \frac{a}{b} = \frac{\text{opposite side}}{\text{adjacent side}} \qquad \cot A = \frac{b}{a} = \frac{\text{adjacent side}}{\text{opposite side}}$$

$$\sec A = \frac{c}{b} = \frac{\text{hypotenuse}}{\text{adjacent side}} \qquad \csc A = \frac{c}{a} = \frac{\text{hypotenuse}}{\text{opposite side}}.$$

The abbreviated names of the trigonometric functions are the ones most often used, and you should remember that they denote certain ratios of lengths. Thus, when someone mentions sin A, you should automatically think "the ratio of a to c" or "side opposite angle A to hypotenuse."

EXAMPLE 2.1

Consider a right triangle whose sides have the values as shown in Figure 2.3. Find the six trigonometric functions for the angle θ.

FIGURE 2.3

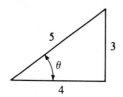

Solution:

$$\sin \theta = \frac{\text{side opposite}}{\text{hypotenuse}} = \frac{3}{5} \qquad \cos \theta = \frac{\text{side adjacent}}{\text{hypotenuse}} = \frac{4}{5}$$

$$\tan \theta = \frac{\text{side opposite}}{\text{side adjacent}} = \frac{3}{4} \qquad \cot \theta = \frac{\text{side adjacent}}{\text{side opposite}} = \frac{4}{3}$$

$$\sec \theta = \frac{\text{hypotenuse}}{\text{side adjacent}} = \frac{5}{4} \qquad \csc \theta = \frac{\text{hypotenuse}}{\text{side opposite}} = \frac{5}{3}.$$

EXAMPLE 2.2

A man on the ground 50 feet from the foot of a building views an antenna whose top is 150 feet above the ground. Find the sine of the angle of elevation from the observer to the top of the antenna. (The angle of elevation is the angle between the horizontal and the line of sight when looking up to the object.) Ignore the distance from the ground to the man's eye.

FIGURE 2.4

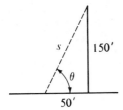

Solution: Figure 2.4 shows the situation. From the Pythagorean theorem, the slant distance to the top of the antenna may be computed

$$s^2 = 150^2 + 50^2$$
$$= 22,500 + 2,500$$
$$= 25,000.$$

Hence, $s \approx 158$. From this, $\sin \theta = \dfrac{150}{158} \approx 0.95$.

EXERCISES FOR SECTION 2.1

Draw right triangles whose sides have the following values and find the six trigonometric functions of the angle A.

1. $a = 4, b = 3, c = 5$
2. $a = 3, b = 2, c = \sqrt{13}$
3. $a = 12, b = 5, c = 13$
4. $a = 1, b = \frac{1}{2}$
5. $a = 2, b = 1$
6. $a = 2, c = 7$
7. $a = 1, b = 2$
8. $a = 1, c = 2$
9. $a = 1, b = 1$
10. $a = \sqrt{2}, c = \sqrt{10}$

11. A 6 foot man casts a shadow of 4 feet. Find the tangent of the angle that the rays of the sun make with the horizontal.

12. A wire 30 feet long is used to brace a flagpole. If the wire is attached to the pole 25 feet above the level ground, what is the cosine of the angle made by the wire with the ground?

13. The line of sight distance to the top of a 100 foot high building is 300 feet. What is the tangent of the angle of elevation?

14. Suppose that a boy is flying a kite at the end of a 100 foot string which makes an angle of 45° with the ground. Find the cosine of the angle which the string makes with the ground.

15. A man on a 100 foot cliff looks down on a rowboat known to be 30 feet from the base of the cliff. What is the sine of the angle of depression? (The angle of depression is defined as the angle between the horizontal and the line of sight when looking down on an object.)

39

2.2   FUNCTIONS OF COMPLEMENTARY ANGLES

The definitions of the trigonometric functions were given in terms of the angle A in Figure 2.1. The complementary angle, B, has trigonometric ratios associated with it, too.

EXAMPLE 2.3

Find $\sin B$, $\cos B$ and $\tan B$ if $a = 3$ and $b = 2$ (see Figure 2.5).

FIGURE 2.5

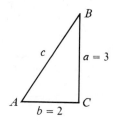

Solution: $c = \sqrt{3^2 + 2^2} = \sqrt{13}$.
Then,

$$\sin B = \frac{\text{side opposite } B}{\text{hypotenuse}} = \frac{b}{c} = \frac{2}{\sqrt{13}},$$

$$\cos B = \frac{\text{side adjacent to } B}{\text{hypotenuse}} = \frac{a}{c} = \frac{3}{\sqrt{13}},$$

$$\tan B = \frac{\text{side opposite } B}{\text{side adjacent to } B} = \frac{b}{a} = \frac{2}{3}.$$

Trigonometric ratios for complementary angles have an interesting relationship. Using triangle ABC and the definitions of $\sin B$, $\cos B$, and $\tan B$, we see that

$$\sin B = \frac{\text{side opposite } B}{\text{hypotenuse}} = \frac{\text{side adjacent to } A}{\text{hypotenuse}} = \cos A,$$

$$\cos B = \frac{\text{side adjacent to } B}{\text{hypotenuse}} = \frac{\text{side opposite } A}{\text{hypotenuse}} = \sin A,$$

$$\tan B = \frac{\text{side opposite } B}{\text{side adjacent to } B} = \frac{\text{side adjacent to } A}{\text{side opposite } A} = \cot A.$$

Similarly,

$$\cot B = \tan A, \quad \sec B = \csc A, \quad \csc B = \sec A.$$

These relations involving the trigonometric functions of complementary angles is one of the main reasons that the sine and cosine are called *complementary functions* or *cofunctions*. Similarly, the tangent and cotangent are complementary and the secant and cosecant are complementary. Making use of the fact that $B = 90° - A$, we have:

$$\sin A = \cos (90° - A) \qquad \cos A = \sin (90° - A)$$
$$\tan A = \cot (90° - A) \qquad \cot A = \tan (90° - A)$$
$$\sec A = \csc (90° - A) \qquad \csc A = \sec (90° - A)$$

or, in general,

(2.2) $\quad$ **Trigonometric function of an acute angle A** $\quad = \quad$ **Complementary function of $(90° - A)$.**

EXAMPLE 2.4

(a) $\sin 30° = \cos (90° - 30°) = \cos 60°$. As we will learn in Section 2.4, $\sin 30° = \frac{1}{2}$. Hence, $\cos 60° = \frac{1}{2}$.

(b) $\tan 50° = \cot (90° - 50°) = \cot 40°$. The value of $\tan 50°$ is 1.1918. Hence, $\cot 40° = 1.1918$.

2.3 FUNDAMENTAL RELATIONS

The values of the six trigonometric functions are interrelated by some very simple formulas. From the definitions, we have:

(2.3)
$$\sin \theta = \frac{\text{opposite}}{\text{hypotenuse}} = \frac{1}{\text{hypotenuse/opposite}} = \frac{1}{\csc \theta},$$
$$\cos \theta = \frac{\text{adjacent}}{\text{hypotenuse}} = \frac{1}{\text{hypotenuse/adjacent}} = \frac{1}{\sec \theta},$$
$$\tan \theta = \frac{\text{opposite}}{\text{adjacent}} = \frac{1}{\text{adjacent/opposite}} = \frac{1}{\cot \theta}.$$

These three relations are called the *reciprocal relationships* for the trigonometric functions. Further,

(2.4) $\quad$ $$\tan \theta = \frac{\text{opposite}}{\text{adjacent}} = \frac{\text{opposite/hypotenuse}}{\text{adjacent/hypotenuse}} = \frac{\sin \theta}{\cos \theta}.$$

As the following two examples are intended to show, a knowledge of one trigonometric ratio for an acute angle of a right triangle is sufficient to determine the other five ratios.

EXAMPLE 2.5

Given that $\sin \beta = \frac{1}{2}$, find the values of the other trigonometric functions. We assume that β is an acute angle.

FIGURE 2.6

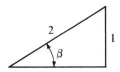

Solution: It is convenient to draw a typical right triangle with $\sin \beta = \frac{1}{2}$. Figure 2.6 is one possibility with the opposite side equal to 1 and the hypotenuse equal to 2. From the Pythagorean theorem, the adjacent side is equal to $\sqrt{3}$. Since the three sides of the right triangle are known, we can write immediately:

$$\cos \beta = \frac{\sqrt{3}}{2}, \ \tan \beta = \frac{1}{\sqrt{3}}, \ \cot \beta = \sqrt{3}, \ \sec \beta = \frac{2}{\sqrt{3}}, \ \csc \beta = 2.$$

As in the previous example, the values of the trigonometric functions are often left in a form involving a radical. If the ratios are actually used for computational purposes, then you will need to convert to approximate decimal values. For instance, in Example 2.5, we would write

$$\cos \beta \approx \frac{1.732}{2} \approx 0.866.$$

EXAMPLE 2.6

Given that $\tan A = \frac{1}{2}$, find $\sin A$ and $\cos A$.

FIGURE 2.7

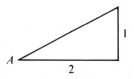

Solution: A typical right triangle is shown in Figure 2.7. The Pythagorean theorem gives the value of the hypotenuse to be $\sqrt{4 + 1} = \sqrt{5}$. Hence,

$$\sin A = \frac{1}{\sqrt{5}}, \ \cos A = \frac{2}{\sqrt{5}}.$$

With the use of the Pythagorean theorem, we can derive a very famous relation between the sine and cosine functions. Consider any right triangle. From the Pythagorean theorem

$$(\text{opposite})^2 + (\text{adjacent})^2 = (\text{hypotenuse})^2.$$

Dividing both sides of this equation by the square of the hypotenuse, we obtain:

$$\left(\frac{\text{opposite}}{\text{hypotenuse}}\right)^2 + \left(\frac{\text{adjacent}}{\text{hypotenuse}}\right)^2 = 1,$$

or, in terms of the trigonometric functions,

$$(\sin \theta)^2 + (\cos \theta)^2 = 1.$$

It is customary to write $(\sin \theta)^2$ as $\sin^2 \theta$ and $(\cos \theta)^2$ as $\cos^2 \theta$. (A similar convention holds for expressing powers of the other trigonometric functions.) Thus the equation reads:

(2.5) $\sin^2\theta + \cos^2\theta = 1,$

a formula that is often called the *Pythagorean relation* of trigonometry.

EXAMPLE 2.7

Given that $\sin \theta = \frac{1}{4}$, use the Pythagorean relation to find $\cos \theta$.

Solution: Solving the Pythagorean relation for $\cos \theta$, we have

$\cos \theta = \sqrt{1 - \sin^2\theta}.$

Therefore,

$\cos \theta = \sqrt{1 - (\frac{1}{4})^2} = \sqrt{1 - \frac{1}{16}} = \frac{\sqrt{15}}{4}.$

EXERCISES FOR SECTIONS 2.2 AND 2.3

Find the trigonometric functions of the angle complementary to θ, if

1. $\cos \theta = 1/2$ 2. $\sin \theta = \sqrt{3}/2$ 3. $\tan \theta = 1$

4. $\sec \theta = 3$ 5. $\cot \theta = 5$ 6. $\sin \theta = 1/\sqrt{3}$

7. $\tan \theta = t$ 8. $\cos \theta = u/v$ 9. $\sin \theta = 1/t$

10. $\csc \theta = 1/t$

Find the other five functions of the acute angle θ.

11. $\cos \theta = 3/5$ 12. $\tan \theta = 2$ 13. $\sin \theta = 1/3$

14. $\sin \theta = 1/2$ 15. $\cos \theta = 1/2$ 16. $\sec \theta = \sqrt{2}$

17. $\sin \theta = u/v$ 18. $\tan \theta = u/v$ 19. $\cos \theta = u$

20. $\sin \theta = 1/v$

21. Given that $\cos \theta = 1/\sqrt{3}$, use the Pythagorean relation to find $\sin \theta$.

22. Repeat Problem 21 if $\cos \theta = \sqrt{3}/2$.

2.4 VALUES OF THE TRIGONOMETRIC FUNCTIONS

The values of the trigonometric functions for some angles can be obtained from some applications of elementary geometry.

EXAMPLE 2.8

Find the values of the trigonometric functions for 45°.

FIGURE 2.8

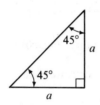

Solution: A 45° acute angle for a right triangle means that the triangle is isosceles, a typical one being shown in Figure 2.8. Using the Pythagorean theorem, the length of the hypotenuse is given by:

$$(\text{hypotenuse}) = \sqrt{a^2 + a^2}$$
$$= a\sqrt{2}.$$

Hence,

$$\sin 45° = \frac{a}{a\sqrt{2}} = \frac{1}{\sqrt{2}} = \frac{\sqrt{2}}{2} \approx 0.707$$

$$\cos 45° = \frac{a}{a\sqrt{2}} = \frac{1}{\sqrt{2}} = \frac{\sqrt{2}}{2} \approx 0.707$$

$$\tan 45° = \frac{a\sqrt{2}}{a\sqrt{2}} = 1$$

$$\cot 45° = 1$$

$$\sec 45° = \sqrt{2} \approx 1.414$$

$$\csc 45° = \sqrt{2} \approx 1.414.$$

EXAMPLE 2.9

Find the trigonometric functions of 60°.

FIGURE 2.9

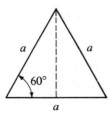

Solution: Consider an equilateral triangle and draw the bisector of one of the angles. This bisector divides the equilateral triangle into two congruent right triangles, as shown in Figure 2.9. The altitude of each of these right triangles is given by

$$h = \sqrt{a^2 - (\tfrac{1}{2}a)^2} = \frac{a\sqrt{3}}{2}.$$

Hence,

$$\sin 60° = \frac{a\sqrt{3}/2}{a} = \frac{\sqrt{3}}{2} \approx 0.866$$

$$\cos 60° = \frac{a/2}{a} = \frac{1}{2} = 0.5$$

$$\tan 60° = \frac{a\sqrt{3}/2}{a/2} = \sqrt{3} \approx 1.732$$

$$\cot 60° = \frac{1}{\sqrt{3}} \approx 0.577$$

$$\sec 60° = \frac{2}{1} = 2$$

$$\csc 60° = \frac{2}{\sqrt{3}} \approx 1.155.$$

The values for an angle of 30° are obtained from the previous example and from the cofunction relation for complementary acute angles.

Table 2.1 summarizes the foregoing discussion. Study it carefully. You should know how to derive it.

TABLE 2.1 Values for Some Important Angles

θ (degrees)	θ(radians)	sin θ	cos θ	tan θ	cot θ	sec θ	csc θ
30	$\pi/6$	$1/2$	$\sqrt{3}/2$	$1/\sqrt{3}$	$\sqrt{3}$	$2/\sqrt{3}$	2
45	$\pi/4$	$\sqrt{2}/2$	$\sqrt{2}/2$	1	1	$\sqrt{2}$	$\sqrt{2}$
60	$\pi/3$	$\sqrt{3}/2$	$1/2$	$\sqrt{3}$	$1/\sqrt{3}$	2	$2/\sqrt{3}$

A remark on a notation convention. If degree measure for an angle is used, it is explicitly mentioned, whereas the fact that radian measure is used is commonly omitted. Thus, the degree notation must be used when writing sin 30°. However, you need not write sin ($\pi/6$ radians) since it is understood that sin $\pi/6$ is that value.

From the nature of the definitions, we can determine how the values of the trigonometric functions change as an angle varies from 0° to 90°. As shown in Figure 2.10, by increasing A, the opposite side increases from a small length to a length equal to that of the hypotenuse; the adjacent side decreases from the size of the hypotenuse to a very small length; and the hypotenuse remains constant.

FIGURE 2.10   Variation of a right triangle as angle A increases (fixed hypotenuse)

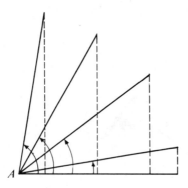

Thus, we can construct the table of variation of the values (Table 2.2). While not giving the exact values, this table tells approximately how the functions vary. (Again, study it carefully and be able to explain the table).

TABLE 2.2   Variation in the Trigonometric Function As A Increases from 0° to 90°

sin A	increases from 0 to 1
cos A	decreases from 1 to 0
tan A	increases from 0 and runs through all real numbers
cot A	decreases to 0, running through all real numbers
sec A	increases from 1, running through all real numbers ≥ 1
csc A	decreases to 1, running through all real numbers ≥ 1

Tables 2.1 and 2.2 are obviously incomplete; the first one is incomplete because it tabulates the functional values corresponding to only three angles; the second, because it gives only a general idea of the nature of the variation. Specific values of the trigonometric ratios for the other angles are computed by methods beyond the scope of this book and, generally, are approximations to the actual values. In this book, we have included two representative tables in the Appendix and Table 2.3 in this

TABLE 2.3   Three Place Table of Trigonometric Functions of Degrees

θ	$\sin\theta$	$\cos\theta$	$\tan\theta$	$\cot\theta$	$\sec\theta$	$\csc\theta$	θ
0°	.000	1.00	.000	—	1.00	—	90°
1°	.018	1.00	.018	57.3	1.00	57.3	89°
2°	.035	.999	.035	28.6	1.00	28.7	88°
3°	.052	.999	.052	19.1	1.00	19.1	87°
4°	.070	.998	.070	14.3	1.00	14.3	86°
5°	.087	.996	.088	11.4	1.00	11.5	85°
6°	.105	.995	.105	9.51	1.01	9.57	~~86°~~ 84°
7°	.122	.993	.123	8.14	1.01	8.21	83°
8°	.139	.990	.141	7.12	1.01	7.19	82°
9°	.156	.988	.158	6.31	1.01	6.39	81°
10°	.174	.985	.176	5.67	1.02	5.76	80°
11°	.191	.982	.194	5.14	1.02	5.24	79°
12°	.208	.978	.213	4.70	1.02	4.81	78°
13°	.225	.974	.231	4.33	1.03	4.45	77°
14°	.242	.970	.249	4.01	1.03	4.13	76°
15°	.259	.966	.268	3.73	1.04	3.86	75°
16°	.276	.961	.287	3.49	1.04	3.63	74°
17°	.292	.956	.306	3.27	1.05	3.42	73°
18°	.309	.951	.325	3.08	1.05	3.24	72°
19°	.326	.946	.344	2.90	1.06	3.07	71°
20°	.342	.940	.364	2.75	1.06	2.92	70°
21°	.358	.934	.384	2.61	1.07	2.79	69°
22°	.375	.927	.404	2.48	1.08	2.68	68°
23°	.391	.921	.425	2.36	1.09	2.56	67°
24°	.407	.914	.445	2.25	1.10	2.46	66°
25°	.423	.906	.466	2.14	1.10	2.37	65°
26°	.438	.899	.488	2.05	1.11	2.28	64°
27°	.454	.891	.510	1.96	1.12	2.20	63°
28°	.470	.883	.554	1.88	1.13	2.13	62°
29°	.485	.875	.532	1.80	1.14	2.06	61°
30°	.500	.866	.577	1.73	1.16	2.00	60°
31°	.515	.857	.601	1.66	1.17	1.94	59°
32°	.530	.848	.625	1.60	1.18	1.89	58°
33°	.545	.839	.649	1.54	1.19	1.84	57°
34°	.559	.829	.675	1.48	1.21	1.79	56°
35°	.574	.819	.700	1.43	1.22	1.74	55°
36°	.588	.809	.727	1.38	1.24	1.70	54°
37°	.602	.799	.754	1.33	1.25	1.66	53°
38°	.616	.788	.781	1.28	1.27	1.62	52°
39°	.629	.777	.810	1.23	1.29	1.59	51°
40°	.643	.766	.839	1.19	1.31	1.56	50°
41°	.656	.755	.869	1.15	1.33	1.52	49°
42°	.669	.743	.900	1.11	1.35	1.50	48°
43°	.682	.731	.933	1.07	1.37	1.47	47°
44°	.695	.719	.966	1.04	1.39	1.44	46°
45°	.707	.707	1.00	1.00	1.41	1.41	45°
θ	$\cos\theta$	$\sin\theta$	$\cot\theta$	$\tan\theta$	$\csc\theta$	$\sec\theta$	θ

chapter. Table 2.3 is tabulated in one degree increments and is accurate to three decimal places. Table A in the Appendix is called a "four place table," meaning that it is accurate to four decimal places. It is tabulated in 10′ increments. Table B, in the Appendix, is given in increments of .01 radian to four decimal places. Note that Table B runs from 0 to 1.57, the radian measure of an acute angle being within these limits.

Table 2.3 is representative of most trigonometry tables that are tabulated in degrees in that it apparently includes only those angles between 0° and 45°. This is so because the values of the functions for angles between 45° and 90° are the same as the values of the cofunction between 0° and 45°. Thus sin 57° = cos (90° − 57°) = cos 33°. Further, most tables that take advantage of this relation between the cofunctions of complementary angles place the complementary angle to the right of the table. The names of the function to be read for that particular angle are then located at the bottom; thus the table does "double duty."

To summarize the use of Table 2.3 in this chapter and Table A in the Appendix:

(1) To find the values of the trigonometric ratios for angles between 0 and 45 degrees, locate the angle at the left hand side of the table and the name of the function at the top of the column.

(2) To find the values of the trigonometric ratios for angles between 45 and 90 degrees, locate the angle at the right hand side of the table and the name of the function at the bottom.

(3) Opposite the angle, in the appropriate column, is found the value of the trigonometric function.

EXAMPLE 2.10

Use Table 2.3 to verify that:

(a) $\sin 34° = 0.559$

(b) $\cos 7° = 0.993$

(c) $\tan 76° = 4.01$

(d) $\sec 21° = 1.07$

(e) $\sin 81° = 0.988$

EXAMPLE 2.11

Use Tables A and B to verify that:

(a) $\sin 34°10′ = 0.5616$

(b) $\cos 54°30′ = 0.5807$

(c) $\tan 65°40′ = 2.2113$

(d) sin 0.72 = 0.6594

(e) cot 1.11 = 0.4964

(f) sec 0.23 = 1.027

In closing this section, we remark that trigonometry tables are used in two ways. The first is to find the value of a trigonometric function if an angle is given. The other is to find the value of the angle when the value of the trigonometric function is known. For example, if you are given that $\cos \theta = \frac{1}{2}$, you know that $\theta = 60°$.

EXAMPLE 2.12

Use Table 2.3 to find the angle θ if $\sin \theta = 0.358$.

Solution: We examine Table 2.3 running down the column headed "$\sin \theta$" until we come to 0.358. Then we read across and find that this corresponds to an angle of 21°. This is written

$\sin \theta = 0.358$

$\theta = 21°$.

EXAMPLE 2.13

Use Table 2.3 to find angle β if $\tan \beta = 1.60$.

Solution: Running down the column headed "tan" at the top of the page we fail to reach 1.60 before coming to 45°; therefore, we continue looking in the column headed "tan" at the bottom until we come to 1.60. Reading "angle" from the right hand column, we find that $\beta = 58°$, that is,

$\tan \beta = 1.60$

$\beta = 58°$.

EXERCISES FOR SECTION 2.4

Using Table 2.3, find the values of the indicated trigonometric functions.

1. sin 13°	2. sin 46°	3. tan 17°
4. cos 61°	5. sec 5°	6. tan 44°
7. cot 17°	8. csc 38°	9. sin 75°
10. cot 56°	11. cos 80°	12. sec 49°

Using Table 2.3, find angle α, if:

13. cos α = 0.974	14. tan α = 0.601	15. cot α = 5.14

16. $\sin \alpha = 0.018$ 17. $\sin \alpha = 0.996$ 18. $\sec \alpha = 1.12$

19. $\csc \alpha = 1.09$ 20. $\cos \alpha = 0.292$ 21. $\tan \alpha = 8.14$

22. $\tan \alpha = 2.05$ 23. $\sec \alpha = 3.63$ 24. $\sin \alpha = 1.000$

Using Tables A and/or B, find the values of the indicated trigonometric functions.

25. $\sin 14°20'$ 26. $\cos 47°40'$ 27. $\sec 64°50'$

28. $\tan 25°30'$ 29. $\cot 57°20'$ 30. $\csc 70°40'$

31. $\tan 1.23$ 32. $\sin 0.54$ 33. $\cot 1.00$

34. $\sec 0.02$ 35. $\cot 0.78$ 36. $\csc 0.50$

Using Table A, find the degree measure of the angle α if:

37. $\sin \alpha = 0.4617$ 38. $\cot \alpha = 0.5354$

39. $\tan \alpha = 3.732$ 40. $\sec \alpha = 2.0957$

Using Table B, find the radian measure of the angle α if:

41. $\sin \alpha = 0.8415$ 42. $\cos \alpha = 0.8253$

43. $\tan \alpha = 4.072$ 44. $\cot \alpha = 1.462$

2.5   INTERPOLATION

Interpolation is a method of estimating a value between two given values. Since all trigonometric tables are tabulated in discrete steps, you will find it necessary to use interpolated values of trigonometric functions for angles between two tabulated values. For example, in Table 2.3, you will need to interpolate to obtain an estimate for those trigonometric ratios corresponding to angles whose measure is not precisely an integer, such as 41.5°. One method, of course, would be to convert 41.5° to 41°30', and then use Table A of the Appendix. But this table would be insufficient for angles such as 41°15'. So unavoidably, you will have to use the method of interpolation.

The type of interpolation that is the easiest to use and understand is called *interpolation by proportional parts* or *linear interpolation*. Although it is only approximately true, we assume that a change in the angular measurement is proportional to a linear change in the value of the trigonometric function.

A graphical display of a typical error introduced by the assumption of linearity is shown in Figure 2.11 for a trigonometric function whose values are increasing from θ_1 to θ_2. The value for the given trigonometric ratio at θ_1 and θ_2 are assumed to be known from a table, and we assume no such tabulated value is known for the angle θ. Hence the necessity to use an interpolated value.

The interpolated value of the function at any θ between θ_1 and θ_2 is the distance from the x-axis to the point P, and the actual value is the distance from the x-axis to the point Q. Thus, the error in using linear inter-

FIGURE 2.11

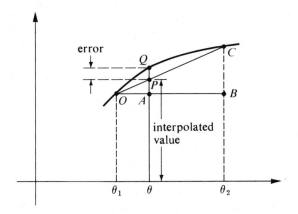

polation is the length of the line segment PQ. As long as the interval from θ_1 to θ_2 is relatively small and the difference in the known tabulated values is not too large, the error introduced will usually be acceptable.

Using Figure 2.11, we can derive an equation for determining the interpolated value in terms of tabulated values. Since triangles OPA and OCB are similar, the corresponding sides are proportional, and hence,

$$\frac{\overline{PA}}{\overline{CB}} = \frac{\theta - \theta_1}{\theta_2 - \theta_1}.$$

In words,

(2.6) $$\frac{\text{interpolated value at } \theta - \text{tabulated value at } \theta_1}{\text{tabulated value at } \theta_2 - \text{tabulated value at } \theta_1} = \frac{\theta - \theta_1}{\theta_2 - \theta_1}.$$

The next few examples will help you to learn the method of linear interpolation.

EXAMPLE 2.14

Use Table 2.3 and the method of linear interpolation to approximate $\sin 31°35'$.

Solution: From Table 2.3, we have $\sin 31° = 0.515$ and $\sin 32° = 0.530$. For an increase of $1°$ in the angle, the sine increases by $0.530 - 0.515 = 0.015$. Then for an angular increase of $35/60$ degree, the sine is assumed to increase by $(35/60)(0.015) = 0.009$. Because $\sin 31°35' > \sin 31°00'$, this correction is *added* to 0.515, giving $\sin 31°35' = 0.524$. The above discussion is summarized in the table below.

			Angle	Sine		
60	$\left[\vphantom{x}\right.$	35 $\left[\vphantom{x}\right.$	31°00'	0.515 $\left.\vphantom{x}\right]$ c		$\left.\vphantom{x}\right]$ 0.015
			31°35'	. . . .		
			32°00'	0.530		

$$\frac{c}{0.015} = \frac{35}{60}$$

$$c = \frac{35}{60}(0.015)$$

$$= 0.009$$

We round off c to three decimal places since this is a three place table. Thus,

$$\sin 31°35' = \sin 31° + 0.009$$
$$= 0.515 + 0.009$$
$$= 0.524.$$

EXAMPLE 2.15

Use Table 2.3 to approximate cos 52°15′.

Solution: The interpolation is shown below.

		Angle	Cosine	
60	15	52°00′	0.616	c
		52°15′	....	0.014
		53°00′	0.602	

$$\frac{c}{0.014} = \frac{15}{60}$$

$$c = \frac{15}{60}(0.014)$$

$$= 0.004$$

Since cos 52°15′ < cos 52°. The correction c is *subtracted* from 0.616. Thus,

$$\cos 52°15' = 0.616 - 0.004 = 0.612.$$

Naturally, an interpolated value will depend on the table used to perform the interpolation. We usually consider an interpolated value to be more accurate if a table with finer divisions is used.

EXAMPLE 2.16

Repeat the previous example using Table A in the Appendix.

Solution: From Table A, cos 52°10′ = 0.6134 and cos 52°20′ = 0.6111.

		Angle	Cosine	
10	5	52°10′	0.6134	c
		52°15′	....	0.0023
		52°20′	0.6111	

$$\frac{c}{0.0023} = \frac{5}{10}$$

$$c = \frac{5}{10}(0.0023)$$

$$= 0.0012$$

Since cos 52°15′ < cos 52°10′, we subtract the correction from 0.6134. Thus,

$$\cos 52°15' = 0.6134 - 0.0012 = 0.6122.$$

Interpolation is also used to approximate the measure of an unknown angle whose trigonometric ratio is given but does not correspond exactly to any of the tabulated values.

EXAMPLE 2.17

Use Table A to find angle θ if tan θ = 0.3.

Solution: From Table A, we find tan 16°40′ = 0.2994 and tan 16°50′ = 0.3026.

	Angle	Tangent	
10	c ⎡ 16°40′ ⎣ .... 16°50′	0.2994 ⎤ 0.0006 0.3000 ⎦ 0.3026	0.0030

$$\frac{c}{10} = \frac{0.0006}{0.0030}$$

$$c = \frac{0.0006}{0.0030}(10) = 2'$$

Adding this 2′ correction to 16°40′, we have $\theta = 16°42′$.

EXAMPLE 2.18

Use Table B to estimate the value of angle θ if cos $\theta = 0.8145$.

Solution: From the table, we have cos 0.61 = 0.8196 and cos 0.62 = 0.8139.

	Angle	Cosine	
0.010	c ⎡ 0.610 ⎣ 0.620	0.8196 ⎤ 0.0051 0.8145 ⎦ 0.8139	0.0057

$$\frac{c}{0.010} = \frac{0.0051}{0.0057}$$

$$c = 0.009$$

The correction c is rounded off to the nearest thousandth to be consistent with the accuracy of the table. Therefore, $\theta = 0.619$ radian.

EXERCISES FOR SECTION 2.5

By interpolation, find the value of the following trigonometric functions. Use Table A in the Appendix.

1. sin 38°38′
2. tan 15°32′
3. cos 26°55′
4. sec 42°15′
5. cot 38°45′
6. csc 70°5′
7. sin 65°26′
8. cos 15°9′
9. tan 50°43′

By interpolation, find the value of the following trigonometric functions. Use Table B in the Appendix.

10. tan 1.425
11. sin $\pi/8$
12. sin 1/8
13. cos $(\sqrt{3}/2)$
14. sec 1.083
15. tan $(\sqrt{2}/2)$
16. sin 0.531
17. cos 0.012
18. cot $(\sqrt{3}/2)$

Use Table A to find the value of θ in degrees and minutes to the nearest minute by interpolation.

19. sin $\theta = 0.776$
20. cos $\theta = 0.3000$
21. tan $\theta = 1.4$
22. cot $\theta = 2$
23. cos $\theta = 0.5108$
24. sin $\theta = 0.4804$
25. tan $\theta = 0.5$
26. cot $\theta = 0.5$
27. sec $\theta = 1.8$
28. tan $\theta = 0.3692$
29. csc $\theta = 4$
30. sin $\theta = 0.1234$

Use Table B to find the radian measure of θ to the nearest thousandth, where θ is a positive acute angle. Use interpolation when necessary.

31. $\sin \theta = 0.1365$ 32. $\cos \theta = 0.7976$ 33. $\tan \theta = 0.4040$

34. $\sin \theta = \pi/6$ 35. $\cos \theta = \pi/8$ 36. $\tan \theta = \pi/3$

37. $\sin \theta = 0.6541$ 38. $\tan \theta = 2$ 39. $\sin \theta = 0.105$

40. $\cot \theta = 0.9602$ 41. $\cos \theta = 0.7$ 42. $\sec \theta = 2$

2.6 SOLUTION OF RIGHT TRIANGLES

One of the principal uses of the trigonometric functions is to compute dimensions of right triangles. This may seem to be largely of academic interest, but, as you will see in this section, the types of applications can be quite modern.

A right triangle is composed basically of six parts, the three sides and the three angles. To *solve a triangle* means that we must find the values of each of these six parts. Of course, they are not all independent. For example, if two of the angles are known, so is the other one. If two of the sides of a right triangle are known, the remaining side is not of arbitrary length. The remaining side must be such that all three sides, together, satisfy the Pythagorean theorem.

When a right triangle is given, the six parts may be completely determined if you know two parts, at least one of which is a side.

(1) If an angle and one of the sides is given, then the third angle is simply the complement of the one given. The other two sides are obtained from the values of the known trigonometric functions.

(2) If two sides are given, the value of the third side is obtained from the Pythagorean theorem. The angles may then be determined by taking ratios of the sides which will uniquely determine the value of some trigonometric function.

Thus, in solving right triangles, we make use of the trigonometric functions, the Pythagorean theorem, and the fact that the two acute angles are complementary. You will usually find it to your advantage to make a rough sketch of the triangle. This will help you to determine what is given and which trigonometric functions must be used to find the unknown parts.

EXAMPLE 2.19

If, in Figure 2.12, angle $\alpha = 27°$, and the side adjacent is 6 units, solve the complete triangle.

FIGURE 2.12

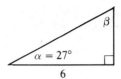

Solution: Since α and β are complementary, $\beta = 90° - 27° = 63°$. Also,

$$\tan \alpha = \frac{\text{side opposite } \alpha}{6},$$

and thus

$$\text{side opposite } \alpha = 6(\tan 27°)$$
$$= 6(.5095) = 3.057.$$

Hence, the hypotenuse is given by

$$\sqrt{6^2 + (3.057)^2} = \sqrt{36 + 9.35} = \sqrt{45.35} \approx 6.7.$$

EXAMPLE 2.20

A ladder of 20 feet is placed to reach a gable of a house 15 feet above the ground. What angle does the ladder make with the level ground?

FIGURE 2.13

Solution: The angle θ is the desired angle. From Figure 2.13, we see that

$$\sin \theta = \frac{\text{side opposite}}{\text{hypotenuse}} = \frac{15}{20} = \frac{3}{4} = 0.75.$$

From Table A, we see that $\sin 48°30' = 0.7490$ and $\sin 48°40' = 0.7509$. Hence, by interpolation,

Angle	Sine
48°30'	0.7490
...	0.7500
48°40'	0.7509

$$\frac{c}{10} = \frac{0.001}{0.0019}$$

$$c = 5'$$

we have $\theta = 48°35'$.

EXAMPLE 2.21

An engineer wishes to know the width of a river at a certain spot. He proceeds as follows: From a point directly across from a tree he walks 100 yards downstream. Then with his transit, he measures the angle that he now makes with the tree and finds it to be 55°. Find the width of the river.

FIGURE 2.14

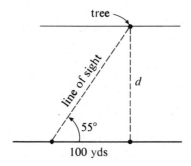

Solution: From Figure 2.14, you can see that this is a typical problem in right triangle trigonometry where the "side opposite" the 55° angle represents the unknown distance across the river. Thus,

$$\frac{d}{100} = \tan 55°$$

from which

$$d = 100(1.4281)$$
$$= 142.81 \text{ yards.}$$

EXAMPLE 2.22

In Figure 2.15, a radar station tracking a missile indicates the angle of elevation to be 20° and the line of sight distance (called the "slant range") to be 40 miles. Determine the altitude and horizontal range of the missile.

FIGURE 2.15

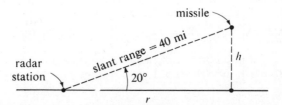

Solution: The altitude is

$h = (40)(\sin 20°)$
$\quad = 13.7 \text{ miles,}$

and the horizontal range is

$r = (40)(\cos 20°)$
$\quad = 37.6 \text{ miles.}$

EXAMPLE 2.23 ⤙

Show how the height of a mountain (or a building) can be obtained by measuring the angle of elevation at two different locations if you measure the distance between the two locations. Another variation on essentially the same problem reads: Two tracking stations d miles apart measure the angle of elevation of a weather balloon to be α and β respectively. Derive a formula for the altitude, h, of the balloon in terms of the angles α and β.

FIGURE 2.16

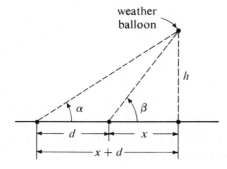

Solution: Figure 2.16 is a picture of the situation. We have two equations:

$$\tan \beta = \frac{h}{x},$$

$$\tan \alpha = \frac{h}{x + d}.$$

The only unknowns in these two equations are x and h. Solving the first for x, we obtain, $x = h \cot \beta$. Using this expression for x in the second equation, we have

$$\tan \alpha = \frac{h}{h \cot \beta + d}.$$

Solving this equation for h:

$h \cot \beta \tan \alpha + d \tan \alpha = h,$

$$h = \frac{d \tan \alpha}{1 - \cot \beta \tan \alpha}$$

$$= \frac{d}{\cot \alpha - \cot \beta}.$$

EXERCISES FOR SECTION 2.6

Solve the following right triangles.

1.

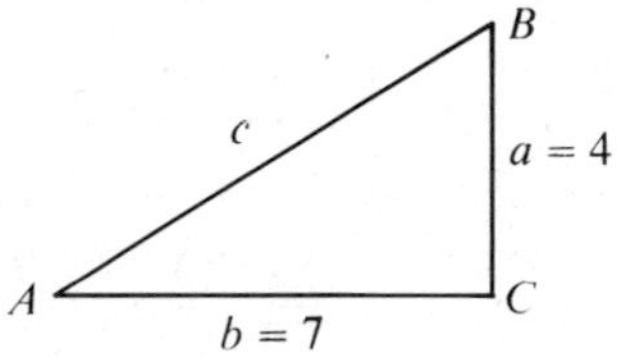

B

c

$a = 4$

A

C

$b = 7$

FIGURE 2.17

2.

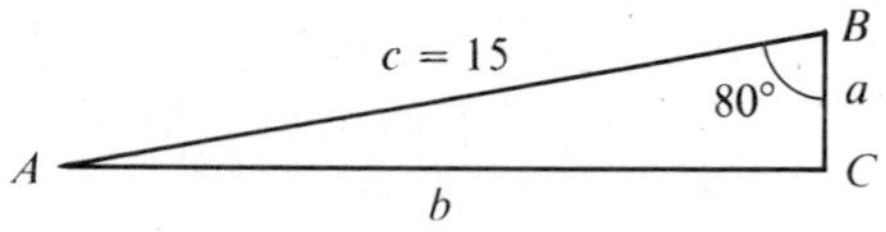

$c = 15$

B

a

80°

A

C

b

FIGURE 2.18

3.

B

$a = 12$

$c = 20$

C

b

A

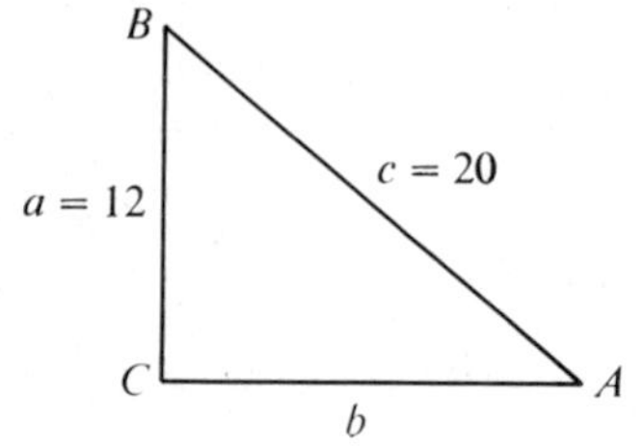

FIGURE 2.19

4.

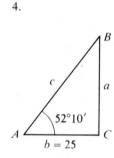

FIGURE 2.20

5.

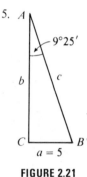

FIGURE 2.21

6. One side of a rectangle is half as long as the diagonal. The diagonal is 5 feet long. How long are the sides of the rectangle?

7. A man is walking along the prairie and stops to measure the angle of inclination to a high mountain. It measures 30°. The man then walks a mile toward the mountain and measures again. This time the angle of inclination is 45°. How high is the mountain?

8. In Japan, it is common to brace trees by means of poles. Suppose that a pole 14 feet long is used to brace a tree standing on level ground. Suppose that the end of the pole touching the ground is 10 feet away from the base of the tree. What is the size of the angle that the pole makes with the ground?

9. One morning, a man 6 feet tall wanted to know the time, but no one in the vicinity had a timepiece of any kind. The man knew that on that day the sun rose at 6:00 A.M. and would be directly overhead at noon. A friend measured the man's shadow which was 10 feet long. Approximately what time was it?

10. A television antenna stands on top of a house which is 20 feet tall. The angle subtended by the antenna from a point 500 feet from the base of the building is 15°. Find the height of the antenna.

11. In designing a steel truss for a bridge as shown in Figure 2.22, it is desired that BC shall be 10 feet and that AC shall be 7 feet. What angle will AB make with AC? With BC?

FIGURE 2.22

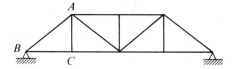

12. At noon in the tropics when the sun is directly overhead, a fisherman holds his 15 foot pole inclined 30° to the horizontal. How long is the shadow of the pole? How high is the tip of the pole above the level of the other end?

13. A boy walking southward along a straight road turns to the left at a point P and continues along a path which runs straight for a distance of 500 feet to a spring S. He then takes another path running at right angles to the road and returns to the road at point Q, which is 190 feet from P. Find the angle at P which the left hand path makes with the road and the angle at S between the two paths.

14. A flagpole broken over by the wind forms a right triangle with the ground. The angle that the broken part makes with the ground is 60°, and the distance from the tip of the pole to the foot is 40 feet. How tall was the pole?

15. The length of each blade of a pair of shears from the pivot to the point is 6 inches. When the points of the open shears are 4 inches apart, what angle do the blades make with each other?

16. In alternating current theory, the impedance, Z, resistance, R, and reactance, X, obey a right triangle relationship as demonstrated in Figure 2.23.

FIGURE 2.23

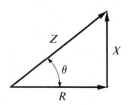

In this problem, solve for the missing components.

a. $R = 30$, $\theta = 60°$	b. $R = 30$, $Z = 60$
c. $Z = 100$, $\theta = 20°$	d. $R = 200$, $X = 100$
e. $Z = 1000$, $X = 800$	f. $X = 25$, $\theta = 30°$

2.7   COMPONENTS OF A VECTOR

The trigonometric ratios have many applications in physics, some of which you will learn in this chapter. In this section, we are interested in applications to *vectors*. Vectors are entities such as velocity and force which require both a magnitude and direction for their description. Graphically, we may think of a vector as an arrow whose length represents the magnitude of the vector and whose angle with a reference line represents its direction. For example, an automobile traveling 60 mph at an angle of 30° north of east can be represented by the vector diagram in Figure 2.24.

FIGURE 2.24   Velocity vector

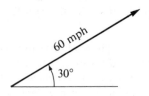

By convention, we usually place vectors with their initial point at the origin of a rectangular coordinate system and use the positive *x*-axis as the reference line for the direction angle. We will designate vectors in bold type. The magnitude of a vector **F** is denoted by $|\mathbf{F}|$.

The projections of the vector onto the *x* and *y* axes are called the *components* of the vector. We say that a vector is resolved into its *x* and *y* components called the horizontal and vertical components of **F** respectively. Resolving a vector into its *x* and *y* components is a simple problem of trigonometry. From Figure 2.25,

$$F_x = x \text{ component of } \mathbf{F} = |\mathbf{F}| \cos \theta,$$
$$F_y = y \text{ component of } \mathbf{F} = |\mathbf{F}| \sin \theta.$$

Obviously,

$$F_x^2 + F_y^2 = |\mathbf{F}|^2.$$

FIGURE 2.25   Components of a vector

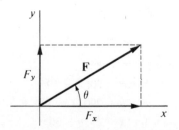

EXAMPLE 2.24

Find the horizontal and vertical components of a force vector of magnitude 15 lbs acting at an angle of 30° to the horizontal.

Solution:

$$F_x = |\mathbf{F}| \cos \theta = (15)(0.866) = 13$$
$$F_y = |\mathbf{F}| \sin \theta = (15)(0.5) = 7.5$$

EXAMPLE 2.25

Find the magnitude and direction of the vector whose components are shown in Figure 2.26.

FIGURE 2.26

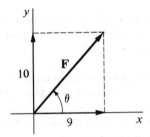

Solution: The magnitude is

$$|\mathbf{F}| = \sqrt{10^2 + 9^2} = \sqrt{181} \approx 13.4$$

The angle that the vector makes with the horizontal is determined from

$$\tan \theta = \frac{10}{9} = 1.111$$
$$\theta \approx 48°.$$

EXAMPLE 2.26

Two wires act on a weight as shown in Figure 2.27. If the tension in the

FIGURE 2.27

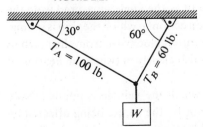
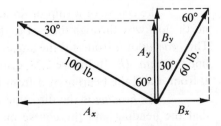

wires is measured at 100 lbs and 60 lbs, what is the cumulative horizontal and vertical effect?

Solution: The components of the 100 lb force are:

Horizontal: $A_x = 100 \cos 30° = 86.6$ lbs to the left;
Vertical: $A_y = 100 \sin 30° = 50.0$ lbs upward.

The components of the 60 lb force are:

Horizontal: $B_x = 60 \cos 60° = 30.0$ lbs to the right;
Vertical: $B_y = 60 \sin 60° = 52.0$ lbs upward.

Hence, the net force in each direction is:

Horizontal: $A_x - B_x = 86.6 - 30.0 = 56.6$ lbs to the left;
Vertical: $A_y + B_y = 50.0 + 52.0 = 102.0$ lbs upward.

EXAMPLE 2.27 ⟲

A boat that can travel at the rate of 3 mph in still water is pointed directly across a stream having a current of 4 mph. What will be the actual speed of the boat, and in which direction will the boat go?

Solution: In still water, the boat would go at right angles to the bank at the rate of 3 mph. But the current carries it downstream 4 units for every 3 units that it goes across. Thus, 4 is the X component of velocity and 3 is the Y component. Hence, the magnitude of the velocity is 5. Let θ be the angle that the velocity vector makes with the bank. Then

$$\tan \theta = \tfrac{3}{4},$$

and hence,

$$\theta \approx 37°.$$

In summary, the boat will travel at 5 mph at an angle of 37° with the bank.

2.8   APPLICATIONS TO NAVIGATION

In some special fields, it has long been the custom to measure direction clockwise directly from a meridian; in particular, in navigation the north line is the reference.

The *course* of a ship or an aircraft is the angle measured from the north clockwise through the east to the direction in which the ship is sailing. The *bearing* of B from A is the angle measured clockwise from the north to line segment AB. In Figure 2.28, distinguish clearly between the bearing of B from A and the bearing of A from B.

The *heading* is the direction in which the vehicle is pointed. Note that the heading and the course may not be the same, being affected by "winds aloft" in the case of aircraft and by the current in the case of ships.

FIGURE 2.28

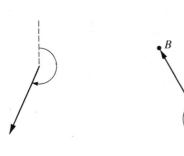

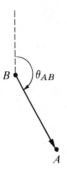

Course Angle   Bearing Angle   Bearing Angle
                  of B from A   of A from B

The heading vector, the course vector and the wind vector comprise a right triangle as shown in Figure 2.29.

FIGURE 2.29

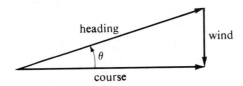

heading

wind

θ

course

EXAMPLE 2.28

A ship sails 15 miles on course 125°. It then sails 30 miles on course 215°. What course must it then sail to return to its starting point? Assume that the course and heading are identical.

FIGURE 2.30

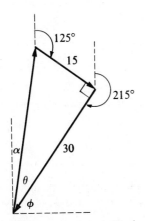

125°

15

215°

α

30

θ

ϕ

Solution: From Figure 2.30, we conclude that

$$\tan \theta = \frac{15}{30} = \frac{1}{2}$$

which means that

$$\theta = 26.5°$$

It is fairly easy to show that angle $\phi = 55°$. Hence the course angle α is given by

$$\alpha = 90° - 26.5° - 55°$$
$$= 8.5°.$$

EXAMPLE 2.29

Consider a flight from Chicago to Boston to be along a west to east direction, with an airline distance of 870 statute miles (see Figure 2.31). A light plane having an airspeed of 180 mph makes the round trip. How many flying hours does it take for the round trip with a constant southerly wind of 23 mph? What are the headings for the two parts of the round trip?

FIGURE 2.31

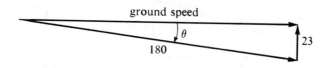

ground speed

θ

180   23

Solution: Let θ be the angle necessary to compensate for the wind. Then

$$\sin \theta = \frac{23}{180} = 0.128$$

and

$$\theta = 7°21'.$$

Hence the ground speed of the plane is

$$(\cos 7°21')(180 \text{ mi/hr}) = 179 \text{ mi/hr}.$$

The round trip will take

$$\frac{1,740 \text{ mi}}{179 \text{ mi/hr}} = 9.72 \text{ hr or about 9 hr 43 min}.$$

The heading for the trip from west to east is $90° + 7°21'$ or $97°21'$, and the heading for the trip from east to west is $270° - 7°21'$, or $262°39'$.

EXERCISES FOR SECTIONS 2.7–2.8

1. The north and west components of the velocity of an aircraft are 300 mph and 900 mph respectively. What is the magnitude of the velocity? What is the course of the aircraft?

2. Find the horizontal and vertical components of a force of 200 lbs acting at 50° to the horizontal.

3. A balloon is rising at the rate of 20 feet per second and is being carried horizontally by a wind that has a velocity of 25 mph. Find its actual velocity and the angle that its path makes with the vertical (60 mph = 88 fps).

4. A boat travels at the rate of 5 mph in still water and is pointed directly across a stream having a current of 3 mph. What will be the actual speed of the boat, and in which direction will the boat go?

5. In which direction must the boat of the preceding exercise be pointed so that the boat will go straight across the stream?

6. An airplane is flying at 500 mph with a windspeed of 150 mph at right angles to it. Compute the angle between course and heading.

7. A ship is sailing due east at a constant speed. At noon, a lighthouse is observed on a bearing of 180° at a distance of 15 nautical miles. At 1 P.M. the bearing is 210°. Find the rate at which the ship is sailing and the bearing of the lighthouse at 3 P.M.

8. How far north does an airplane traveling 1000 mph fly in 1 hour if it is on a course of 300°?

2.9   APPLICATIONS TO SPACE-RELATED SCIENCES

In space-related sciences, trigonometry has many important applications ranging from solutions of right triangles to problems of a complex analytical nature. The following material is, to a large extent, taken from *Space Mathematics*, published by the National Aeronautics and Space Administration and with permission of that organization. In Chapter 4, several similar applications are presented.

FIGURE 2.32

The weight of an astronaut on the moon is one-sixth his weight on Earth. This fact has a marked effect on such simple acts as walking, running, jumping, and the like. To study these effects and to train astronauts for working under lunar gravity conditions, scientists at NASA Langley Research Center have designed an inclined plane apparatus to simulate reduced gravity.

The apparatus consists of an inclined plane and a sling that holds the astronaut in a position perpendicular to the inclined plane as shown in Figure 2.32. The sling is attached to one end of a long cable that runs parallel to the inclined plane. The other end of the cable is attached to a trolley that runs along a track high overhead. This device allows the astronaut to move freely in a plane perpendicular to the inclined plane.

EXAMPLE 2.30 ⇌

Let W be the weight of the astronaut and θ the angle between the inclined plane and the ground. Make a vector diagram to show the tension in the cable and the force exerted by the inclined plane against the feet of the astronaut.

Solution: The weight of the astronaut is resolved into two components, one parallel to the inclined plane, the other perpendicular to it. These components are $W \sin \theta$ and $W \cos \theta$, respectively. To be in equilibrium, the component $W \sin \theta$ must be balanced by the tension in the cable, and the component $W \cos \theta$ must be balanced by the force exerted by the inclined plane (see Figure 2.33).

FIGURE 2.33

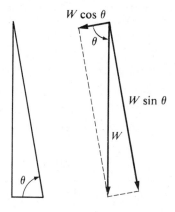

EXAMPLE 2.31 ⇌

From the point of view of the astronaut in the sling, the inclined plane is the ground and his weight; that is, the downward force against the inclined plane, is $W \cos \theta$. What is the value of θ required to simulate lunar gravity? What is the tension in the cable?

Solution: To simulate lunar gravity, we must have $W \cos \theta = W/6$. Thus,

$\cos \theta = 1/6 = 0.1667$
$\theta = 80°24'$ to the nearest minute.

The tension in the cable is

$W \sin 80°24' = 0.986 \, W$.

A parallel of latitude on the Earth's surface is a circle in a plane parallel to the equatorial circle. The latitude angle is the angle made by the radius from the midpoint of the equator and the equator itself (see Figure 2.34).

FIGURE 2.34

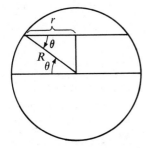

EXAMPLE 2.32

Show that the length of any parallel of latitude around Earth is equal to the equatorial distance around Earth times the cosine of the latitude angle.

Solution: By the definition of the cosine function,

$\cos \theta = r/R$ or $r = R \cos \theta$.

Let the length of the parallel of latitude be C_p. If C_e denotes the average circumference of Earth, then

$C_p = 2\pi r$
$\quad = 2\pi R \cos \theta$
$\quad = C_e \cos \theta$.

An interesting method of measuring the height of clouds is shown in Figure 2.35. A sweeping light beam is placed at point A, and a light source detector is placed at point B. The axis of the detector is maintained vertical, and the light beam is made to sweep from the horizontal ($\alpha = 0°$) to the vertical ($\alpha = 90°$). When the beam illuminates the base of the clouds directly above the detector, as shown in the figure, the detector is activated, and the angle α is read. Since d is known, the height h can be computed.

FIGURE 2.35

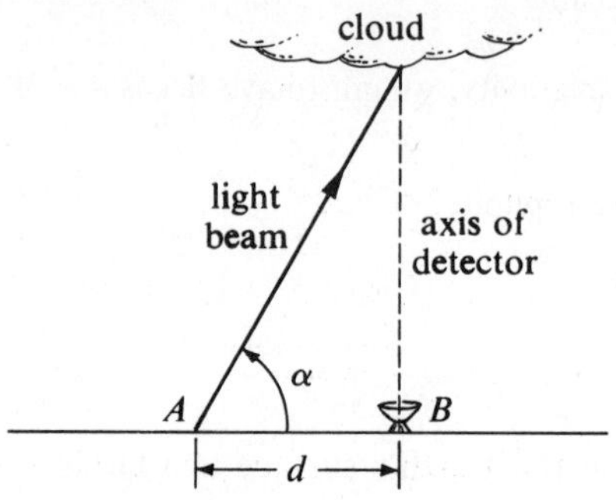

cloud

light
beam

axis of
detector

α

A B

$\longleftarrow d \longrightarrow$

EXAMPLE 2.33

If the height of the cloud is 2,050 feet and the distance d is 1,000 feet, compute the angle α.

Solution: Using the relation $\dfrac{h}{d} = \tan \alpha$, we have

$$2{,}050 \text{ feet} = (1{,}000 \text{ feet})(\tan \alpha)$$
$$2.050 = \tan \alpha.$$
$$\alpha = 64°.$$

The light source of the system must be reasonably close to the detector so that the illumination of the cloud above the detector is sufficiently strong to be detected. At many U.S. National Weather Service stations two beam sources are used, one 800 feet and the other 1600 feet from the detector. To have reliable readings, α may not exceed 85°.

Our last example of this section deals with design of a lunar lander. Surprisingly, it is an application of trigonometry that gives the necessary design goal for construction of the legs of the lander. Since three points determine a plane, spacecraft that are designed to land on the moon are designed with three legs.

EXAMPLE 2.34

A spacecraft designed to soft land on the moon has three feet that form an equilateral triangle on level ground and each of the three legs make an

FIGURE 2.36

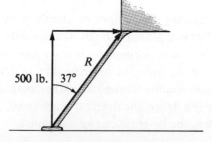

500 lb.   37° R

angle of 37° with the vertical. If the impact force of 1500 lbs is evenly distributed, find the force on each leg. (Figure 2.36.)

Solution: Consider one leg. Five hundred pounds is the vertical component of force **R** acting at 37° from the vertical. Thus,

$$\cos 37° = \frac{500 \text{ lb}}{|\mathbf{R}|},$$

$$|\mathbf{R}| = \frac{500}{\cos 37°}$$

$$= 626 \text{ lbs.}$$

EXERCISES FOR SECTION 2.9

1. What is the angle of the inclined plane used to simulate gravity for a 200 lb astronaut walking on an asteroid whose gravity is $\frac{1}{8}$ that of Earth?

2. If the plane used to simulate gravity were inclined at 60°, what percentage of the astronaut's weight would bear against the plane?

3. Find the length of the 30° parallel, north or south latitude. (Assume $C_e = 25,000$ miles.)

4. Determine the length of the Arctic Circle (66°33'N).

5. How far is it "around the world" along the parallel of 80°N latitude?

'6. Using the cloud altitude detector, compute the height of the cloud if the light source is 100 feet from the detector and the angle is 45°.

7. Find the angle α when clouds are 1000 feet high and the light source is located 100 feet from the detector.

8. If $\alpha = 85°$ and $d = 1600$ feet, compute the height of the cloud.

9. If $d = 1000$ feet, compute the difference of the height of intersection of the beam with the axis of the detector for $\alpha = 20°$ and $\alpha = 25°$.

10. Suppose the Moonlander is to be designed for an impact force of double that mentioned in Example 2.34. How does this affect the force on each leg?

11. In determining the height of a cloud, the light source 800 feet from the detector makes an angle of 85° with the horizontal. Find the corresponding angle for the light source at 1600 feet.

3

TRIGONOMETRIC
FUNCTIONS
FOR ANY ANGLE

3.1   EXTENDING THE BASIC DEFINITIONS

The definitions of the six basic ratios given in the preceding chapter are adequate as long as we limit the study of trigonometry to the solution of right triangles. In order to include some of the more important applications of trigonometry, it is necessary to generalize the basic definitions. We begin by redefining the six trigonometric functions in terms of an angle in standard position* in the coordinate plane.

FIGURE 3.1

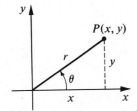

Consider an angle θ in standard position in the coordinate plane as shown in Figure 3.1. The terminal side of θ could obviously lie in any one of the four quadrants. Let P be a point on the terminal side of the angle θ, having coordinates (x, y), and let the distance from the origin to the point P be r. This line segment, called the *radius vector*, is always considered to have a positive length. By the Pythagorean theorem, we know that

$$r = \sqrt{x^2 + y^2}.$$

To be consistent with the definitions of Chapter 2, the trigonometric functions of the angle θ in Figure 3.1 must then be given by

(3.1)

$$\sin \theta = \frac{\text{ordinate of P}}{\text{radius vector}} = \frac{y}{r} \qquad \csc \theta = \frac{\text{radius vector}}{\text{ordinate of P}} = \frac{r}{y}$$

$$\cos \theta = \frac{\text{abscissa of P}}{\text{radius vector}} = \frac{x}{r} \qquad \sec \theta = \frac{\text{radius vector}}{\text{abscissa of P}} = \frac{r}{x}$$

$$\tan \theta = \frac{\text{ordinate of P}}{\text{abscissa of P}} = \frac{y}{x} \qquad \cot \theta = \frac{\text{abscissa of P}}{\text{ordinate of P}} = \frac{x}{y}.$$

Note that each of the functions is expressed in the terminology of the rectangular Cartesian coordinate plane. Using this terminology to state the definitions of the six trigonometric functions of an angle in standard position, the formulas of Equation 3.1 are the extensions of formulas in (2.1)

---

*Recall that an angle is in standard position if its initial side is along the positive *x*-axis. See Section 1.7.

to angles greater than 90°. To write the values for the trigonometric functions of any angle, we need to know the abscissa, ordinate, and radius vector of a point on the terminal side of the angle.

EXAMPLE 3.1

An angle θ in standard position has the point (6, 3) on its terminal side. Find the values of the six trigonometric functions of the angle θ. (See Figure 3.2.)

FIGURE 3.2

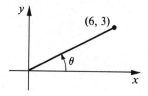

Solution: Using Equation 3.1 with $x = 6$, $y = 3$, and $r = \sqrt{6^2 + 3^2} = \sqrt{45} = 3\sqrt{5}$,

$$\sin \theta = \frac{y}{r} = \frac{3}{3\sqrt{5}} = \frac{1}{\sqrt{5}} = \frac{\sqrt{5}}{5} \qquad \csc \theta = \frac{r}{y} = \frac{3\sqrt{5}}{3} = \sqrt{5}$$

$$\cos \theta = \frac{x}{r} = \frac{6}{3\sqrt{5}} = \frac{2}{\sqrt{5}} = \frac{2\sqrt{5}}{5} \qquad \sec \theta = \frac{r}{x} = \frac{3\sqrt{5}}{6} = \frac{\sqrt{5}}{2}$$

$$\tan \theta = \frac{y}{x} = \frac{3}{6} = \frac{1}{2} \qquad \cot \theta = \frac{x}{y} = \frac{6}{3} = 2.$$

EXAMPLE 3.2

An angle θ in standard position has its terminal side passing through the point (3, −4). Find the six trigonometric functions of the angle. (See Figure 3.3.)

FIGURE 3.3

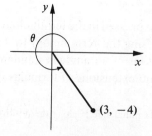

Solution: Using Equation 3.1 with $x = 3$, $y = -4$, and $r = \sqrt{3^2 + (-4)^2} = 5$,

$$\sin \theta = \frac{y}{r} = \frac{-4}{5} = -\frac{4}{5} \qquad \csc \theta = \frac{r}{y} = \frac{5}{4} = -\frac{5}{4}$$

$$\cos \theta = \frac{x}{r} = \frac{3}{5} \qquad \sec \theta = \frac{r}{x} = \frac{5}{3}$$

$$\tan \theta = \frac{y}{x} = \frac{-4}{3} = -\frac{4}{3} \qquad \cot \theta = \frac{x}{y} = \frac{3}{-4} = -\frac{3}{4}.$$

The interesting thing about Example 3.2 is that four of the six values are negative. Remembering that r is always positive, it should be clear to you that the signs of the trigonometric functions depend upon the signs of x and y.

The sine function is the ratio of y to r, which means that it is positive for angles in the first and second quadrant and negative for those in the third and fourth. This is because y is positive above the x-axis and negative below.

The cosine function, which is the ratio of x to r, is positive for angles in the first and fourth quadrants and negative in the second and third. This is because x is positive to the right of the y-axis and negative to the left.

The tangent function, which is the ratio of y to x, is positive in the first and third quadrants because y and x have the same signs in these quadrants. The tangent is negative in the second and fourth quadrants. The signs of the remaining three functions can be analyzed in the same way. Table 3.1 summarizes the results for all six functions.

TABLE 3.1

Quadrant	Positive Functions	Negative Functions
I	All	None
II	sine cosecant	cosine, secant tangent, cotangent
III	tangent cotangent	sine, cosine secant, cosecant
IV	cosine secant	sine, cosecant tangent, cotangent

The definitions of the trigonometric functions of any angle show that the functional values are completely determined by the location of the terminal side when the angle is in standard position. Thus, *coterminal angles have equal functional values.* For instance, since $30°$ and $390°$ are coterminal, $\sin 30° = \sin 390°$, $\cos 30° = \cos 390°$, $\tan 30° = \tan 390°$, etc. Thus, in finding values of trigonometric functions, we need only consider angles between $0°$ and $360°$.

An angle whose terminal side lies on a coordinate axis is called a *quadrantal angle*. Angles of 0°, ±90°, ±180°, etc. are examples. For these angles, one of the coordinates of a point on the terminal side must be zero. Since division by zero is undefinable, two of the six trigonometric functions will be undefined at each quadrantal angle.

EXAMPLE 3.3

Find the trigonometric functions of an angle θ whose terminal side passes through the point $(-1, 0)$ as shown in Figure 3.4.

FIGURE 3.4

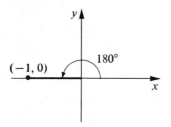

Solution: In this case $x = -1$, $y = 0$, and $r = 1$. Since $\theta = 180°$, we write

$$\sin 180° = \frac{y}{r} = \frac{0}{1} = 0 \qquad \csc 180° = \frac{r}{y} = \frac{1}{0} \text{ (undefined)}$$

$$\cos 180° = \frac{x}{r} = \frac{-1}{1} = -1 \qquad \sec 180° = \frac{r}{x} = \frac{1}{-1} = -1$$

$$\tan 180° = \frac{y}{x} = \frac{0}{-1} = 0 \qquad \cot 180° = \frac{x}{y} = \frac{-1}{0} \text{ (undefined)}.$$

The preceding example exhibits the values for a quadrantal angle of 180°, or one coterminal with it. The values of the other quadrantal angles can be found by a similar procedure and are listed for your reference in Table 3.2.

TABLE 3.2

Deg.	Rad.	$\sin \theta$	$\cos \theta$	$\tan \theta$	$\cot \theta$	$\sec \theta$	$\csc \theta$
0	0	0	1	0	undefined	1	undefined
90	$\pi/2$	1	0	undefined	0	undefined	1
180	π	0	-1	0	undefined	-1	undefined
270	$3\pi/2$	-1	0	undefined	0	undefined	-1

EXERCISES FOR SECTION 3.1

Find the values of the trigonometric functions at an angle in standard position whose terminal side passes through the given point.

1. $(2, 4)$ 2. $(-1, 5)$ 3. $(-9, 16)$ 4. $(3, 1)$

5. $(2, -7)$ 6. $(-1, -1)$ 7. $(3, -1)$ 8. $(1, -1)$

9. $(-\sqrt{3}, -1)$

10. Show that the values of the trigonometric functions are independent of the choice of the point P on its terminal side.

11. In which quadrants must the terminal side of θ lie for $\sin \theta$ to be positive? $\cos \theta$? $\tan \theta$?

12. Find the six trigonometric functions of $90°$ by noticing that $(0, 1)$ lies on the terminal side of the angle of $90°$ when it is placed in standard position.

13. Show that $\sin 60° = \sin 420°$.

14. Find the six trigonometric functions of $0°$. Use $(1, 0)$ as a point on the terminal side.

15. Find the six trigonometric functions of $270°$. Use $(0, -1)$ as a point on the terminal side.

16. For which values of θ are each of the trigonometric functions defined?

17. For which values of θ is $\sin \theta = 1$? For which values is $\cos \theta = 1$?

3.2   ELEMENTARY RELATIONS

From the definitions given in the previous section you can see that the same reciprocal relationships hold for the general trigonometric functions as in Chapter 2. Thus

$$\sin \theta = \frac{1}{\csc \theta}, \qquad \cos \theta = \frac{1}{\sec \theta}, \qquad \tan \theta = \frac{1}{\cot \theta}.$$

Also, the fact that $\tan \theta = y/x$ enables us to write

$$\tan \theta = \frac{y}{x} = \frac{y/r}{x/r} = \frac{\sin \theta}{\cos \theta}.$$

Because of this and the reciprocal relations, the values of all six trigonometric functions can be determined if you know the value of one of them and the quadrant of the terminal side of the angle. If the quadrant is not given, two sets of values are possible.

EXAMPLE 3.4

Given that $\tan \theta = -4/3$ and that θ in standard position has its terminal side in quadrant II, find the values of the other five trigonometric functions.

FIGURE 3.5

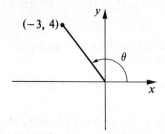

Solution: We choose a convenient point on the terminal side, in this case (−3, 4) as shown in Figure 3.5. (If we had been told to locate the point in quadrant IV, it would be the point (3, −4).) The desired trigonometric functions for the given angle are

$$\sin \theta = \frac{4}{5}, \qquad \cos \theta = \frac{-3}{5}, \qquad \cot \theta = \frac{-3}{4},$$

$$\sec \theta = \frac{5}{-3}, \qquad \csc \theta = \frac{5}{4}.$$

EXAMPLE 3.5

Given that $\cos \theta = -5/13$, find the values of the other trigonometric functions. (See Figure 3.6.)

FIGURE 3.6

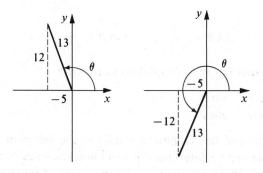

Solution: Since the quadrant is not specified, two angles between 0 and 2π will satisfy the given condition. One is in the second quadrant and the other in the third quadrant. For the second quadrant angle:

$$\sin \theta = \frac{12}{13}, \qquad \tan \theta = -\frac{12}{5}, \qquad \cot \theta = -\frac{5}{12},$$

$$\sec \theta = -\frac{13}{5}, \qquad \csc \theta = \frac{13}{12}$$

For the third quadrant angle:

$$\sin \theta = -\frac{12}{13}, \quad \tan \theta = \frac{-12}{-5} = \frac{12}{5}, \quad \cot \theta = \frac{-5}{-12} = \frac{5}{12},$$

$$\sec \theta = -\frac{13}{5}, \quad \csc \theta = -\frac{13}{12}.$$

3.3 APPROXIMATING THE VALUES OF THE TRIGONOMETRIC FUNCTIONS

Suppose that a radius vector *one* unit long is chosen for the terminal side of an angle θ in standard position, then

$$\sin \theta = \frac{y}{r} = \frac{y}{1} = y,$$

$$\cos \theta = \frac{x}{r} = \frac{x}{1} = x.$$

FIGURE 3.7

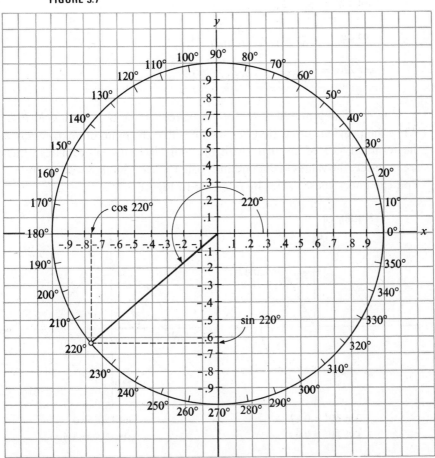

That is, the values of sin θ and cos θ are equal to the y and x coordinates of the end point of the unit radius vector. Thus, the coordinates of the points on a circle of radius 1 centered at the origin are identified with the trigonometric functions. In Figure 3.7, you see such a circle with angles from 0° to 360° marked off in 10° increments. The y coordinate of a point on the circle corresponds to sin θ and the x coordinate corresponds to cos θ. Using this circle, you can approximate the values of the trigonometric functions for any angle θ.

EXAMPLE 3.6

Find the values of the trigonometric functions of 220°.

Solution: With reference to Figure 3.7, we estimate sin 220° to be −0.64 and cos 220° to be −0.77. Therefore,

$$\sin 220° = -0.64$$

$$\cos 220° = -0.77$$

$$\tan 220° = \frac{\sin 220°}{\cos 220°} = \frac{-0.64}{-0.77} = 0.83$$

$$\cot 220° = \frac{1}{\tan 220°} = \frac{1}{0.83} = 1.2$$

$$\sec 220° = \frac{1}{\cos 220°} = \frac{1}{-0.77} = -1.3$$

$$\csc 220° = \frac{1}{\sin 220°} = \frac{1}{-0.64} = -1.6$$

A circle centered at the origin of radius one is called a *unit circle*. What the previous discussion has shown is that the point of intersection of the terminal side of an angle with the unit circle has coordinates which are precisely the values of the sine and cosine. Figure 3.8 shows six examples. You can check these values by referring to Figure 3.7.

FIGURE 3.8

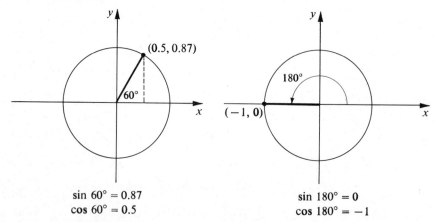

$$\sin 60° = 0.87$$
$$\cos 60° = 0.5$$

$$\sin 180° = 0$$
$$\cos 180° = -1$$

FIGURE 3.8 con't

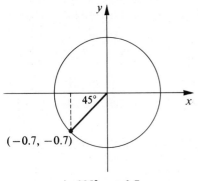

sin 225° = −0.7
cos 225° = −0.7

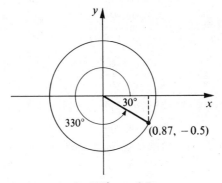

sin 330° = −0.5
cos 330° = 0.87

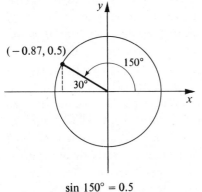

sin 150° = 0.5
cos 150° = −0.87

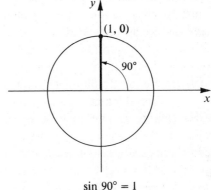

sin 90° = 1
cos 90° = 0

EXERCISES FOR SECTIONS 3.2 AND 3.3

Find the trigonometric functions at an angle θ that satisfies the given conditions.

1. $\tan \theta = \frac{3}{4}$ in Q I
2. $\sec \theta = -3$
3. $\tan \theta = \frac{3}{4}$ in Q III
4. $\tan \theta = \frac{1}{2}$
5. $\cos \theta = -1$
6. $\cot \theta = \pi$
7. $\sin \theta = 0$
8. $\sin \theta = \sqrt{3}/2$
9. $\sin \theta = -\frac{1}{2}$ in Q III
10. $\sin \theta = \frac{1}{5}$
11. $\tan \theta = 10$ in Q I
12. $\csc \theta = 2$

Use Figure 3.7 to approximate the values of the following trigonometric functions.

13. sin 70°

14. cos 35°

15. tan 10°

16. sin 125°

17. sin 155°

18. tan 130°

19. cos 165°

20. sin 110°

21. sin 215°

22. sin $\pi/4$

23. tan 345°

24. cos 345°

25. sec 250°

26. sin 300°

27. cos $2\pi/3$

28. csc 200°

29. sin 315°

30. tan $5\pi/4$

31. Use the definitions of the trigonometric functions for any angle to show that $\sin^2\theta + \cos^2\theta = 1$.

3.4 THE USE OF TABLES FOR ANGLES THAT ARE NOT ACUTE

As you learned in the previous section, the values of the trigonometric functions may be found for any angle. However, since graphical methods lack the precision needed for most applications, you must also learn how to use trigonometric tables to find values for angles greater than 90°. The process is not difficult, but it does require some explanation since trigonometric tables are traditionally tabulated from 0° to 90°.

Consider angles α, β, γ, and δ, in standard position, whose terminal sides each lie in a different quadrant as shown in Figure 3.9a. To find the values of the trigonometric functions for each of these angles, we must first find the measure of the acute angle made by the terminal side of the given angle and the x-axis. This angle is called the *reference angle* for the given angle. In Figure 3.9a, each reference angle is denoted with a prime and can be found by using the following rules.

(1) First Quadrant Angle: $\alpha' = \alpha$

(2) Second Quadrant Angle: $\beta' = 180° - \beta$

(3) Third Quadrant Angle: $\gamma' = \gamma - 180°$

(4) Fourth Quadrant Angle: $\delta' = 360° - \delta$ ·

FIGURE 3.9a

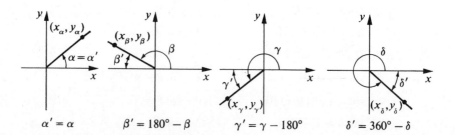

FIGURE 3.9b

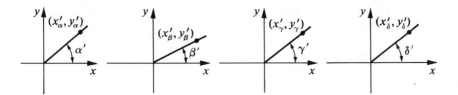

The reference angles found in Figure 3.9a are shown in standard position in Figure 3.9b. The coordinates of the intersection of the terminal side of each angle in Figure 3.9a with a circle of radius r are numerically equal (i.e., except for sign) to those obtained for the reference angles placed in standard position. It follows then that, except possibly for numerical sign, any trigonometric function of an angle has the identical value as the same function of the reference angle. For example, we find that

$$\tan \alpha = \frac{y_\alpha}{x_\alpha} = \frac{y'_\alpha}{x'_\alpha} = \tan \alpha'$$

$$\tan \beta = \frac{y_\beta}{x_\beta} = \frac{y'_\beta}{-x'_\beta} = -\tan \beta'$$

$$\tan \gamma = \frac{y_\gamma}{x_\gamma} = \frac{-y'_\gamma}{-x'_\gamma} = \tan \gamma'$$

$$\tan \delta = \frac{y_\delta}{x_\delta} = \frac{-y'_\delta}{x'_\delta} = -\tan \delta'.$$

Notice that these results agree with those given in Table 3.1 with respect to the numerical sign of the tangent in each quadrant.

Thus the functional values of the reference acute angle determine completely the values of the trigonometric functions of an angle in standard position. The algebraic sign is determined by the quadrantal location of the terminal side. In summary, to determine values of the trigonometric functions for any angle, proceed as follows:

(1) Determine the positive coterminal angle with measure between $0°$ and $360°$ corresponding to the given angle.

(2) Sketch the angle in standard position.

(3) Determine the reference acute angle.

(4) Find the value of the trigonometric function of the reference acute angle, usually from the Tables in the Appendix.

(5) The value of the trigonometric function of the reference acute angle is the same as the value of the trigonometric function of the given angle except perhaps for the sign. The sign is determined from the location of the terminal side of the given angle.

EXAMPLE 3.7

Find cos 145°20'. (See Figure 3.10.)

FIGURE 3.10

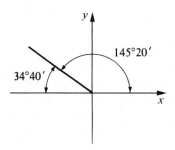

Solution: We see that 145°20' is a second quadrant angle, and, therefore, the reference angle is

$\theta' = 180° - 145°20' = 34°40'$.

The reference angle is indicated in the figure. Remembering that the cosine function is negative in the second quadrant, we have

cos 145°20' = −cos 34°40'
           = −0.8225. (Table A, Appendix)

EXAMPLE 3.8

Find tan 4. (See Figure 3.11.)

FIGURE 3.11

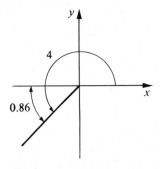

Solution: An angle of 4 radians lies in the third quadrant as shown in the figure. The reference angle is then

$\theta' = 4 - \pi = 4 - 3.14 = 0.86$.

Since the tangent function is positive in the third quadrant, we have

tan 4 = tan 0.86
    = 1.16.   (Table B, Appendix)

EXAMPLE 3.9

Find sin 1000 and sin 1000°.

Solution: Dividing 1000 by 6.28, we find that the angle of 1000 radians is coterminal with the angle of 1.48 radians. Since this is a first quadrant angle,

sin 1000 = sin 1.48
       = 0.9959.   (Table B)

Since $1000°/360° = 2$ with a remainder of 280°, the angle of 1000° is coterminal with a fourth quadrant angle. The reference acute angle is 80°. Hence,

sin 1000° = sin 280°
        = −sin 80°
        = −0.9848.   (Table A)

EXAMPLE 3.10

Find tan $100\pi/3$.

Solution: Dividing the given angle by 2π we obtain

$$\frac{100}{3}\pi \div 2\pi = 16 \text{ with a remainder of } \frac{4}{3}\pi.$$

Since $4\pi/3$ is a third quadrant angle and since the reference acute angle is $\pi/3$:

$$\tan\frac{100}{3}\pi = \tan\frac{4}{3}\pi$$

$$= \tan\frac{1}{3}\pi = \sqrt{3}.$$

EXAMPLE 3.11

Find $\cos(-527°)$.

Solution: This angle is coterminal with $-167°$ which in turn is coterminal with 193°. This angle, being in the third quadrant, has a reference acute angle of 13°. Hence,

$\cos(-527°) = \cos 193°$
         $= -\cos 13°$
         $= -0.9744.$

83

By considering cases where the angle θ has, in turn, its terminal side in each of the four quadrants, the following general relations may be shown:

$$\sin \theta = -\sin(-\theta) \qquad \cos \theta = \cos(-\theta)$$
$$\sin(\pi - \theta) = \sin \theta \qquad \cos(\pi - \theta) = -\cos \theta$$
$$\sin(\pi + \theta) = -\sin \theta \qquad \cos(\pi + \theta) = -\cos \theta$$
$$\sin(2\pi - \theta) = -\sin \theta \qquad \cos(2\pi - \theta) = \cos \theta.$$

You should not attempt to memorize this type of relation but rather be able to work out any of the results listed by the methods of this section.

EXERCISES FOR SECTION 3.4

Express the given trigonometric function in terms of the same function of a positive acute angle.

1. cos 125°
2. tan 94°
3. sin 225°
4. csc 252°28′
5. tan 1243°
6. tan 100
7. sec 10
8. sin 90
9. cos 45
10. cos 5

Evaluate:

11. sin 154°
12. sin 333°
13. tan 96°
14. cos 205°
15. sec 163°20′
16. tan 200°35′
17. cos 285°50′
18. csc 261°
19. sin 247°36′
20. cos 108°29′

Evaluate:

21. sin 100
22. tan −100
23. sin 4.22
24. cos 5.16
25. csc 20
26. sec (−4)
27. cot 1.335
28. tan −2.745
29. cos 3.01
30. cos −7.485

Evaluate:

31. $\sin 13\pi/3$
32. $\csc 41\pi/4$
33. $\tan 69\pi/6$
34. $\cos 19\pi/6$
35. $\tan 22\pi/3$
36. $\cot 27\pi/4$
37. $\cos 61\pi/2$
38. $\sin(-35\pi/6)$
39. $\sec 43\pi/6$
40. $\sin 1000\pi$

Find θ where $0 \leq \theta < 2\pi$.

41. $\sin \theta = -0.6157$, $\cos \theta > 0$
42. $\cos \theta = 0.4226$, $\tan \theta < 0$

43. $\cot \theta = 0.9004,$ $\qquad \sin \theta < 0$

44. $\cos \theta = 0.8241,$ $\qquad \sin \theta > 0$

45. $\tan \theta = -1.804,$ $\qquad \sec \theta > 0$

Find θ where $0 \le \theta < 360°$.

46. $\sin \theta = 0.4331,$ $\qquad \cos \theta < 0$

47. $\sin \theta = -0.4253,$ $\qquad \tan \theta < 0$

48. $\cos \theta = -0.8635,$ $\qquad \cot \theta > 0$

49. $\cot \theta = 3.0326,$ $\qquad \csc \theta < 0$

50. $\cos \theta = 0.9012,$ $\qquad \sec \theta > 0$

51. $\tan \theta = -6.8269,$ $\qquad \csc \theta > 0$

52. Complete Table 3.3 with the exact values of the trigonometric functions. Use your knowledge of the special angles. Do not use the Trigonometric Tables.

TABLE 3.3

Radians	Degrees	$\sin \theta$	$\cos \theta$	$\tan \theta$	$\cot \theta$	$\sec \theta$	$\csc \theta$
0	0	0	1	0	undef.	1	undef.
$\pi/6$	30°	1/2	√3/2	√3/3	√3	2√3/3	2
$\pi/4$	45°	√2/2	√2/2	1	1	√2	√2
$\pi/3$	60°	√3/2	1/2	√3	√3/3	2	2√3/3
$\pi/2$	90°	1	0	undef.	0	undef.	1
$2\pi/3$	120°	1/2	-√3/2	-√3/3	-√3	-2√3/3	2
$3\pi/4$	135°	√2/2	-√2/2	-1	-1	-√2	√2
$5\pi/6$	150°	√3/2	-1/2	-√3	-√3/3	-2	2√3/3
π	180°	0	-1	0	undef.	-1	undef.
$7\pi/6$	210°	-1/2	-√3/2	√3/3	√3	-2√3/3	-2
$5\pi/4$	225°	-√2/2	-√2/2	1	1	-√2	-√2
$4\pi/3$	240°	-√3/2	-1/2	√3	√3/3	-2	-2√3/3
$3\pi/2$	270°	-1	0	undef.	0	undef.	-1
$5\pi/3$	300°	-1/2	√3/2	-√3/3	-√3	2√3/3	-2
$7\pi/4$	315°	-√2/2	√2/2	-1	-1	√2	-√2
$11\pi/6$	330°	-√3/2	1/2	-√3	-√3/3	2	-2√3/3
2π	360°	0	1	0	undef.	1	undef.

4

THE SOLUTION
OF
OBLIQUE
TRIANGLES

4.1   OBLIQUE TRIANGLES

Any triangle which is not a right triangle is called *oblique*: hence, in an oblique triangle, none of the angles are equal to 90°. In Section 2.6, you learned that a right triangle is uniquely determined by two of its five unknown parts, if at least one of the two is the length of a side. In this chapter, we study conditions under which an oblique triangle is solvable and arrive at roughly the same conclusion: a knowledge of at least three of the six parts is necessary to solve the general triangle.

The three parts needed to solve a triangle are not completely arbitrary. For example, if the three angles of a triangle are given, no unique solution is possible. This is because many triangles can be constructed having these angles but different side lengths. All such triangles would be *similar* but not *congruent*.* As the chapter develops, you will discover other more subtle cases in which three parts assigned arbitrarily yield impossible or ambiguous situations. The question we wish to answer is "what information is necessary and sufficient to obtain a unique solution of an oblique triangle?" The answer is contained in the following theorems from plane geometry dealing with congruent triangles.

THEOREM 4.1

Two triangles are congruent if and only if two sides and the included angle of one are equal respectively to two sides and the included angle of the other.

THEOREM 4.2

Two triangles are congruent if and only if three sides of one are equal respectively to three sides of the other.

THEOREM 4.3

Two triangles are congruent if and only if two angles and the included side of one are equal respectively to two angles and the included side of the other.

From the perspective of solving oblique triangles, the preceding theorems say that a triangle is uniquely determined if:

Case 1:   Two sides and the included angle are given.

---

*The word *congruent* means of the same shape and size. Thus, two triangles that are congruent coincide exactly in all their parts if placed properly one upon the other.

Case 2: Three sides are given.

Case 3: Two angles and the included side are given.

A fourth case that arises in solving oblique triangles is important even though the information given does not necessarily yield a unique solution.

Case 4: Two sides and an angle opposite one of the sides are given.

This case is sometimes referred to as the *ambiguous* case since two triangles, one triangle, or no triangles may result from data given in this form. For instance, Figure 4.1 shows two triangles that can be obtained from the given information $a = 15$, $b = 20$, and $A = 20°$. In Section 4.4, we will discuss this case in detail. For the present, you should understand that it is possible for two noncongruent triangles to have the same "Case 4" data.

FIGURE 4.1

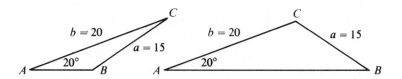

The theorems or *laws* that allow us to solve oblique triangles are derived in Sections 4.2 and 4.3 by subdividing a general oblique triangle into two right triangles. The following three examples will give you an idea of how this subdivision works. The proofs of the theorems are then generalizations of this procedure.

EXAMPLE 4.1

Solve triangle ABC with $b = 5$, $c = 3$, and $A = 30°$.

FIGURE 4.2

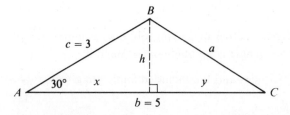

Solution: Drop a perpendicular from the vertex at B to the opposite side as in Figure 4.2. Then, it is easy to see that

$$h = 3 \sin 30° = 3\left(\frac{1}{2}\right) = \frac{3}{2},$$

$$x = 3 \cos 30° = 3\left(\frac{\sqrt{3}}{2}\right) = \frac{3\sqrt{3}}{2},$$

$$y = 5 - x = 5 - \frac{3\sqrt{3}}{2}.$$

The unknown side a is calculated from the Pythagorean theorem:

$$a^2 = h^2 + y^2$$
$$= \frac{9}{4} + \left(5 - \frac{3\sqrt{3}}{2}\right)^2$$
$$= \frac{9}{4} + 25 - 15\sqrt{3} + \frac{27}{4}$$
$$= 8.02.$$

Hence,

$$a = \sqrt{8.02} = 2.83.$$

The angle with vertex at C may be determined from the relation

$$\sin C = \frac{h}{a} = \frac{1.5}{2.83} = 0.5300$$

from which

$$C = 32°.$$

The remaining angle is determined from the fact that the sum of the three angles in a triangle is 180°. Thus,

$$B = 180° - 30° - 32°$$
$$= 118°.$$

EXAMPLE 4.2

Solve the triangle shown in Figure 4.3.

FIGURE 4.3

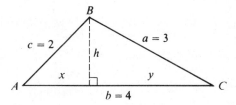

Solution: As in the previous example, we drop a perpendicular from the vertex at B. Then we have the following three equations:

$$h^2 + y^2 = 9,$$
$$h^2 + x^2 = 4,$$
$$x + y = 4.$$

Eliminating h^2 from the first two of these equations gives

$y^2 - x^2 = 5.$

Using the fact that $x = 4 - y$, we obtain

$y^2 - (4 - y)^2 = 5.$

After simplifying this, we obtain

$y = 2.62.$

Then, $x = 1.38$, and hence,

$$\cos A = \frac{x}{2} = \frac{1.38}{2} = 0.690, \qquad \cos C = \frac{y}{3} = \frac{2.62}{3} = 0.873.$$

From Table A,

$A = 46°22', \qquad C = 29°11'.$

Since the sum of the angles must be 180°,

$B = 180° - 46°22' - 29°11'$
$\quad = 104°27'.$

EXAMPLE 4.3

Find the length of the side c in the triangle of Figure 4.4.

FIGURE 4.4

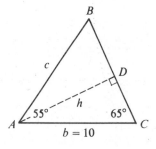

Solution: Drop a perpendicular from vertex A to the opposite side. Then since $B = 180° - 55° - 65° = 60°$, we conclude that

$h = 10 \sin 65°$ (from right triangle ACD)

and

$h = c \sin 60°$ (from right triangle ABD)

from which

$c \sin 60° = 10 \sin 65°$

or $\quad c = 10 \dfrac{\sin 65°}{\sin 60°}$

$$= 10\frac{0.9063}{0.8666}$$

$$= 10.46.$$

As a point of information, we note that the generalization of the technique exhibited in Examples 4.1 and 4.2 leads to what is known as the Law of Cosines (Section 4.2). Generalizing the procedure of Example 4.3 yields what is known as the Law of Sines (Section 4.3).

EXERCISES FOR SECTION 4.1

Solve the following triangles by subdividing them into two right triangles.

1. $A = 30°, B = 70°, c = 15$ 2. $a = 4, b = 7, c = 5$

3. $A = 50°, b = 3, c = 4$ 4. $A = 60°, b = 20, c = 30$

5. $A = 45°, C = 70°, b = 100$

6. Two planes leave New York at the same time, one flying to Boston at 300 mph the other to Cleveland at 400 mph. The angle between their flight plans is approximately 45°. How far apart are they at the end of two hours?

7. At a certain point, the angle of elevation of the top of a flagpole which stands on level ground is 30°. At a point 100 feet nearer the pole, the angle of elevation is 58°. How high is the pole?

8. From a helicopter the angles of depression of two successive milestones on a level road below are 15° and 30° respectively. Find the height of the helicopter.

9. In measuring the height of a bell tower with a transit set 5 feet above the ground, a student finds that from a point A the angle of elevation of the top of the tower is 45°. After moving the transit 50 feet in a straight line toward the tower, he finds the angle to be 60°. Find the height of the bell tower.

4.2   THE LAW OF COSINES

The *Law of Cosines* is a formula that enables us to solve an oblique triangle when two sides and the included angle are given, as shown in Case 1, or where three sides are given as shown in Case 2. The derivation of the Law of Cosines is a generalization of the methods used in Examples 4.1 and 4.2.

Consider any oblique triangle ABC; either of the triangles shown in Figure 4.5 will do. Drop a perpendicular from the vertex B to side AC or its extension. Call the length of this perpendicular h. In either case, we obtain $h = c \sin A$, and hence,

$$h^2 = c^2 \sin^2 A.$$

FIGURE 4.5   Law of Cosines

(a)

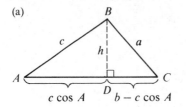

$c \cos A$ $b - c \cos A$

(b)

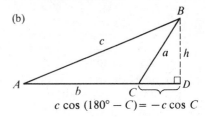

$c \cos (180° - C) = -c \cos C$

Or, using

$$\sin^2 A + \cos^2 A = 1,$$

we have

$$h^2 = c^2(1 - \cos^2 A).$$

Referring to Figure 4.5, we also have from right triangle BCD that

$$h^2 = a^2 - (b - c \cos A)^2.$$

Equating the right hand sides of the two preceding equations, we get

$$c^2(1 - \cos^2 A) = a^2 - (b - c \cos A)^2,$$
$$c^2 - c^2 \cos^2 A = a^2 - b^2 + 2bc \cos A - c^2 \cos^2 A.$$

By simplifying this expression, we arrive at

(4.1) $a^2 = b^2 + c^2 - 2bc \cos A.$

In a similar manner, it can be shown that

$$b^2 = a^2 + c^2 - 2ac \cos B$$

and

$$c^2 = a^2 + b^2 - 2ab \cos C.$$

Each of these formulas is a statement of the Law of Cosines. In words, it says that the square of any side of a triangle is equal to the sum of the squares of the other two sides minus twice their product and the cosine of the angle between them. If the angle is 90°, the Law of Cosines reduces to the Theorem of Pythagoras so that it is quite properly considered as an extension of that famous theorem.

The Law of Cosines gives the relationship between three sides and one of the angles of any triangle. Thus, if you are given any of these three parts, you can compute the remaining parts or show that such a triangle is impossible. For example, if three sides of a triangle are given, angle A may be found from Equation 4.1 by solving for $\cos A$ to obtain an alternate form of the Law of Cosines:

(4.2) $\cos A = \dfrac{b^2 + c^2 - a^2}{2bc}.$

Similar formulas may be obtained for cos *B* and cos *C*. Note that in this form the law says that the cosine of an angle may be found by computing a fraction, whose numerator is the sum of squares of the adjacent sides minus the square of the opposite side, and whose denominator is twice the product of the adjacent sides.

EXAMPLE 4.4

Solve the triangle with side $a = 5$, side $b = 6$ and angle $C = 60°$ as shown in Figure 4.6.

FIGURE 4.6

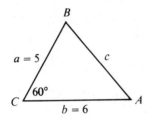

Solution:

$c^2 = a^2 + b^2 - 2ab \cos C$
$\quad = 25 + 36 - 60 \cos 60°$
$\quad = 31.$

Therefore,

$c = \sqrt{31} \approx 5.6.$

To solve for angle *A*, we use Equation 4.2 of the Law of Cosines:

$\cos A = \dfrac{b^2 + c^2 - a^2}{2bc}$

$\quad = \dfrac{36 + 31 - 25}{67}$

$\quad = \dfrac{42}{67} = 0.6268.$

Therefore,

$A = 51°11'.$

The remaining angle could also be found from the Law of Cosines, but since the sum of the angles is 180°,

$B = 180° - 60° - 51°11'$
$\quad = 68°49'.$

EXAMPLE 4.5

Two airplanes leave an airport at the same time; one going Northeast at 400 mph, and the other directly west at 300 mph. How far apart are they two hours after leaving?

FIGURE 4.7

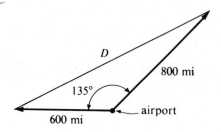

Solution: From Figure 4.7 and from the Law of Cosines,

$$D^2 = 600^2 + 800^2 - 2(600)(800)\cos 135°.$$

Notice that

$$\cos 135° = -\cos 45° = -0.707.$$
$$D^2 = 360,000 + 640,000 - (960,000)(-0.707)$$
$$= 1,678,720,$$
$$D \approx 1295 \text{ miles.}$$

EXAMPLE 4.6

In a steel bridge, one part of a truss is in the form of an isosceles triangle as shown in Figure 4.8. At what angles do the sides of the truss meet?

FIGURE 4.8

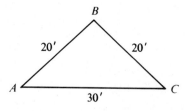

Solution:

$$\cos A = \frac{20^2 + 30^2 - 20^2}{(2)(20)(30)} = \frac{900}{1200} = 0.75.$$

Hence,

$$A = 41°25'.$$

This is also the value of angle C since the triangle is isosceles. Then,

$B = 180° - 82°50'$
$\quad = 97°10'.$

Suppose we had decided to use the Law of Cosines to find angle B. Then,

$$\cos B = \frac{20^2 + 20^2 - 30^2}{(2)(20)(20)} = \frac{800 - 900}{800} = -\frac{1}{8} = -0.125.$$

The fact that $\cos B$ is negative tells us that angle B is greater than $90°$ and less than $180°$. The angle whose cosine is 0.125 is $82°50'$, and therefore,

$B = 180° - 82°50' = 97°10'.$

This agrees with the previous result. Notice how the determination of angle B was affected by the fact that $\cos B$ was negative.

EXAMPLE 4.7

A satellite traveling in a circular orbit 1000 miles above Earth passes directly over a tracking station at noon. Assume that the satellite takes 2 hours to make an orbit and that the radius of Earth is 4,000 miles. Find the distance between the satellite and tracking station at 12:03 P.M.

FIGURE 4.9

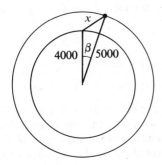

Solution: From Figure 4.9, we see that the angle β must be computed. Since the angular velocity is $3°$ per minute, a total of $9°$ is traveled in 3 minutes. Hence, $\beta = 9°$. By the Law of Cosines,

$x^2 = (4,000)^2 + (5,000)^2 - 2(4,000)(5,000) \cos 9°$
$\quad = 16 \times 10^6 + 25 \times 10^6 - 39.51 \times 10^6$
$\quad = 1.49 \times 10^6,$
$x = 1.22 \times 10^3 = 1,220$ miles.

Thus, the distance between the satellite and the tracking station is 1,220 miles.

The form of the Law of Cosines as in Equation 4.2 further allows you to see that information given on the sides of triangles is not arbitrary.

For example, if you are given that $a = 1, b = 3, c = 1$, then using Equation 4.2,

$$\cos A = \frac{(3)^2 + (1)^2 - (1)^2}{2(3)(1)} = \frac{9}{6} = \frac{3}{2}.$$

However, this is impossible since $|\cos A| \leq 1$. Hence, no such triangle exists.

EXERCISES FOR SECTION 4.2

In each of the following exercises, use the Law of Cosines to find the unknown side.

1. $a = 45, b = 67, C = 35°$ 2. $a = 20, b = 40, C = 28°$

3. $a = 10, b = 40, C = 120°$ 4. $b = 10, c = 10, B = 30°$

5. $b = 38, c = 42, A = 135°$ 6. $a = 3.49, b = 3.54, C = 5°24'$

In each of the following exercises, use the Law of Cosines to find the largest angle.

7. $a = 7, b = 6, c = 8$ 8. $a = 16, b = 17, c = 18$

9. $a = 18, b = 14, c = 10$ 10. $a = 3, b = 5, c = 6$

11. $a = 17, b = 25, c = 12$ 12. $a = 56, b = 67, c = 82$

In each of the following exercises, use the Law of Cosines to solve the triangles.

13. $a = 4, b = 1, C = 30°$ 14. $a = 5, b = 5, C = 60°$

15. $a = 120, b = 145, C = 94°25'$ 16. $a = 9, b = 7, c = 5$

17. $a = 2, b = 3, c = 4$ 18. $a = 5, c = 5, B = 28°$

19. In a triangular lot ABC, the stake that marked the corner C has been lost. By consulting his deed to the property, the owner finds that $AB = 80$ feet, $BC = 50$ feet, and $CA = 40$ feet. At what angle with AB should he run a line so that by laying off 40 feet along this line he can locate corner C?

FIGURE 4.10

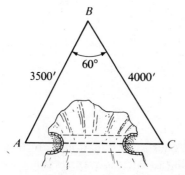

20. An airplane flying directly north toward a city C alters its course toward the northeast at a point 100 miles from C and heads for city B, approximately 50 miles away. If B and C are 60 miles apart, what course should the airplane fly to get to B?

21. In planning a tunnel under a hill, an engineer lays out the triangle ABC as shown in Figure 4.10 in order to determine the course of the tunnel. If $AB = 3500$ feet, $BC = 4000$ feet, and angle $B = 60°$, what are the sizes of the angles A and C and the length of AC?

22. If two forces, one of 500 pounds and the other of 400 pounds, act from a point at an angle of 60° with each other, what is the size of the resultant? (See Figure 4.11.)

FIGURE 4.11

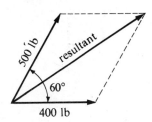

23. In order to measure the distance between two points, A and B, on opposite sides of a building, a third point C is chosen such that the following measurements can be made: $CA = 200$ feet, $CB = 400$ feet, and the angle ACB measures 60°. What is the distance between A and B?

24. Show that for any triangle ABC,

$$\frac{a^2 + b^2 + c^2}{2abc} = \frac{\cos A}{a} + \frac{\cos B}{b} + \frac{\cos C}{c}.$$

4.3 THE LAW OF SINES

You may have noticed that the Law of Cosines cannot be used to solve triangles for which two angles and one side are given. Triangles of this type may be solved using a formula known as the *Law of Sines*. This formula in conjunction with the Law of Cosines enables us to solve any triangle for

FIGURE 4.12   Law of Sines

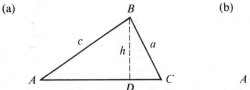
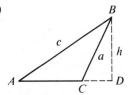

which we are given three parts, or at least to declare that no solution is possible.

Consider either triangle shown in Figure 4.12. By drawing a perpendicular h from the vertex B to side b or its extension, we see from Figure 4.12a that

$$h = c \sin A \text{ and } h = a \sin C.$$

Equating these two expressions, we get

$$c \sin A = a \sin C$$

or, rearranging terms,

$$\frac{a}{\sin A} = \frac{c}{\sin C}$$

In a similar manner, we can show that

$$\frac{a}{\sin A} = \frac{b}{\sin B}.$$

Hence,

$$(4.3) \qquad \frac{a}{\sin A} = \frac{b}{\sin B} = \frac{c}{\sin C}.$$

Equation 4.3 is called the *Law of Sines*. In words, it states that, in any triangle, the ratios formed by dividing the sides by the sine of the angle opposite them are equal.

Combinations of any two of the three ratios given in Equation 4.3 will yield an equation with four parts. Obviously, if we know three of these parts, we can find the fourth.

EXAMPLE 4.8

Given that $c = 10$, $A = 40°$, and $B = 60°$, find a, b, and C. (See Figure 4.13.)

FIGURE 4.13

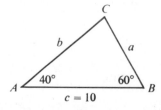

$c = 10$

Solution: We begin by observing that

$$C = 180° - (A + B) = 180° - (60° + 40°) = 80°.$$

Using the Law of Sines, we have

$$\frac{a}{\sin 40°} = \frac{10}{\sin 80°} \text{ or } a = \frac{10(0.6428)}{0.9848} = 6.53$$

and

$$\frac{b}{\sin 60°} = \frac{10}{\sin 80°} \text{ or } b = \frac{10(0.8660)}{0.9848} = 8.79.$$

EXAMPLE 4.9

A surveyor desires to run a straight line from A in the direction AB, as shown in Figure 4.14, but finds that an obstruction interferes with the line of sight. He, therefore, lays off the line segment $\overline{BX}$ for a distance of 150 feet in such a way that angle $ABX = 135°$ and runs XY at an angle of 75° with $\overline{BX}$. At what distance from X in this line should he take the point C from which to run a line CD in prolongation of AB?

FIGURE 4.14

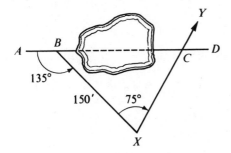

Solution: Since angle $CBX = 45°$, we have from the Law of Sines:

$$\frac{\sin 45°}{\overline{CX}} = \frac{\sin 60°}{150'}.$$

Hence,

$$\overline{CX} = \frac{\sin 45°}{\sin 60°} 150'$$

$$= \frac{\sqrt{2}/2}{\sqrt{3}/2} 150 = \frac{\sqrt{2}}{\sqrt{3}} 150 \approx \frac{1.414}{1.732} 150 = 122.4'.$$

The next two examples involve triangles in which two sides and an angle opposite one of them is given (Case 4). You will recall that data such as this may define one, two, or no triangles. For simplicity, we restrict the following discussion to examples in which a unique triangle is defined by the given data. The discussion of the ambiguous case is presented in the next section.

EXAMPLE 4.10

A satellite traveling in a circular orbit 1,000 miles above Earth is due to pass directly over a tracking station at noon. Assume that the satellite takes 2 hours to make an orbit and that the radius of Earth is 4,000 miles. If the tracking antenna is aimed 30° above the horizon, at what time will the satellite pass through the beam of the antenna? (See Figure 4.15.)

FIGURE 4.15

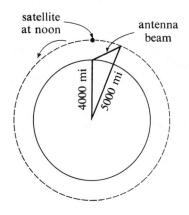
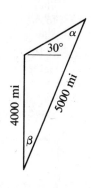

Solution: From the Law of Sines,

$$\frac{\sin \alpha}{4{,}000} = \frac{\sin 120°}{5{,}000},$$

$$\sin \alpha = \frac{4{,}000 \sin 120°}{5{,}000} = 0.693.$$

Hence,

$$\alpha = 43.9°,$$

and

$$\beta = 180° - (120° + 43.9°) = 16.1°.$$

Time between $\beta = 16.1°$ and $\beta = 0.0°$ is $(16.1°/360°)(120 \text{ min}) = 5.4 \text{ min}$. Thus, the satellite will pass through the beam of the antenna at $12{:}00 - 5.4$ minutes or $11{:}54.6$ A.M.

EXAMPLE 4.11

Consider a flight from Chicago to Boston and a return, which is a one-way airline distance of 870 miles. A light plane having an airspeed of 180 mph makes the round trip. How many flying hours will it take for the round trip with a constant southwest wind* of 23 miles per hour? What headings will the pilot use for the two parts of the trip?

---

*Wind direction is conventionally specified by the direction from which the wind is blowing. Thus, a "southwest wind" means the wind is blowing from the Southwest.

Solution: For the eastbound trip, shown in Figure 4.16, the Law of Sines is applied to determine θ.

FIGURE 4.16 Eastbound trip

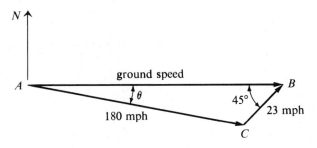

$$\sin \theta = \frac{23}{180} \sin 45° = 0.090$$

$$\theta = 5°10'.$$

Applying the Law of Sines again, the ground speed represented by $\overline{AB}$ is determined as follows:

$$\frac{\overline{AB}}{\sin C} = \frac{180}{\sin B} \quad \text{or} \quad \overline{AB} = \frac{\sin 129°50'}{\sin 45°} \cdot 180 \text{ mi/hr} = 197 \text{ mi/hr}.$$

Thus, the time required for the eastbound trip is

$$\frac{870 \text{ mi}}{197 \text{ mi/hr}} = 4.42 \text{ hr}.$$

For the westbound trip, shown in Figure 4.17, θ is again $5°10'$, and the ground speed is found by use of the Law of Sines.

FIGURE 4.17 Westbound trip

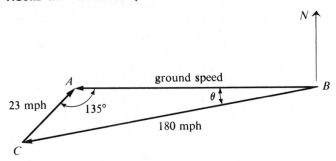

$$\overline{AB} = \frac{\sin 39°50'}{\sin 135°} \cdot 180 \text{ mi/hr} = 163 \text{ mi/hr},$$

and the time required is

$$\frac{870 \text{ mi}}{163 \text{ mi/hr}} = 5.34 \text{ hr}.$$

Thus, the total time for the round trip is 9.76 hours, or 9 hours 46 minutes. The heading for the eastbound trip is 90° + 5°10′, or 95°10′, and the heading for the westbound trip is 270° − 5°10′, or 264°50′.

EXAMPLE 4.12 ↵

A satellite C in an equatorial orbit is being tracked by two stations A and B both located on the Equator. (See Figure 4.18.)

FIGURE 4.18

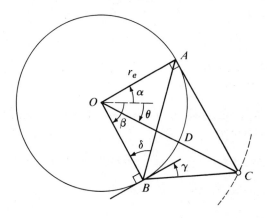

Given r_e = 4,000 miles, α = 30°, β = 50°, and γ = 30°, compute the height h of the satellite C above the Equator, by following these steps:

(a) Notice that triangle AOB is isosceles. Compute the length $\overline{AB}$ using the Law of Sines and the fact that 2δ = 180° − (α + β) = 100°.

(b) Compute the length $\overline{AC}$. The angle ABC at B is 90° − δ + γ = 70°, and angle OAC is a right angle.

(c) Now use the Pythagorean theorem in triangle ACO to compute the length $\overline{OC}$.

(d) Compute the altitude h.

Solution:

(a) 2δ = 180° − (α + β) = 180° − 80° = 100°
     δ = 50°

From the given data, it is known that angle AOB = α + β = 80°. (See Figure 4.19.) Now, by the Law of Sines,

$$\frac{\overline{AB}}{\sin 80°} = \frac{4,000 \text{ mi}}{\sin 50°},$$

$$\overline{AB} = \frac{(4,000 \text{ mi})(0.985)}{0.766}$$

$$= 5,140 \text{ mi.}$$

FIGURE 4.19

4.3 THE LAW OF SINES

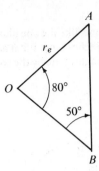

(b) We know that $\angle BAC = 90° - \angle OAB$, but $\angle OAB = \delta = 50°$. Thus, $\angle BAC = 40°$, and $\angle ACB = 180° - (70° + 40°) = 70°$. (See Figure 4.20.) We see that triangle $AB\overset{\frown}{C}$ is isosceles, therefore $\overline{AB} = \overline{AC} = 5,140$ miles.

FIGURE 4.20

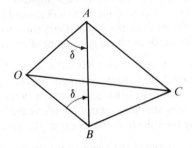

(c) By the Pythagorean theorem,

$$(\overline{OC})^2 = (\overline{AO})^2 + (\overline{AC})^2$$
$$= (4,000 \text{ mi})^2 + (5,140 \text{ mi})^2$$
$$= 16,000,000 \text{ mi}^2 + 26,420,000 \text{ mi}^2$$
$$= 42,420,000 \text{ mi}^2,$$
$$\overline{OC} = 6,513 \text{ mi}.$$

(d) The height h of the satellite above the Equator is represented by CD, which is

$$\overline{OC} - \overline{OD} = 6,513 \text{ mi} - 4,000 \text{ mi}$$
$$= 2,513 \text{ mi}.$$

EXERCISES FOR SECTION 4.3

Solve the oblique triangle in which:

1. $A = 32°, B = 48°, a = 10$ 2. $A = 60°, B = 45°, b = 3$

3. $A = 45°, a = 8, b = 5$ 4. $A = 75°, a = 20, b = 10$

103

5. $A = 30°, b = 10, a = 5$ 6. $A = 30°, b = 10, a = 20$

7. $A = 120°, a = 6, b = 5$

8. The crank and connecting rod of an engine, like the one illustrated in Figure 4.21, are respectively 12 inches and 40 inches long. What angle does the crank make with the horizontal when the angle made by the connecting rod is 12°?

FIGURE 4.21

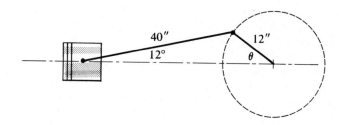

9. From a given position, an observer notes that the angle of elevation of the top of an antenna is 45°. After walking 1000 feet toward the base of the antenna up a slope of 30°, he finds the angle of elevation to be 75°. Find the vertical height of the antenna above each point of observation.

10. A satellite, traveling in a circular orbit 1500 miles above Earth, is due to pass directly over a tracking station at noon. Assume that the satellite takes 90 minutes to make an orbit and that the radius of the Earth is 4000 miles. If the tracking antenna is aimed 20° above the horizon, at what time will the satellite pass through the beam of the antenna?

11. In the previous exercise, determine the angle above the horizon that the antenna should be pointed so that its beam will intercept the satellite at 12:05 P.M.

12. Consider a flight from Miami to New York to be along a north-south direction with an airline distance of approximately 1000 miles. A jetliner, having an airspeed of 500 mph, makes the round trip. If there is a constant northwest wind of 100 mph, how long will it take for the round trip? What headings will the pilot use for the two parts of the trip?

4.4   THE AMBIGUOUS CASE

We are now ready to analyze how to solve those triangles for which the measure of two sides and an angle opposite one of them is given. For ease of discussion, suppose that two sides a and b and an angle A are given. As indicated previously, there may be one, two, or no triangles with these measurements.

$A < 90°$:   Perhaps the best way to make the situation clear, when angle A is acute, is to draw a figure. Let us construct a line segment having a length of b units along one side of angle A to locate the vertex C. Then it is obvious from Figure 4.22 that the length of side a determines whether there are one, two, or no triangles. In Figure 4.22a, only one triangle is possible since a > b. In Figure 4.22b, two triangles are possible by swinging an arc of length a from C so that it intersects side c at two points. In Figure 4.22c, the length of side a is such that it intersects side c at one point to form a single right triangle. Finally, in Figure 4.22d, the length of side a is too short to intersect side c and therefore no triangle can be formed.

FIGURE 4.22 Ambiguous case, $A \leqq 90°$

(a)
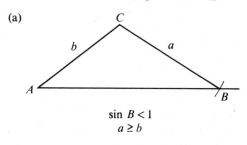
$$\sin B < 1$$
$$a \geq b$$

(b)
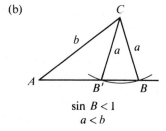
$$\sin B < 1$$
$$a < b$$

(c)
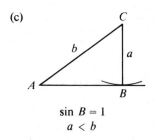
$$\sin B = 1$$
$$a < b$$

(d)
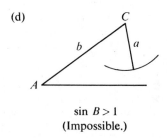
$$\sin B > 1$$
(Impossible.)

The situations, described graphically in Figure 4.22, can be stated analytically by solving

$$\frac{a}{\sin A} = \frac{b}{\sin B}$$

for sin B, and noting that:

(1) If $a < b$ and $\sin B > 1$, then B cannot exist, so there is no triangle.

(2) If $a < b$ and $\sin B = 1$, then $B = 90°$, so there is one right triangle.

(3) If $a < b$ and $\sin B < 1$, then two angles at B are possible; the acute angle B from the tables and the obtuse angle $B' = 180° - B$.

(4) If $a \geq b$, then there is only one triangle.

105

$A \geq 90°$: The case in which angle A is greater than or equal to 90° is much easier to analyze as shown in Figure 4.23. As you can see in Figure 4.23a, if $a \leq b$, there is no triangle. If $a > b$, there is one triangle as shown in Figure 4.23b.

FIGURE 4.23 Ambiguous case, $A > 90°$

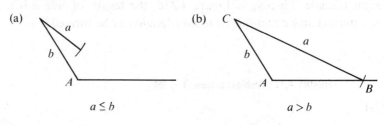

$a \leq b$ $a > b$

EXAMPLE 4.13

How many triangles can be formed if $a = 4$, $b = 10$, and $A = 30°$?

Solution: Using the Law of Sines, we have

$$\frac{\sin B}{10} = \frac{\sin 30°}{4} \text{ or } \sin B = \frac{10(0.5)}{4} = 1.25.$$

Since $\sin B > 1$, we conclude that no triangle corresponds to this given information. (See Figure 4.24.)

FIGURE 4.24

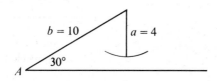

EXAMPLE 4.14

Verify that two triangles can be drawn for $a = 9$, $b = 10$, and $A = 60°$ and then solve each triangle.

Solution: Substituting the given values in the Law of Sines, we get

$$\frac{\sin B}{10} = \frac{\sin 60°}{9} \text{ or } \sin B = \frac{10(0.8660)}{9} = 0.9622.$$

Since $\sin B < 1$ and $a < b$, we conclude that there are two possible solutions. This is shown in Figure 4.25. One triangle is ABC and the other is $AB'C'$. From the table we find that

$B = 74°10'$.

FIGURE 4.25

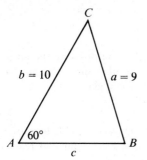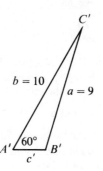

Therefore, angle B' is given by

$B' = 180° - B = 180° - 74°10' = 105°50'.$

To solve triangle ABC, we note that angle C is given by

$C = 180° - (A + B) = 180° - (60° + 74°10') = 45°50'.$

Hence,

$$\frac{c}{\sin 45°50'} = \frac{9}{\sin 60°} \text{ or } c = \frac{9(0.7173)}{0.8660} = 7.41.$$

Similarly in triangle $AB'C'$, we have

$C' = 180° - (A + B') = 180° - (60° + 105°50') = 14°10'.$

So,

$$\frac{c'}{\sin 14°10'} = \frac{9}{\sin 60°} \text{ or } c' = \frac{9(0.2447)}{0.8660} = 2.54.$$

EXAMPLE 4.15

Verify that only one triangle can be drawn for the case in which $b = 10$, $A = 60°$, and $a = 11$.

FIGURE 4.26

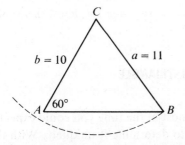

Solution: Figure 4.26 depicts the information given. Applying the Law of Sines, we get

$$\frac{11}{0.866} = \frac{10}{\sin B}$$

from which $\sin B = 0.7873$. Since the side opposite the given angle is greater than the side adjacent, there is only one solution. Notice that had we missed the fact that $a > b$, we would get

$$B = 51°55' \text{ and } B' = 128°05'.$$

However, the "solution" of $B' = 128°05'$ is impossible because a triangle with an angle of $60°$ and $128°05'$ cannot exist. Thus, we reach the same conclusion as before.

This last example shows how important it is to continually check that the information being given and being calculated is consistent and not giving impossible situations.

It is really not necessary to memorize the facts for the ambiguous case since, for any specific problem, the ambiguity or nonsolvability will become evident when the solution is attempted. For example, if in the course of solving a triangle, you find that $\sin B > 1$, this will mean that no triangle exists corresponding to the data given. If $\sin B < 1$, there are two angles which satisfy this particular inequality, but you will also have to watch for the limitation that the sum of the angles is less than $180°$.

EXERCISES FOR SECTION 4.4

In Exercises 1–5 state whether the triangle has one solution, two solutions, or no solutions, given that $A = 30°$, $b = 4$, and:

1. $a = 1$ 2. $a = 2$ 3. $a = 3$ 4. $a = 4$ 5. $a = 5$

For the following triangles, find all the unknown measurements or show that no such triangle exists.

6. $a = 20, b = 10, A = 35°40'$ 7. $a = 2, b = 6, A = 26°20'$

8. $a = 4, b = 8, A = 30°$ 9. $a = 15, c = 8, A = 150°$

10. $a = 50, b = 19, B = 22°30'$ 11. $b = 60, c = 74, B = 140°$

12. $a = 50, c = 10, A = 48°$ 13. $C = 28°, a = 20, c = 15$

14. $B = 40°, a = 12, b = 10$ 15. $A = 30°, b = 400, a = 300$

4.5   ANALYSIS OF THE GENERAL TRIANGLE

In Section 4.1, we mentioned that most of the time you could expect three parts of a triangle to be sufficient to determine it uniquely. With the aid of the two fundamental laws derived in Sections 4.2 and 4.3, we are now in a position to summarize the approach.

Case 1: *Two sides and an included angle given.*
Use the Law of Cosines to obtain the third side. A second angle may be obtained using either the Law of Cosines or the Law of Sines. The third angle is computed as 180° minus the sum of the other two.

Case 2: *Three sides given.*
Use the Law of Cosines to obtain one of the angles, preferably the largest one. A second angle may be obtained using either the Law of Cosines or Sines, and the third one may be obtained from the fact that the sum of the angles must be 180°.

Case 3: *Two angles and an included side given.*
The two given angles must have a sum less than 180° otherwise no such triangle is possible. Use the Law of Sines to determine the two unknown sides.

Case 4: *Two sides and a nonincluded angle are given.*
If two sides a and b and an angle A are given, there may be two, one, or no triangles with these measurements. A carefully drawn figure will usually make the situation clear. Analytically we have,

(1) If A is acute, then there is no, one, or two solutions depending on whether $a < b \sin A$, $a = b \sin A$ or $a > b \sin A$, unless $a \geq b$ in which case there is only one solution.

(2) If A is obtuse, there is no or one solution corresponding to $a \leq b$ or $a > b$.

EXERCISES FOR SECTION 4.5

Solve the following triangles, or show that no such triangle exists.

1. $A = 60°, B = 75°, a = 600$
2. $A = 75°, a = 120, b = 75$
3. $B = 15°, C = 105°, a = 4$
4. $A = 30°, b = 60, c = 50$
5. $a = 8, b = 2, c = 6$
6. $C = 15°, b = 15, c = 10$
7. $C = 30°, a = 300, b = 500$
8. $a = 2,000, b = 1,000, c = 2,500$
9. $B = 120°, a = 60, b = 25$
10. $B = 30°, a = 500, b = 400$
11. $B = 70°, a = 12, b = 6$
12. $A = 20°, a = 2, b = 3$

13. From a window 35 feet above the street, the angle of depression of the curb on the other side of the street is 15°, and, on the near side, the angle of depression is 45°. How wide is the street?

14. At successive milestones on a straight road leading to a mountain,

readings of the angle of elevation to the top of the mountain are made of 30° and 45° respectively. What is the line of sight distance to the top of the mountain from the nearest milestone?

15. Two forces, one of 75 lbs and the other of 100 lbs act at a point. If the angle between the forces is 60°, find the magnitude and direction of the resultant force. Give the direction as the angle between the resultant and the 100 lb force.

16. The air speed of a plane is 400 mph, and there is a 75 mph wind from the northeast at a time when the heading of the plane is due east. Find the ground speed and direction of the path of the plane.

4.6 AREA FORMULAS

As you undoubtedly know, the area of a triangle is given by one-half the product of any base with the corresponding altitude. With the use of the Law of Cosines and the Law of Sines, we can derive some equivalent expressions for area for which the height need not be specifically computed. In this section we examine three such formulas.

Consider the triangle in Figure 4.27. The altitude from the vertex B to side b is given by $h = c \sin A$. Hence, the area S is given by

(4.4) $S = \frac{1}{2}bc \sin A.$ AreA

This procedure could be repeated for each vertex to give equivalent formulas. In general: the area of a triangle is equal to one-half the product of the lengths of any two sides and the sine of the included angle.

FIGURE 4.27

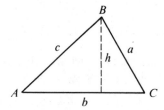

EXAMPLE 4.16

Find the area of a triangle with $a = 3$, $b = 5$, and $C = 48°$.

Solution: Since C is the angle between sides a and b, the area is given by

$S = \frac{1}{2}(3)(5) \sin 48°$

$\quad = (7.5)(0.7431)$

$\quad = 5.57.$

The expression for area may be altered further by using the Law of Sines. Since $c = b \sin C/\sin B$, we have from Equation 4.4:

(4.5) $\quad S = \dfrac{b^2}{2} \dfrac{\sin A \sin C}{\sin B}$.

Thus, the area may be calculated if one of the sides and two of the angles are given (since the third angle may then be easily found).

EXAMPLE 4.17

Find the area of a triangle with two angles and an included side given by 30°, 45°, and 3, respectively.

Solution: The remaining angle is 105°. Hence,

$$S = \frac{9}{2} \frac{\sin 30° \sin 45°}{\sin 105°},$$

$$S = \frac{9}{2} \frac{(1/2)(\sqrt{2}/2)}{0.9659}$$

$$= 1.64.$$

A formula for the area may be derived from Equation 4.4, which is an expression in terms of the length of the sides.

$$S^2 = \tfrac{1}{4}b^2c^2 \sin^2 A$$
$$= \tfrac{1}{4}b^2c^2(1 - \cos^2 A)$$
$$= (\tfrac{1}{2}bc)(\tfrac{1}{2}bc)(1 - \cos A)(1 + \cos A).$$

Now, from the Law of Cosines, we have that

$$\tfrac{1}{2}bc(1 + \cos A) = \tfrac{1}{2}bc\left(1 + \frac{b^2 + c^2 - a^2}{2bc}\right)$$
$$= \frac{2bc + b^2 + c^2 - a^2}{4}$$
$$= \frac{(b + c)^2 - a^2}{4}$$
$$= \frac{(b + c - a)(b + c + a)}{4}.$$

Similarly, we could obtain:

$$\tfrac{1}{2}bc(1 - \cos A) = \frac{(a - b + c)(a + b - c)}{4}.$$

Therefore, the expression S^2 becomes:

$$S^2 = \frac{(b + c - a)(a + b + c)(a - b + c)(a + b - c)}{16}$$

$$= \tfrac{1}{4}\sqrt{(b + c - a)(a + b + c)(a - b + c)(a + b - c)}.$$

Sometimes we express this formula in terms of the perimeter,

$$P = a + b + c:$$

(4.6) $$S = \tfrac{1}{4}\sqrt{P(P - 2a)(P - 2b)(P - 2c)}.$$

EXAMPLE 4.18

Find the area of the triangle whose sides are 2, 2, and 3.

Solution: Since the perimeter is 7, we have

$$S = \tfrac{1}{4}\sqrt{7(7 - 4)(7 - 4)(7 - 6)} = \tfrac{1}{4}\sqrt{63} = \tfrac{3}{4}\sqrt{7} = 1.99.$$

Note from Equation 4.6 that the lengths of the sides of a triangle are inherently limited. For example, no triangle exists whose sides are 1, 2, and 3.

EXERCISES FOR SECTION 4.6

Find the area of a triangle with the following measurements.

1. $a = 15, b = 5, C = 30°$ 2. $a = 12, b = 10, c = 5$

3. $a = 10, A = 60°, B = 45°$ 4. $a = 10, A = 120°, B = 30°$

5. $a = 3, b = 4, c = 5$

6.   Why is it impossible to express the area of a triangle only in terms of its angles?

7.   How are the areas of similar triangles related?

8.   Workmen need a triangular steel plate which is 12, 16, and 24 inches, respectively, along the sides. What is the area of such a plate?

9.   If the plate mentioned in Exercise 8 is made of sheet steel weighing 0.9 oz per square inch of surface, how much does the plate weigh?

10.   A farmer has a field shaped as shown in Figure 4.28. Find the area of the field.

FIGURE 4.28

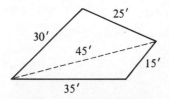

5

ANALYTICAL
TRIGONOMETRY

5.1   TRIGONOMETRIC FUNCTIONS OF REAL NUMBERS

In Chapter 3 the domain of the trigonometric functions was defined as the set of all angles with most of the discussion being limited to the interior angles of a triangle. Because of this restriction, you may think that the trigonometric functions are important only for angles less than 180°. This is far from the case; as a matter of fact, some of the important applications of trigonometry have nothing to do with triangles.

Previously we pointed out that modern trigonometry consists of two, more or less, distinct branches. The study of the six ratios and their application to problems involving triangles is one branch, called *triangle trigonometry*. The other branch is concerned with the general functional behavior of the six ratios, especially with respect to the nature of their variation and their graphs. This branch is often called *analytical trigonometry*.

In analytical trigonometry, we consider the six trigonometric functions to be functions of real numbers in addition to being functions of angles. The discussion in this section will show that the extension of the domain of the trigonometric functions to include real numbers is a rather simple matter of matching real numbers with the radian measure of angles.

Recall that the radian measure of an angle is the ratio of the length of the arc of a circle subtended by the angle to radius. Referring to Figure 5.1a, we have θ (radians) $= s/r$. If $r = 1$, the radian measure of a central angle θ is numerically equal to the arc length s. Thus, if a real number is represented by arc length on the *unit* circle, it will correspond directly to the radian measure of some central angle.

FIGURE 5.1   Representative arc

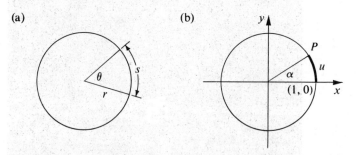

(a)

(b)

It is customary to represent a real number, u, on the unit circle by an arc beginning at (1, 0) and equal in length to the real number, as shown in Figure 5.1b. For positive real numbers this so-called *representative arc* is laid off in a counterclockwise sense while negative numbers are laid off in a clockwise direction. The point P at the terminal end of the representative arc determines an angle α in standard position. The angle with this radian measure is said to be *associated* with the real number u.

EXAMPLE 5.1

Sketch the angles associated with the real numbers 2, 2π, 10, -10, and 6.

Solution: See Figure 5.2.

FIGURE 5.2

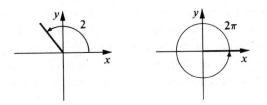

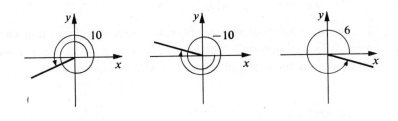

By using this natural association of real numbers with angles we may define the trigonometric functions for any real number u. If θ is the angle associated with u, then we have:

$$
\begin{array}{lll}
\sin u = \sin \theta, & \cos u = \cos \theta, & \tan u = \tan \theta \\
\sec u = \sec \theta, & \csc u = \csc \theta, & \cot u = \cot \theta.
\end{array}
$$

(5.1)

To clearly understand what has been accomplished by these definitions, you must keep in mind that u is a real number and not an angle. As a result of these definitions, the discussion of trigonometric functions can take place independent of the concept of angle.

The following example illustrates some practical applications of trigonometric functions in which the argument has nothing to do with angles.

EXAMPLE 5.2

(a) A weight hanging on a certain vibrating spring has a velocity described by $\sin 3t$. In this case, the argument is $3t$, where t is the time in seconds.

(b) The instantaneous voltage for certain electrical systems is given by $156 \sin 377t$, where t is the value of the time in seconds.

(c) The equation of motion of a shaft with flexible bearings is given by $x = x_0 \sin (\pi/2L)x$, where x and L are given in inches.

The trigonometric functions were defined in Chapters 2 and 3 as ratios of numerical values. The extension to real numbers shows how these same functions are related to a circle. Hence, the trigonometric functions are often called the "circular" functions.

Since it is customary not to write the dimension of radians, it will be impossible (and immaterial) to determine the distinction between an argument of a real number and an argument of an angle in radians. Care must be taken to indicate the correct units of measurements only if the argument is an angle measured in degrees, minutes, and seconds. Otherwise, by convention, the argument is an angle measured in radians or is a real number. Thus, sin 30° means the sine of an angle of 30° but sin 30 means either of the following two concepts, both of which give equal numerical values:

(1) the sine of an angle of 30 radians,

(2) the sine of the real number 30.

Using multiples of π to express real numbers in connection with the argument of a trigonometric function is common practice since it is then easy to determine the representative arc and the associated angle.

EXAMPLE 5.3

Evaluate $\sin \frac{1}{6}\pi$.

Solution: Note that we need not say "$\frac{1}{6}\pi$ what?" For in this case "$\frac{1}{6}\pi$" could mean either $\frac{1}{6}\pi$ radians, or merely the real number $\frac{1}{6}\pi$. Either way, the same numerical value is obtained. Hence,

$\sin \frac{1}{6}\pi = \frac{1}{2}.$

The values of the trigonometric functions for real numbers may be found from Table B in the Appendix, by considering the real number as an angle expressed in radians. Table B, may be interpreted either as a table of trigonometric functions of angles measured in radians or of trigonometric functions of real numbers.

EXAMPLE 5.4

Find cos 0.5, sin 1.4, tan 0.714.

Solution: From Table B,

cos 0.5 = 0.8776,
sin 1.4 = 0.9854.

Tan 0.714 must be approximated by interpolation. From Table B,

tan 0.71 = 0.8595,
tan 0.72 = 0.8771,

and thus,

$$\tan 0.714 \approx (0.4)(.0176) + 0.8595 \approx 0.8665.$$

The names of the trigonometric functions are the same regardless of whether they are being used in the sense of ratios or in a wider functional sense. However, by writing $y = \sin x$ or $f(x) = \sin x$ you will be obviously emphasizing the functional concept of the sine function. Further, do not be misled into believing that there is some convention for the letter used for the argument of the trigonometric functions; any convenient letter or symbol can be used for the argument. Thus, $\sin x$, $\sin u$, $\sin \theta$, $\sin v$, etc. all mean exactly the same thing. Only the application will tell you if the argument is to be interpreted as an angle or as a real number.

EXERCISES FOR SECTION 5.1

1. Sketch the angle associated with each of the following real numbers.

   a. 1   b. 2   c. 3   d. 10

   e. 3π f. -4 g. -4π h. $\frac{1}{3}\pi$

   i. $\frac{1}{3}$ j. $\frac{1}{2}$ k. $\frac{1}{2}\pi$

2. In calculus the ratio $\sin x/x$ is important. Using Table B find the values of the ratio for the following values of x.

   a. 0.3   b. 0.2   c. 0.1   d. 0.05   e. 0.01

   What value do you think $\sin x/x$ approaches as x approaches 0? What is $\sin x/x$ when $x = 0$?

3. If $f(x) = \sin x$ and $g(x) = \cos x$, show that $[f(x)]^2 + [g(x)]^2 = 1$.

If $f(x) = \sin x$, find the following values.

4. $f(\frac{1}{2}\pi)$ 5. $f(\pi)$ 6. $f(100)$ 7. $f(-10)$

8. $f(3\pi)$ 9. $f(\frac{1}{6}\pi)$ 10. $f(2\pi)$

If $g(x) = \cos x$, find the following values.

11. $g(0)$ 12. $g(\frac{1}{3}\pi)$ 13. $g(\pi)$ 14. $g(25)$

15. $g(-10)$ 16. $g(5\pi)$ 17. $g(5)$

18. If $f(x) = \sin x$, solve the equation $f(x) = 0$.

19. If $g(x) = \cos x$, solve the equation $g(x) = 0$.

20. For which values of x is $\sin x = 1$?

21. For which values of x is $\cos x = 1$?

22. For which values of x is $\sec x = \frac{1}{2}$?

23. Solve the inequality, $\cos x \leq \sec x$.

24. Solve the inequality $\sin x > \csc x$.

25. Solve the inequality $\sin x \geq 1$.

A *zero* of a function $f(x)$ is a value $x = x_0$ such that $f(x_0) = 0$.

26. What are the zeros of sin x?

27. What are the zeros of cos x?

28. Which pairs of functions have the same zeros?

5.2 PERIODIC PHENOMENA

Saying that something is *periodic* means that it repeats itself at regular intervals. Examples of periodic phenomena such as the motion of a pendulum, alternating current, or the vibration of a tuning fork, occur throughout the physical sciences. It may surprise you that it is often some variety of trigonometric function which plays the important role of describing this periodicity.

Before discussing the periodic nature of the trigonometric functions, we make the following precise but general definition of a periodic function.

DEFINITION 5.1

A function f is said to be *periodic* if there exists a number $p > 0$, such that

$$(5.2) \quad \mathbf{f(x) = f(x + p)}$$

for all x in the domain of the function. If there is a smallest number p for which this expression is true, then p is called the *period* (or the *fundamental period*) of the function.

FIGURE 5.3 Periodic functions

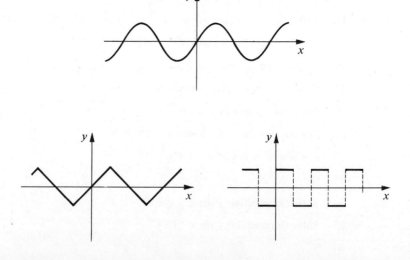

Figure 5.3 has several examples of periodic functions. A periodic function is completely described by giving its period and the functional values over one period interval. The next example illustrates this.

EXAMPLE 5.5

Sketch the graph of the function defined over $0 < x < 1$ by

$$f(x) = x^2$$

and which is periodic with period one.

Solution: We need only sketch the graph of the function on $0 < x < 1$, and then repeat this for all other intervals. (See Figure 5.4.)

FIGURE 5.4

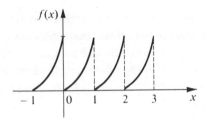

If a function is periodic with period p, then it is also periodic with period $2p, 3p, \ldots, np, \ldots$ that is,

$$f(x) = f(x + p) = f(x + 2p) = f(x + 3p) = \cdots = f(x + np) = \cdots$$

However, only the value p is considered to be *the* period of the function.

To see how trigonometry is used to describe periodic phenomena, you must first clearly understand the nature of the periodicity of the trigonometric functions. The general definitions of the trigonometric functions are given in terms of the values of the coordinates of the point of intersection of the terminal side of an angle with a circle of radius r. Since two angles that differ by 2π radians are coterminal, it follows that the values of the trigonometric functions are the same for any two numbers differing by 2π. Thus, we say that the trigonometric functions are periodic with period 2π. (In terms of degrees, the trigonometric functions have a period of $360°$.)

That 2π is the *smallest* period, and thus the fundamental period for the sine and cosine functions, is obvious merely by observing that the algebraic sign of these two functions does not repeat in any regular pattern for an interval less than 2π. The sign of the tangent function repeats every π, and, since the values of the tangent in the third and fourth quadrants are numerically the same as the values of the tangent in the first and second quadrants, the tangent function is periodic with fundamental period π. (In terms of degrees, the period of tan x is 180°). In summary, we have the following periodic conditions for the trigonometric functions:

$$\sin x = \sin(x + 2n\pi)$$
$$\cos x = \cos(x + 2n\pi)$$
$$\tan x = \tan(x + n\pi)$$
$$\cot x = \cot(x + n\pi)$$
$$\sec x = \sec(x + 2n\pi)$$
$$\csc x = \csc(x + 2n\pi)$$

where n is a positive integer.

5.3   BOUNDEDNESS

Most realistic physical phenomena tend to be constrained within certain limits or bounds. Phenomena of this type are described mathematically by functions called *bounded* functions. A function is bounded if there is a number M for which $|f(x)| \leq M$ for all x in the domain of the function. For example, the functions whose graphs are in Figure 5.5 are bounded while those of Figure 5.6 are unbounded.

FIGURE 5.5   Bounded functions

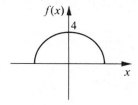
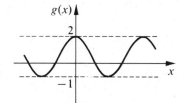

FIGURE 5.6   Unbounded functions

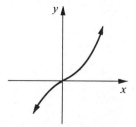
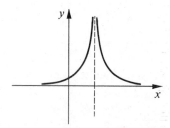

If a function is bounded, it will have many bounds. But in describing the property of boundedness, we will usually give the two extremes of the functional values, both the lower and upper. For example, the function f

of Figure 5.5a varies between 0 and 4 so we write $0 \leq f(x) \leq 4$, and, in Figure 5.5b, the boundedness of g is described by $-1 \leq g(x) \leq 2$.

A function which is bounded between c and d has a graph which is constrained between the lines $y = c$ and $y = d$, whereas the graph of an unbounded function is unlimited in its vertical extent.

Since the sine and cosine functions may be conceived as coordinates of points on a unit circle, and since these coordinates are constrained to lie between -1 and 1, the sine and cosine functions are bounded by -1 and 1. Thus the graphs of the sine and cosine lie between the lines $y = 1$ and $y = -1$. The other four trigonometric functions are unbounded and, therefore, have graphs that are unlimited in vertical extent.

5.4   EVEN AND ODD FUNCTIONS

Some functions have the property that their functional values are unchanged when the sign of the independent variable is changed. For example, if $f(x) = x^2$, then $f(-x) = (-x)^2 = x^2$. In general, we denote this by

$$(5.3) \quad f(x) = f(-x).$$

Functions which have this property are called *even* functions.

Likewise there are functions which obey the rule: when the sign of the independent variable changes, so does the sign of the dependent variable, leaving the numerical value unchanged. For example, if $f(x) = x^3$, then $f(-x) = (-x)^3 = -x^3$. This is written in general as

$$(5.4) \quad f(-x) = -f(x).$$

Functions which obey this rule are called *odd* functions.

The graphs of even and odd functions have an interesting kind of geometric symmetry.

(1)   For an even function, $y = f(x)$, if the point (x, y) is on the graph of the function, so is $(-x, y)$

Graphs which have this property are said to be *symmetric with respect to the y-axis*. (See Figure 5.7.)

FIGURE 5.7   Symmetry with respect to y-axis

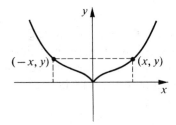

(2)   For odd functions, $y = f(x)$, if the point with coordinates (x, y) is on the graph of the function, so is the point $(-x, -y)$.

Graphs which have this property are said to be *symmetric with respect to the origin*. (See Figure 5.8.)

FIGURE 5.8   Symmetry with respect to origin

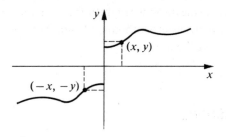

Usually, of course, a function is neither even nor odd, but, surprisingly it can be proved that every function may be expressed as the sum of an even and an odd function (see exercises).

By reasoning analogous to that of Section 3.4, we know that the trigonometric functions obey the following formulas:

$$\sin x = -\sin(-x)$$
$$\cos x = \cos(-x)$$
$$\tan x = -\tan(-x)$$
$$\cot x = -\cot(-x)$$
$$\sec x = \sec(-x)$$
$$\csc x = -\csc(-x)$$

and thus, the sine, tangent, cotangent and cosecant functions are odd functions while the cosine and cosecant functions are even functions. Thus, their graphs will have the symmetry properties described above.

5.5   VARIATION OF THE TRIGONOMETRIC FUNCTIONS

As an angle increases from 0 to 2π, its terminal side rotates in a counter-clockwise sense and during this interval all values of the trigonometric functions are included. Table 5.1 shows the variation of the values of the trigonometric functions during one revolution of the terminal side. Because of the property of periodicity the pattern in Table 5.1 will be repeated for $2\pi \leq x \leq 4\pi$, for $4\pi \leq x \leq 6\pi$, etc.

TABLE 5.1   Variation of the Trigonometric Functions

When x increases from:	$\sin x$	$\cos x$	$\tan x$	$\cot x$	$\sec x$	$\csc x$
0 to $\dfrac{\pi}{2}$	increases from 0 to 1	decreases from 1 to 0	increases from 0 to become unbounded	decreases from large values to 0	increases from 1 to become unbounded	decreases from large values to 1
$\dfrac{\pi}{2}$ to π	decreases from 1 to 0	decreases from 0 to -1	increases from unbounded negative to 0	decreases from 0 to unbounded negative numbers	increases from large negative numbers to 1	increases from 1 to large positive values
π to $\dfrac{3\pi}{2}$	decreases from 0 to -1	increases from -1 to 0	increases from 0 to become unbounded	decreases from large values to 0	decreases from -1 to unbounded negative numbers	increases from large negative numbers to -1
$\dfrac{3\pi}{2}$ to 2π	increases from -1 to 0	increases from 0 to 1	increases from unbounded negative numbers to 0	decreases from 0 to unbounded negative numbers	decreases from large positive numbers to 1	decreases from -1 to unbounded negative numbers

5.6   GRAPHS OF THE SINE AND COSINE FUNCTIONS

The graph of any function $y = f(x)$ is the set of points in the plane with the coordinates $(x, f(x))$. In general, such a graph is obtained by tabulating values and plotting the corresponding points. But, in particular cases, the task can be significantly shortened by using some general properties of the given function.

We first examine the graphs of the sine and cosine functions considered as functions of *real numbers*. These two graphs have significance in many unrelated areas and the job of graphing either the sine or the cosine is almost identical.

We first summarize some of the analytical properties previously discussed.

(1)   Both $\sin x$ and $\cos x$ are *bounded*, above by 1 and below by -1. Thus, the graph of each of the functions lies between the lines $y = 1$ and $y = -1$.

(2)   Both $\sin x$ and $\cos x$ are *periodic* with period 2π. Thus only one interval of length 2π need be considered when graphing the two functions under consideration. Outside this interval, the graph repeats itself.

123

(3)   The sine function is odd, i.e., $\sin x = -\sin(-x)$. Thus the graph of $\sin x$ is symmetric about the origin.
The cosine function is even, i.e., $\cos x = \cos(-x)$. Thus, its graph is symmetric about the y-axis.

(4)   Sin $x = 0$ for $x = 0$, $\pm\pi$, $\pm 2\pi$, $\pm 3\pi$ etc.
Cos $x = 0$ for $x = \pm\frac{1}{2}\pi$, $\pm\frac{3}{2}\pi$, $\pm\frac{5}{2}\pi$, etc.
In each case, these are the intercepts on the x-axis.

(5)   The numerical values of the sine and cosine functions for $0 \leq x \leq \frac{1}{2}\pi$ correspond to the values of $\sin x$ and $\cos x$ in the first quadrant. The other three quadrants yield values numerically the same with, at most, a difference in sign.

To obtain the specific graph we need a reasonable number of points for $0 < x < \frac{1}{2}\pi$. Then a smooth curve can be drawn through these points after which the general properties may be used to obtain the remainder of the curve. Usually we emphasize certain "special" points corresponding to $x = 0, \frac{1}{2}\pi, \pi, \frac{3}{2}\pi$, and 2π.

Figure 5.9 shows the graph of one period of the sine function. To the left of the graph is a circle of radius 1. The sine function has values numerically equal to the y coordinates of points on this circle. This figure displays the relationship between points on the unit circle and corresponding points on the graph of the function.

FIGURE 5.9

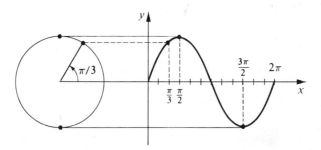

Figure 5.10 shows a graph of several periods of the function $y = \sin x$, and Figure 5.11 shows several periods of the cosine function. The preceding graphs have been terminated, but, in reality, they continue indefinitely. To emphasize this indefinite continuation, a statement of the period is often included with the graph.

The graph of the sine function is sometimes called a *sine wave* or a *sinusoid*. A *cycle* is the shortest segment of the graph which includes one period. The *frequency* of the sinusoid is defined to be the reciprocal of the period. It represents the number of cycles of the sine function in each unit interval. The graphs of the sine and cosine functions should clearly demonstrate their boundedness, their periodicity, and their zeros.

FIGURE 5.10

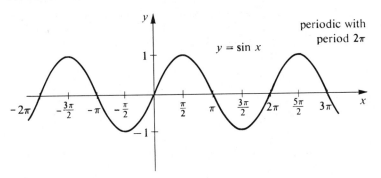

periodic with
period 2π

$y = \sin x$

FIGURE 5.11

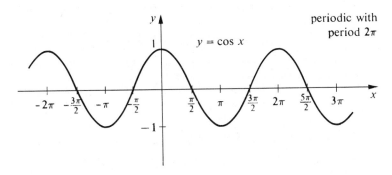

periodic with
period 2π

$y = \cos x$

You might also notice that the graphs of the sine and cosine functions are quite similar. In fact, the graph of the cosine function may be obtained by shifting the graph of the sine function $\pi/2$ units to the left. (See Exercise 13.)

EXERCISES FOR SECTIONS 5.2–5.6

1. Give the domain and range for each of the six trigonometric functions.

2. For which values is the tangent function undefined?

3. Discuss the symmetry of the graphs of the sine and cosine functions with respect to the line $x = \frac{1}{2}\pi$. With respect to $x = \pi$.

4. Determine which of the following statements are true.
   a. If $-\pi/2 < x_1 < x_2 < 0$, then $\sin x_1 < \sin x_2$.
   b. If $2\pi < x_1 < x_2 < 5\pi/2$, then $\cos x_1 < \cos x_2$.
   c. If $3\pi < x_1 < x_2 < 4\pi$, then $\cos x_1 < \cos x_2$.
   d. If $2\pi < x_1 < x_2 < 3\pi$, then $\sin x_1 < \sin x_2$.

125

5. Discuss the symmetry of the tangent and cotangent functions.

6. Discuss the symmetry of the cosecant and secant functions.

7. Sketch the graphs of $y = x$ and $y = \sin x$ on the same axes and convince yourself that $\sin x < x$, if $x > 0$.

8. Determine which of the following define even functions.

    a. $x + x\sqrt{2}$ b. $\csc x$

    c. $x \sin x$ d. $x \cos x$

    e. $\sin x \cos x$ f. $\sin^2 x$

9. Which of the functions of Exercise 8 describe odd functions?

10. a. Show that the product of two even functions is even.

     b. Show that the product of two odd functions is even.

     c. Show that the product of an even and an odd function is odd.

11. What can you say about the symmetry of the graphs of the following functions?

    a. $\sin x \cos x$ b. $x \sin x$ c. $x \cos x$

12. Show that every function may be expressed as the sum of an even and an odd function.

13. Prove the last statement of Section 5.6.

14. The function $f(x) = |\sin x|$ is called the *full wave rectified sine wave*. Make a sketch of its graph. What is its period?

15. Make a sketch of the *half-wave rectified sine wave* defined by

$$f(x) = \sin x, \qquad 0 \le x \le \pi$$
$$= 0, \qquad\quad \pi \le x \le 2\pi$$

and periodic with period 2π.

16. Sketch the function $f(x) = |\cos x|$.

5.7   MORE ON THE SINE AND COSINE FUNCTIONS

Instead of $\sin x$ and $\cos x$, you will frequently encounter functions like $\sin 2x$, $4 \cos x$, $\cos (x + \pi)$, etc. Modified functions of this type are easy to graph if you are familiar with the properties of $\sin x$ and $\cos x$.

    In practice we must deal with the basic trigonometric functions altered in three ways:

(1) multiplication of the function by a constant

(2) multiplication of the argument by a constant

(3) addition of a constant to the argument

We will use $y = \sin x$ to determine each of these cases with the understanding that the results apply also to $y = \cos x$.

(1)   *Multiplication of the Function by a Constant*

We have seen that the values of the sine function oscillate between $+1$ and -1. If we multiply $\sin x$ by a positive constant A, we then write $y = A \sin x$. Since

$$-1 \leq \sin x \leq 1$$

it follows that, when multiplying through by A,

$$-A \leq A \sin x \leq A.$$

The value of A is called the *amplitude* of the sine wave. If A is greater than one, the amplitude of the basic sine wave is increased; if A is less than one, the amplitude is decreased. Sometimes A is called the *maximum*, or *peak* value of the function. Figure 5.12 shows the graph of $y = A \sin x$ for $A = 1, 1/2,$ and 2.

FIGURE 5.12

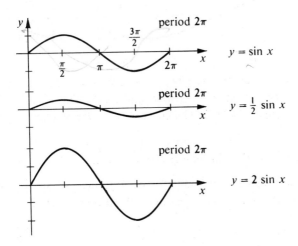

(2)   *Multiplication of the Argument by a Constant*

If $\sin x$ has its argument multiplied by a constant B, the function becomes $\sin Bx$. The graph of this function remains sinusoidal in form but since the argument is Bx and since the sine function repeats itself for every increase in the argument of 2π, we can see that one period of $\sin Bx$ is contained in the interval

$$0 \leq Bx \leq 2\pi,$$

that is, for

$$0 \leq x \leq \frac{2\pi}{B}.$$

Therefore, multiplying the argument by a constant has the effect of altering the period to be $2\pi/B$. Thus, the period of $\sin 2x$ is π. The period of $\sin \frac{1}{2}x$ is 4π. Graphically, increasing B has the effect of squeezing the sine curve together like an accordion. Decreasing B has the effect of pulling it apart. (See Figure 5.13.)

FIGURE 5.13

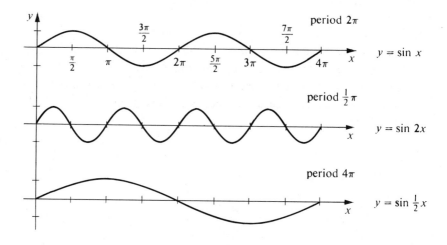

On a fundamental interval, the sine curve is 0 at $x = 0$, π, and 2π. The curve $y = \sin Bx$ is 0 at $x = 0$, π/B, and $2\pi/B$. The basic sine curve reaches a maximum at $y = \pi/2$. The curve $y = \sin Bx$ reaches a maximum at $y = \pi/(2B)$.

(3) Addition of a Constant to the Argument

The addition of a constant to the argument of $\sin x$ is written $\sin(x + C)$. The constant C has the effect of shifting the graph of the sine

FIGURE 5.14

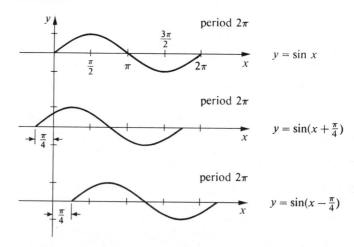

function to the right or to the left. Notice that $\sin(x + C)$ is zero when $x + C = 0$, that is for $x = -C$. This value of x for which the argument of the sine function is zero is called the *phase shift*. If C is positive the shift is to the left and if C is negative, the shift is to the right. Figure 5.14 shows three sine waves with phase shifts of 0, $\frac{1}{4}\pi$, and $-\frac{1}{4}\pi$.

In the more general case, the effects of changes in amplitude, period and phase shift are all combined. The function

$$y = A \sin(Bx + C)$$

has an amplitude of A, a period of $2\pi/B$ and a phase shift corresponding to the value of x given by $Bx + C = 0$, that is $x = -C/B$. Figure 5.15 shows a graph of the basic sine curve and the graph of $y = 3 \sin(2x - \frac{1}{3}\pi)$.

FIGURE 5.15

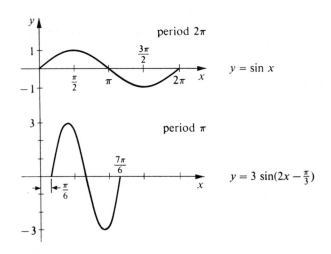

EXAMPLE 5.6

Sketch the graph of $y = 2 \sin(\frac{1}{3}x + \frac{1}{9}\pi)$.

Solution: The amplitude of the graph is 2, the period is $2\pi/(1/3) = 6\pi$, and the phase shift is $-\frac{1}{3}\pi$. (See Figure 5.16.)

FIGURE 5.16

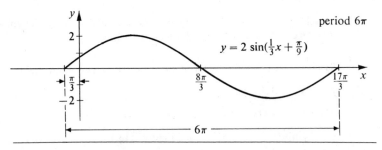

In all cases, the distinctive shape of the sine curve remains unaltered. This basic shape is expanded or contracted vertically by the multiplication by the amplitude constant A, expanded or contracted horizontally by the constant B, and shifted to the right or left by the constant C.

A similar analysis could be made for the cosine function. We will not discuss in detail the function $y = A \cos(Bx + C)$, but the constants A, B, and C alter the basic cosine function in a manner quite similar to that described for the sine function.

EXAMPLE 5.7

Sketch the graph of $y = 3 \cos(\frac{1}{2}x + \frac{1}{4}\pi)$.

Solution: The amplitude is 3 since the basic cosine function is multiplied by 3. The period is $2\pi/(1/2) = 4\pi$. The phase shift is found from the equation $\frac{1}{2}x + \frac{1}{4}\pi = 0$, that is for $x = -\pi/2$. Hence the phase shift is $\pi/2$ units to the left. The graph of this function and the basic cosine function are shown in Figure 5.17.

FIGURE 5.17

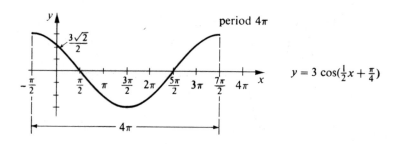

If the function is multiplied by a negative constant, you may use one of the relationships of Section 3.4 to put the expression into a more standard form.

EXAMPLE 5.8

Sketch $y = -2 \sin(3x + 1)$ by first expressing it in the form $y = A \sin(Bx + C)$ where A and B are both positive.

Solution: By using the fact that $\sin x = -\sin(-x)$, we have that

$y = 2 \sin(-3x - 1)$.

Then, since $\sin(x + \pi) = \sin(-x)$, we have

$y = 2 \sin[(3x + 1) + \pi]$.   (See Figure 5.18.)

FIGURE 5.18

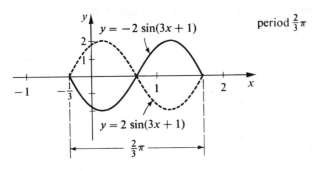

$y = -2\sin(3x + 1)$

period $\frac{2}{3}\pi$

$y = 2\sin(3x + 1)$

$\frac{2}{3}\pi$

Another method of graphing the above function is to initially sketch the function $y = 2\sin(3x + 1)$, and then reflect that graph in the x-axis.

EXERCISES FOR SECTION 5.7

Sketch the graphs of the given functions. In each case, give the amplitude, period, and phase shift.

1. $y = 3\sin x$
2. $y = \frac{1}{2}\sin x$
3. $y = \cos(x + \frac{1}{3}\pi)$
4. $y = 2\sin\frac{1}{3}x$
5. $y = 2\cos(\frac{1}{2}x - \frac{1}{2}\pi)$
6. $y = \sin 2(x + \frac{1}{6}\pi)$
7. $y = \cos(2x + \pi)$

Write the following expressions in the form $A\sin(Bx + C)$ where A and B are positive, and then sketch.

8. $-\sin(x + 1)$
9. $-\sin(-2x + 3)$
10. $-\sin(2\pi x + \frac{1}{2})$
11. $3\cos(2\pi x + \pi)$
12. $-\cos(\pi x + 1)$

Write the equation of the following sinusoids.

13.
14.

FIGURE 5.19

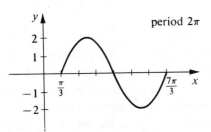

period 2π

FIGURE 5.20

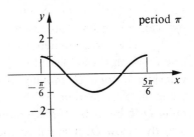

period π

131

15.

FIGURE 5.21

16.

FIGURE 5.22

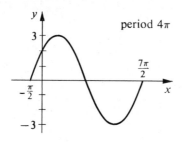

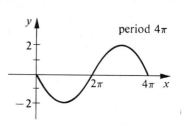

17. The equation for the voltage drop across the terminals of an ordinary electric outlet is given approximately by

$$E = 156 \sin(110\pi t).$$

Sketch the voltage curve for several cycles.

18. If B is small the equation $y = \sin Bx$ approximates the shape of ocean waves. Sketch several cycles of an ocean wave

$$y = \sin \frac{1}{20} \pi x.$$

19. It is always possible to express functions of the type $A \sin(Bx + C)$ and $A \cos(Bx + C)$ in the form $A' \sin(B'x + C')$ where A', B', and C' are positive. Prove this.

20. How are the graphs of $y = \sin(-t)$ and $y = \sin(t)$ related?

21. How are the graphs of $\cos(-t)$ and $\cos(t)$ related?

22. How are the graphs of $\sin(t)$ and $\cos(\frac{1}{2}\pi - t)$ related?

5.8 HARMONIC MOTION

Imagine an object hanging on a spring as shown in Figure 5.23. If the object is pulled down and released, it will oscillate up and down about the rest or *equilibrium* point. Assuming there is no frictional force, this oscillatory motion will continue indefinitely. Vibratory motion of this type is called *simple harmonic motion*. Simple harmonic motion can be described mathematically using sine and cosine functions.

The correspondence between simple harmonic motion and the co-sine function is established by referring to the circle drawn in Figure 5.23. Consider a point Q, moving at a constant angular velocity of ω rad/sec along the circumference of the circle and suppose the initial position of the point Q to be $(r, 0)$. If P is a point on the horizontal diameter of the circle, directly below Q, it is called the *projection* of Q on the diameter. As Q

FIGURE 5.23 **Simple harmonic motion**

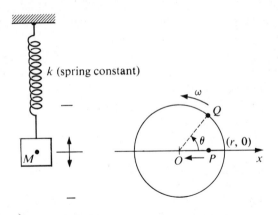

revolves, the point P moves back and forth along the diameter of the circle in the same way that the object attached to the spring moves, the only difference being that the movement of the object is vertical and that of P is horizontal. Thus, the point P moves with simple harmonic motion. If we can represent the motion of point P by a mathematical function, we have analytically described simple harmonic motion.

The displacement of P from its starting point at any time t is the distance $OP = x$. If θ represents the angle which OQ makes with the horizontal diameter, we have

$$x = r \cos \theta.$$

More commonly we write this expression as a function of time by replacing θ with ωt, to get

$$x = r \cos \omega t.$$

as the description of the simple harmonic motion.

If the object is displaced through a distance y from its equilibrium position and released with an initial velocity, its motion is described by the equation

$$y = A \cos(\omega_0 t + C)$$

where ω_0 is called the *natural angular frequency* and is given by the formula $\omega_0 = \sqrt{k/M}$. In this formula, k is a constant called the spring constant, and M is the mass of the object. The period of the motion is $2\pi/\omega_0$. The amplitude and phase shift are determined from the "initial conditions," that is, the initial displacement and initial velocity. The fact that the motion is harmonic means that the mass will oscillate about its equilibrium point with bounds set by the constant A with frequency $\omega_0/2\pi$ cycles per second. In the more realistic physical case the motion would tend to decrease in amplitude due to some sort of "damping" until it eventually ceased to oscillate.

Other phenomena described by simple harmonic motion include the motion of a particle in a guitar string that has been compressed or elongated and then released, the motion of a particle of air brought about by certain sound waves, and certain radio and television devices.

Motion described by a product of a sine wave and a nonconstant factor is called *damped harmonic motion*. The nonconstant factor is called a *damping factor*, and the most relevant case is when the damping factor decreases to zero for large values of the independent variable.

EXAMPLE 5.9 ⇌

Sketch the damped harmonic motion described by $y = 2^{-x}\sin 2x$.

Solution: The graphs of 2^{-x} and -2^{-x} is shown along with the complete graph in Figure 5.24. The sine wave has varying amplitude and touches the two curves (called "envelopes") while oscillating between them.

FIGURE 5.24

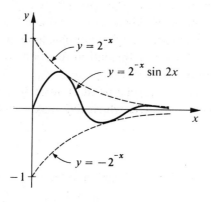

EXERCISES FOR SECTION 5.8

➤ 1. A piston is connected to the rim of a wheel as shown in Figure 5.25. The radius of the wheel is 2 feet and the length of the connecting rod

FIGURE 5.25

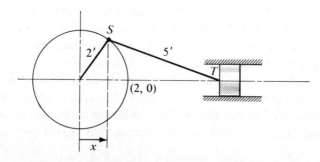

ST is 5 feet. The wheel rotates counterclockwise at the rate of one revolution per second. Find a formula for the position of the point S, t seconds after it has coordinates $(2, 0)$. Find the position of the point S when $t = \frac{1}{2}, \frac{3}{4}$, and 2.

2. One end of a shaft is fastened to a piston that moves vertically. The other end is connected to the rim of the wheel by means of prongs as shown in Figure 5.26. If the radius of the wheel is 2 feet and the shaft is 5 feet long, find a formula for the distance d feet between the bottom of the piston and the x-axis, t seconds after P is at $(2, 0)$. Assume the wheel rotates at 2 revolutions per second.

FIGURE 5.26

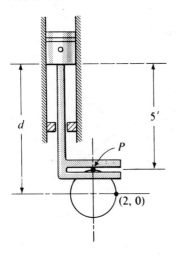

3. How does the mass in Figure 5.23 affect the amplitude of the motion? the period?

4. How does the spring constant affect the period?

5. Give the natural angular frequency of a spring-mass system if $M = 2$ and $k = 3$.

6. Sketch the graph of $x \sin x$ for $0 < x < 4\pi$.

7. Sketch the graph of $3^{-x} \cos x$ for $0 < x < 2\pi$.

8. Sketch the graph of $2^x \cos x$ for $0 < x < 2\pi$.

5.9   ADDITION OF ORDINATES

Functions such as

$$y_1 = \sin x + \cos x$$

and

$$y_2 = x + \sin x,$$

which are written as a sum of more elementary functions, occur frequently. It can be a very tedious process to graph such functions if you use the method of substituting values of x and determining corresponding ordinates. Sometimes a technique called *addition of ordinates* can be useful in plotting such functions. Thus, suppose $h(x) = f(x) + g(x)$. We sketch the graphs of $f(x)$ and $g(x)$ on the same coordinate system as in Figure 5.27. Then for particular values of x, such as x_1, we find $h(x_1)$ as the sum of $f(x_1)$ and $g(x_1)$. A vertical line is usually drawn at the point $(x_1, 0)$ and then the ordinates $f(x_1)$ and $g(x_1)$ are added by using a set of dividers, or by markings on the edge of a strip of paper. This process is repeated as often as necessary to get a representation of the desired graph.

FIGURE 5.27   Addition of ordinates

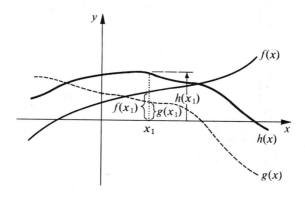

EXAMPLE 5.10

Use the method of addition of ordinates to sketch the function $y = \sin x + \cos 2x$.

FIGURE 5.28

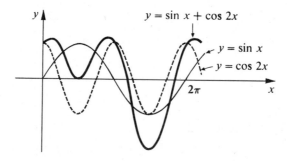

Solution: In Figure 5.28, both $\sin x$ and $\cos 2x$ are sketched along with their sum. The period of the given function is 2π even though that of $\cos 2x$ is π.

EXAMPLE 5.11

Sketch the graph of $y = x + \sin x$.

FIGURE 5.29

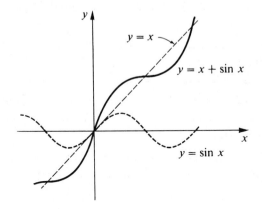

Solution: See Figure 5.29. In this case the basic sine curve oscillates about the curve $y = x$. Note that the given function is *not* periodic and is *not* bounded.

EXERCISES FOR SECTION 5.9

By the method of addition of ordinates, sketch graphs of the following functions. In each case, tell if the function is periodic.

1. $y = \sin x + \cos x$ 2. $y = \sin 2x + 2 \sin x$

3. $y = \sin \frac{1}{2}x - 2 \cos x$ 4. $y = x - \sin x$

5. $y = \sin x + 2$ 6. $y = \cos x - x$

7. Compare the graph of the function $y = \sqrt{2} \sin(x + \frac{1}{4}\pi)$ with the graph of the function $y = \cos x + \sin x$.

8. Compare the graph of the function $y = \cos^2 x$ with the graph of $y = \frac{1}{2} + \frac{1}{2} \cos 2x$.

5.10   GRAPHS OF THE TANGENT AND COTANGENT FUNCTIONS

The analytical properties of the tangent and cotangent functions have been discussed previously and are summarized here. Each of the properties influences the nature of the graph in a very important manner.

137

(1) Both tan x and cot x are periodic with period π. Thus, only an interval of length π need be analyzed for purposes of graphing the two functions, for example $-\frac{1}{2}\pi < x < \frac{1}{2}\pi$ or $0 < x < \pi$.

(2) Both tan x and cot x are *unbounded*, which means their values become arbitrarily large. Tan x becomes unbounded near odd multiples of $\frac{1}{2}\pi$ while cot x becomes unbounded near multiples of π.

(3) Both tan x and cot x are odd since they are quotients of an odd function and an even function. Thus, their graphs are symmetric with respect to the y-axis.

(4) Tan x is zero for $x = 0$, $\pm\pi$, $\pm2\pi$, etc. Cot x is zero at $x = \pm\frac{1}{2}\pi$, $\pm\frac{3}{2}\pi$, $\pm\frac{5}{2}\pi$, etc. These are the places where the graph crosses over the x-axis.

(5) Numerically (ignoring sign) the values of both functions are completely determined in the first quadrant, that is for $0 < x < \frac{1}{2}\pi$.

FIGURE 5.30

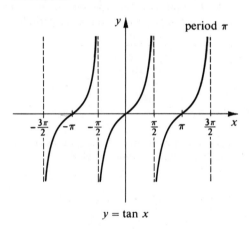

$y = \tan x$

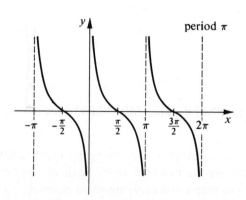

$y = \cot x$

Figure 5.30 shows a graph of several periods of the tangent function and of the cotangent function. For purposes of graphing, the places where the graphs cross the x-axis and the places where the functions become unbounded are emphasized. The places where the functions become unbounded are called *vertical asymptotes*. Thus, the asymptotes for $\tan x$ are $x = \pm\frac{1}{2}\pi,\ \pm\frac{3}{2}\pi,\ \pm\frac{5}{2}\pi$, etc. The asymptotes for $\cot x$ are $x = 0, \pm\pi, \pm 2\pi, \pm 3\pi$, etc.

The graphs of the more general functions $y = A\tan(Bx + C)$ and $y = A\cot(Bx + C)$ are analyzed in a manner similar to that of Section 5.7.

In the case of $y = A\tan x$, we do not call A the amplitude because this would imply that the function is bounded. The constant A, then, multiplies each functional value but has no other graphical significance.

The period of $\tan Bx$ is π/B. Thus, if $B > 1$, the period is shortened; if $B < 1$, the period is larger than that of the basic tangent function.

The constant C is a phase shift constant and acts to translate the basic function to the right or left.

EXAMPLE 5.12

Sketch the function $y = \tan(4x - \frac{1}{3}\pi)$.

Solution: The period of this function is $\frac{1}{4}\pi$. The phase shift is located by determining where the argument $4x - \frac{1}{3}\pi$ is equal to zero. Thus the phase shift is $\frac{1}{12}\pi$. The graph is shown in Figure 5.31.

FIGURE 5.31

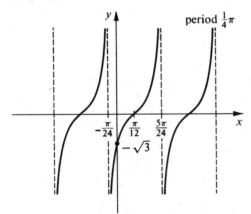

5.11 GRAPHS OF THE SECANT AND COSECANT FUNCTIONS

The graphs of $\sec x$ and $\csc x$ can be sketched directly from that of the $\cos x$ and $\sin x$ since they are reciprocals of the respective functions. You should, of course, note their important general properties.

(1) Both functions are unbounded. In fact, since sin x and cos x are both bounded by ± 1, the graphs of csc x and sec x lie above $y = 1$ and below $y = -1$.

(2) Both sec x and csc x are periodic with period 2π.

(3) The secant function is even and the cosecant function is odd.

(4) Sec x and csc x are never 0.

(5) Numerically, the functional values are determined for $0 < x < \pi/2$.

Both functions are sketched in Figure 5.32. In each case, their reciprocal functions are sketched lightly on the same coordinate system to show the relationship between the two.

FIGURE 5.32

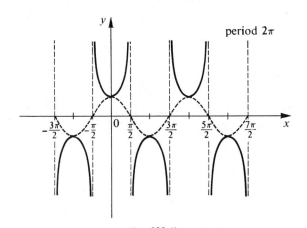

$y = \sec x$

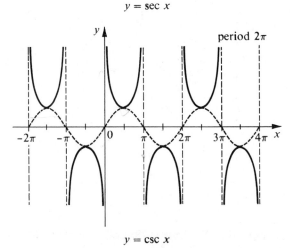

$y = \csc x$

The manner of sketching the more general functions $y = A \sec(Bx + C)$ and $y = A \csc(Bx + C)$ is similar to that discussed for the other functions. Suffice it to say, that the basic waveforms remain the same, but the constants A and B exert a kind of vertical and horizontal stretching while C effects a horizontal translation.

EXERCISES FOR SECTIONS 5.10 AND 5.11

Sketch the graphs of the given functions, over at least 2 periods. Give the period and the phase shift. List the asymptotes.

1. $y = \tan 2x$ 2. $y = \tan(x + \frac{1}{2}\pi)$

3. $y = \cot(\frac{1}{4}\pi - x)$ 4. $y = 2\sec(x - \frac{1}{2}\pi)$

5. $y = \tan(2x + \frac{1}{3}\pi)$ 6. $y = 2\csc 2x$

7. $y = \csc(2x - 3\pi)$ 8. $y = \sec(x + \frac{1}{3}\pi)$

9. $y = -\tan(x - \frac{1}{4}\pi)$

10. Does $\tan x$ exist at its asymptote?

11. How are the graphs of $\tan x$ and $\cot x$ related?

12. How are the graphs of $\sec x$ and $\csc x$ related?

13. How are the zeros of the tangent function related to the asymptotes of the cotangent function?

14. How are the zeros of the sine function and the asymptotes of the cosecant function related?

5.12 A FUNDAMENTAL INEQUALITY

The inequality

$$\sin x < x < \tan x$$

is fundamental to trigonometric analysis since it relates the arc length on the unit circle to two of the trigonometric functions. To demonstrate the

FIGURE 5.33

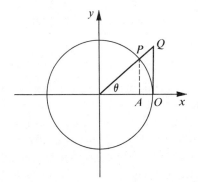

validity of this inequality, construct a unit circle as shown in Figure 5.33. From the figure, it is obvious that the length of AP is less than the length of the arc OP which in turn is less than OQ.

$$\overline{AP} < \overset{\frown}{OP} < \overline{OQ}.$$

Since the circle has radius of 1, $\sin x = \sin \theta = \overline{AP}$, $\tan x = \tan \theta = \overline{OQ}$, and hence,

$$\sin x < x < \tan x.$$

Figure 5.34 shows the three functions, $y = \sin x$, $y = x$, and $y = \tan x$, and, at the same time, exhibits the fact that the inequality is true only for $0 < x < \frac{1}{2}\pi$.

FIGURE 5.34

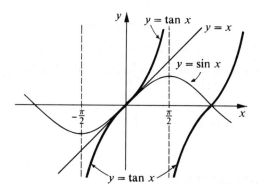

The ratio $\sin x/x$ is important in calculus. In the exercises for Section 5.1, you were asked to compute the values of this ratio for a few values of x near zero. You should have found that this ratio is just slightly less than 1 when x is a very small number. Using the fundamental inequality, we can show this a bit more rigorously. Divide the members of the fundamental inequality by $\sin x$ to obtain

$$1 < \frac{x}{\sin x} < \frac{1}{\cos x}, \qquad \text{(we are assuming } x \text{ is positive).}$$

Inverting and reversing the sense of the inequalities, we obtain

$$\cos x < \frac{\sin x}{x} < 1.$$

Since $\cos x$ is near to 1 when x is small and since the ratio is trapped between two functions close to 1, it follows that it also has values close to 1. (A similar argument for negative x leads to the same conclusion.)

The function $\sin x/x$ is undefined for $x = 0$, but if we sketch its graph it will look as though its value "should be" 1. (See Figure 5.35.)

FIGURE 5.35

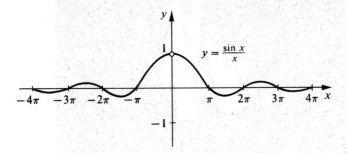

$$y = \frac{\sin x}{x}$$

One of the side results of the fact that sin x/x is close to 1 for x close to zero is that for small values of x, sin $x \approx x$. Thus, in some applications, if the variation in x is small, sin x is replaced by x.

EXERCISES FOR SECTION 5.12

1. By carefully examining the graphs of $y = 2x/\pi$ and $y = \sin x$, convince yourself that $2x/\pi \leq \sin x \leq 1$ for $0 < x < \pi/2$.

2. What are the zeros of sin x/x?

3. Sketch the function $f(x) = \sin 2x/x$ for $x \neq 0$. What do you think the values of the function are approaching when x is near 0?

6

EQUATIONS,
IDENTITIES,
AND
INEQUALITIES

Any combination of trigonometric functions such as $3 \sin x + \cos x$ or $\sec^2 x + \tan^2 x + 2 \sin x$ is called a trigonometric expression. One of the important things you will learn in this book is how to simplify or alter the form of trigonometric expressions using certain fundamental trigonometric relations.

There are eight *fundamental* relations or identities that you should know if you are to work effectively in the remainder of this book. You are already familiar with most of these relations but they are listed here for completeness. The fundamental relations fall into three groups as shown below.

The Reciprocal Relations

$$(6.1) \quad \sin \theta = \frac{1}{\csc \theta}$$

$$(6.2) \quad \cos \theta = \frac{1}{\sec \theta}$$

$$(6.3) \quad \tan \theta = \frac{1}{\cot \theta}$$

We establish Equation 6.1 by observing for any angle θ in standard position

$$\sin \theta \csc \theta = \left(\frac{y}{r}\right)\left(\frac{r}{y}\right) = 1.$$

Therefore,

$$\sin \theta = \frac{1}{\csc \theta}.$$

The other two relations are established in a similar manner.

The Quotient Relations

$$(6.4) \quad \tan \theta = \frac{\sin \theta}{\cos \theta}$$

$$(6.5) \quad \cot \theta = \frac{\cos \theta}{\sin \theta}$$

To establish Equation 6.4, we note that

$$\cos \theta \tan \theta = \left(\frac{x}{r}\right)\left(\frac{y}{x}\right) = \frac{y}{r} = \sin \theta.$$

Therefore,

$$\tan \theta = \frac{\sin \theta}{\cos \theta}$$

The Pythagorean Relations

(6.6) $\sin^2 \theta + \cos^2 \theta = 1$

(6.7) $\tan^2 \theta + 1 = \sec^2 \theta$

(6.8) $\cot^2 \theta + 1 = \csc^2 \theta$

We prove Equation 6.6 by dividing $x^2 + y^2 = r^2$ by r^2 to get

$$\frac{x^2}{r^2} + \frac{y^2}{r^2} = 1.$$

Then, since

$$\sin \theta = \frac{y}{r} \text{ and } \cos \theta = \frac{x}{r},$$

we have

$$\cos^2 \theta + \sin^2 \theta = 1.$$

Note that Equation 6.7 is derived from Equation 6.6. By dividing both sides of 6.6 by $\cos^2 \theta$, we get

$$\frac{\sin^2 \theta}{\cos^2 \theta} + 1 = \frac{1}{\cos^2 \theta}$$

from which, after using the fact that $\dfrac{\sin \theta}{\cos \theta} = \tan \theta$ and $\dfrac{1}{\cos \theta} = \sec \theta$, we have

$$\tan^2 \theta + 1 = \sec^2 \theta.$$

Similarly Equation 6.8 is derived from Equation 6.6 by first dividing both sides by $\sin^2 \theta$ and then applying Equations 6.1 and 6.5.

These eight relations are called the *fundamental identities* of trigonometry because they are valid for all values of the argument for which the functions in the expression have meaning. Also, as before, the variable (often the letter x is chosen instead of θ) may be regarded as either a real number or an angle, the interpretation being chosen from the context.

Using the fundamental identities you can (sometimes ingeniously) manipulate trigonometric expressions into alternative forms.

EXAMPLE 6.1

Write the following expression as a single trigonometric term.

$$\frac{\tan x \csc^2 x}{1 + \tan^2 x}.$$

Solution: From Equation 6.7 the denominator may be written as $\sec^2 x$. Thus,

$$\frac{\tan x \csc^2 x}{1 + \tan^2 x} = \frac{\tan x \csc^2 x}{\sec^2 x}.$$

We now express $\tan x$, $\csc x$, and $\sec x$ in terms of the sine and cosine functions:

$$\frac{\tan x \csc^2 x}{1 + \tan^2 x} = \frac{\dfrac{\sin x}{\cos x} \cdot \dfrac{1}{\sin^2 x}}{\dfrac{1}{\cos^2 x}}$$

$$= \frac{\cos^2 x \sin x}{\sin^2 x \cos x}$$

$$= \frac{\cos x}{\sin x}$$

$$= \cot x.$$

As you can see by this example, a large part of the process is algebraic. The series of steps used in the simplification procedure is not unique. For example, we could have initially expressed the complete expression in terms of the sine and cosine functions. Experience with the use of the eight fundamental relations in simplifying trigonometric expression will give you some facility to choose a reasonable approach. Writing the entire expression in terms of the sine and cosine function is often appropriate but not necessarily the most "economical."

EXAMPLE 6.2

Simplify the expression

$(\sec x + \tan x)(1 - \sin x)$.

Solution: We write each of the functions in terms of the sine and cosine functions:

$$(\sec x + \tan x)(1 - \sin x) = \left(\frac{1}{\cos x} + \frac{\sin x}{\cos x}\right)(1 - \sin x)$$

$$= \frac{(1 + \sin x)(1 - \sin x)}{\cos x}$$

$$= \frac{(1 - \sin^2 x)}{\cos x}$$

$$= \frac{\cos^2 x}{\cos x}$$

$$= \cos x.$$

(What is the domain of this expression?)

EXAMPLE 6.3

Simplify the expression

$(\sin x + \cos x)^2$.

Solution: Note that this is *not* the same expression as $\sin^2 x + \cos^2 x$. By squaring the expression, we obtain:

$$(\sin x + \cos x)^2 = \sin^2 x + 2 \sin x \cos x + \cos^2 x$$
$$= 1 + 2 \sin x \cos x.$$

EXAMPLE 6.4

Simplify the expression

$$\sin^4 x - \cos^4 x + \cos^2 x.$$

Solution: We write the expression in a form involving only the cosine function. Thus,

$$\sin^4 x - \cos^4 x + \cos^2 x = (1 - \cos^2 x)^2 - \cos^4 x + \cos^2 x$$
$$= 1 - 2 \cos^2 x + \cos^4 x - \cos^4 x + \cos^2 x$$
$$= 1 - \cos^2 x$$
$$= \sin^2 x.$$

Certain algebraic expressions encountered in calculus are often transformed into trigonometric expressions in which, after simplification, "hard to handle" terms such as radicals disappear.

EXAMPLE 6.5

By using the substitution $x = 2 \sin \theta$, simplify the expression $\sqrt{4 - x^2}$ and determine an interval for the variable θ which corresponds to $0 \leq x \leq 2$ in a one-to-one manner. What is $\tan \theta$?

Solution: Substituting $x = 2 \sin \theta$ into the radical, we have:

$$\sqrt{4 - x^2} = \sqrt{4 - 4 \sin^2 \theta}$$
$$= \sqrt{4(1 - \sin^2 \theta)}$$
$$= |2 \cos \theta| = 2|\cos \theta|.$$

When $x = 0$, $\theta = 0$ and when $x = 2$, $\theta = \frac{1}{2}\pi$ so that the interval $0 \leq x \leq 2$

FIGURE 6.1

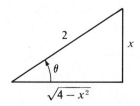

$$\sqrt{4 - x^2}$$

corresponds to $0 \leq \theta \leq \frac{1}{2}\pi$. On this interval $\cos \theta \geq 0$ so that $|\cos \theta| = \cos \theta$. Hence,

$$\sqrt{4 - x^2} = 2 \cos \theta \text{ for } 0 \leq x \leq 2 \text{ and } 0 \leq \theta \leq \frac{1}{2}\pi.$$

Since $\sin \theta = x/2$, the right triangle in Figure 6.1 shows the relations necessary to establish that

$$\tan \theta = \frac{x}{\sqrt{4 - x^2}}.$$

EXERCISES FOR SECTION 6.1

Simplify the following expressions.

1. $\cos \theta + \tan \theta \sin \theta$

2. $\csc \theta - \cot \theta \cos \theta$

3. $\tan x + \cot x$

4. $\dfrac{1 + \cos x}{1 + \sec x}$

5. $\dfrac{(\tan x)(1 + \cot^2 x)}{(1 + \tan^2 x)}$

6. $\sec x - \sin x \tan x$

7. $\cos x \csc x$

8. $\cos x(\tan x + \cot x)$

9. $(\cos^2 x - 1)(\tan^2 x + 1)$

10. $\dfrac{(\sec^2 x - 1)}{\sec^2 x}$

11. $\dfrac{\sec x - \cos x}{\tan x}$

12. $\dfrac{1 + \tan^2 x}{\tan^2 x}$

13. $(\sin^2 x + \cos^2 x)^3$

14. $\dfrac{1 + \sec x}{\tan x + \sin x}$

15. $(\csc x - \cot x)^4(\csc x + \cot x)^4$

16. $\dfrac{\sec x}{(\tan x + \cot x)}$

17. $(\tan x)(\sin x + \cot x \cos x)$

18. $1 + \dfrac{\tan^2 x}{1 + \sec x}$

19. $\dfrac{\tan x \sin x}{(\sec^2 x - 1)}$

20. $(\cos x)(1 + \tan^2 x)$

By using the following substitutions, reduce the given expression to one involving only trigonometric functions.

21. $\sqrt{a^2 + x^2}$, let $x = a \tan \theta$. What is $\sin \theta$?

22. $\sqrt{36 + 16x^2}$, let $x = 3/2 \tan \theta$. What is $\sin \theta$?

23. $\dfrac{\sqrt{x^2 - 4}}{x}$, let $x = 2 \sec \theta$.

24. $x^2\sqrt{4 + 9x^2}$, let $x = 2/3 \tan \theta$.

6.2   TRIGONOMETRIC EQUATIONS

A *trigonometric equation* is any statement involving a conditional equality of two trigonometric expressions. A *solution* to the trigonometric equation is a value of the variable (within the domain of the function) which makes the statement true. The *solution set* is the set of all values of the variable which are solutions. To solve a trigonometric equation means to find the solution set for some indicated domain. If no domain is specifically mentioned, the domain is assumed to be all values of the independent variable for which the terms of the equation have meaning.

If the solution set is the null set, the equation is said to have no solution. If the solution set is the complete domain of the independent variable for the functions involved, it is called an *identity*. For example, each fundamental relation given by Equations 6.1–6.8 is called an identity because each is true regardless of the value of the argument.

To solve trigonometric equations, we proceed in a series of steps until a point is reached which allows an explicit determination of the solution set. Usually, some specific knowledge about certain values of the trigonometric functions is necessary to make this determination.

We say that two trigonometric equations are *equivalent* if they have the same solution sets. Any operation on a given equation is *permissible* if the consequence of the operation is an equivalent equation. It can be shown that the permissible operations are: (1) adding or subtracting the same expression to both sides of an equality, and (2) multiplying or dividing both sides by the same nonzero expression.

The most basic type of trigonometric equation is one which is linear in a single trigonometric function of θ. The trigonometric equation in this case is analogous to the linear equation in one variable and can always be put into the form of a trigonometric function equal to a constant. The solution set is then all values of the argument for which the function is equal to this constant.

In most cases, trigonometric equations have an infinite number of solutions. However, we shall find the solution set over *one* period unless specified otherwise. The roots on this interval will be sufficient since the other roots can be obtained by simply adding multiples of the period.

EXAMPLE 6.6

Solve the equation $\cos x = \frac{1}{2}$.

Solution: The period of $\cos x$ is 2π. The only solutions to this equation on the interval $0 \leq x \leq 2\pi$ are $x = \frac{1}{3}\pi$ and $x = \frac{5}{3}\pi$. (We note that the complete solution set is comprised of those values that can be written in the form $\frac{1}{3}\pi + 2n\pi$ and $\frac{5}{3}\pi + 2n\pi$ where n is an integer.) Figure 6.2

illustrates the nature of the solution set as the points of intersection of the curve $y = \cos x$ with the line $y = \frac{1}{2}$.

FIGURE 6.2

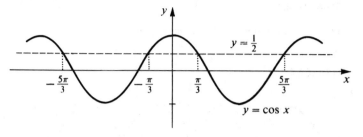

EXAMPLE 6.7

Solve the trigonometric equation $\tan 2x = 1$.

Solution: Since the period of this function is $\frac{1}{2}\pi$, it is sufficient to examine for roots on the interval $0 \leq x \leq \frac{1}{2}\pi$. The value of θ at which $\tan \theta = 1$ is $\theta = \frac{1}{4}\pi$. Hence $\tan 2x = 1$ has the solution $x = \frac{1}{8}\pi$. Figure 6.3 shows a graphical interpretation of the solution set as the intersection of the curve $y = \tan 2x$ with the line $y = 1$.

FIGURE 6.3

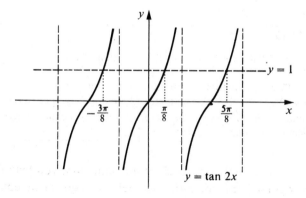

EXAMPLE 6.8

Solve the equation $4 \sin \theta + 1 = 2 \sin \theta$.

Solution:

$$4 \sin \theta + 1 = 2 \sin \theta$$
$$2 \sin \theta = -1$$
$$\sin \theta = -1/2$$

The period of $\sin \theta$ is 2π which means $\theta = \frac{7}{6}\pi$ and $\theta = \frac{11}{6}\pi$ are the desired solutions.

EXAMPLE 6.9

Find the solution set to the equation $|\sin x| = \frac{1}{2}$.

FIGURE 6.4

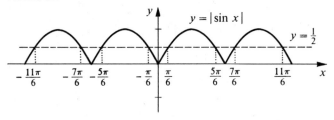

Solution: Figure 6.4 shows the intersection points of the curve $y = |\sin x|$ with $y = \frac{1}{2}$. Since $|\sin x|$ is periodic with period π, we need only find those values of x for which the equation is true on the interval $0 \leq x \leq \pi$. From your knowledge of the sine function, these values are $x = \frac{1}{6}\pi$ and $x = \frac{5}{6}\pi$.

Trigonometric equations which are quadratic in one of the functions can be factored into a product of linear factors. The total solution set is the union of the solution sets to each of the resulting linear equations.

EXAMPLE 6.10

Solve the equation $2\cos^2\theta + 3\cos\theta + 1 = 0$ on $0 \leq \theta \leq 2\pi$.

Solution: This is a quadratic equation in $\cos\theta$ and may be factored as $(2\cos\theta + 1)(\cos\theta + 1) = 0$. The factor $(2\cos\theta + 1)$ is equal to zero when $\theta = \frac{2}{3}\pi$ and $\theta = \frac{4}{3}\pi$. Likewise, the factor $(\cos\theta + 1)$ is equal to zero when $\theta = \pi$. Hence the solution set is $\{\frac{2}{3}\pi, \pi, \frac{4}{3}\pi\}$.

If more than one function occurs in the equation, you may find it helpful to use trigonometric identities to yield an equivalent equation involving only one function.

EXAMPLE 6.11

Solve the equation $2\cos^2 x - \sin x - 1 = 0$.

Solution: Since $\cos^2 x = 1 - \sin^2 x$, we have

$$2(1 - \sin^2 x) - \sin x - 1 = 0,$$
$$2 - 2\sin^2 x - \sin x - 1 = 0,$$
$$2\sin^2 x + \sin x - 1 = 0.$$

Factoring:

$(2 \sin x - 1)(\sin x + 1) = 0.$

The solution set of the original equation is given by the union of the solution sets to the two equations:

$$\left\{ \begin{array}{l} 2 \sin x - 1 = 0 \\ \sin x + 1 = 0 \end{array} \right\}.$$

The solution to $2 \sin x - 1 = 0$ is $x = \frac{1}{6}\pi$ and $x = \frac{5}{6}\pi$, and to $\sin x + 1 = 0$ is $\frac{3}{2}\pi$. Hence, the solution set is

$$\left\{ \; \tfrac{1}{6}\pi, \; \tfrac{5}{6}\pi, \; \tfrac{3}{2}\pi \; \right\}.$$

In solving trigonometric equations, the following is normally a good procedure:

(1) Gather the entire expression to one side of the equality.

(2) Use the fundamental identities to express this conditional equality in terms of one function, or, failing this, as a product of two expressions each involving one function.

(3) Use some knowledge from algebra, such as the quadratic formula or techniques of factoring, to write as a product of linear factors.

(4) The zeros (if there are any) of each of the linear factors should be recognizable by inspection. The total solution set is the union of these sets.

EXAMPLE 6.12

Solve the equation $2 \tan x \sec x - \tan x = 0$ on the interval $(0, 2\pi)$.

Solution: Factoring, we have: $\tan x(2 \sec x - 1) = 0$, which means that the solution set is given by the union of the solution sets to the two equations $\tan x = 0$ and $2 \sec x - 1 = 0$. The second of these has a solution set equal to the null set since $\sec x \geq 1$. On the interval $(0, 2\pi)$, $\tan x$ is zero at $x = 0$ and $x = \pi$. Thus the solution set is $\{0, \pi\}$.

Note that squaring both sides of an equality is not a "permissible" operation since it does not necessarily yield an equivalent equation. In practice you need not restrict yourself to permissible operations, but when other operations, such as squaring both sides, are used, you should be aware that nonequivalent equations may result. For example, if you divide two sides of an equation by $\sin x$, at least a mental note must be made of the fact that $\sin x = 0$ for values of x of the form $x = n\pi$. Then you must try these values in the original expression to see if they are members of the solution set.

EXAMPLE 6.13

Solve the equation $\sin x + \cos x = 1$ on $(0, 2\pi)$.

Solution: If we square both sides of this equation we get

$\sin^2 x + 2 \sin x \cos x + \cos^2 x = 1$

from which, after using the fact that $\sin^2 x + \cos^2 x = 1$, we have

$\sin x \cos x = 0$

The solution set to this equation is the set of values of x for which $\sin x = 0$, (that is, $x = 0$ and π), and the values of x for which $\cos x = 0$ (that is, $x = \frac{1}{2}\pi$, and $\frac{3}{2}\pi$). Hence, the possible solutions are

$\{0, \frac{1}{2}\pi, \pi, \frac{3}{2}\pi\}$.

Since the squaring operation does not yield an equivalent equation, you must check the values in this set to determine if they are truly solutions to the original equation. (You can be sure that the solution set is a *subset* of this set). It is easy to show that only $x = 0$ and $x = \frac{1}{2}\pi$ are valid solutions. Thus, the solution set to the given equation is

$\{0, \frac{1}{2}\pi\}$.

EXAMPLE 6.14

Solve the equation $2 \sin x \cos x = \cos x$ for $0 \leq x \leq 2\pi$.

Solution: Rather than divide both sides by $\cos x$, (which is zero at certain points), we transpose $\cos x$ to the left hand side. Then we factor to obtain

$\cos x (2 \sin x - 1) = 0$

from which we have the two equations $\cos x = 0$ and $2 \sin x - 1 = 0$. On the interval of interest the solutions to the first of these equations is $x = \frac{1}{2}\pi$ and $x = \frac{3}{2}\pi$. The second equation is valid for $x = \frac{1}{6}\pi$ and $\frac{5}{6}\pi$. Hence the solution set is

$\{\frac{1}{6}\pi, \frac{1}{2}\pi, \frac{5}{6}\pi, \frac{3}{2}\pi\}$.

EXERCISES FOR SECTION 6.2

Solve the following equations over one period of the function. Make a sketch showing the solution set as the intersection of a line with the graph of some trigonometric function.

1. $\sin x = \frac{1}{2}$

2. $\cos 2x = \frac{1}{2}\sqrt{2}$

3. $\tan x = \sqrt{3}$

4. $\cos x = 1$

5. $\sin x = \frac{1}{2}\sqrt{3}$

6. $\cos(3x + \frac{1}{6}\pi) = \frac{1}{2}$

7. $\sin(2x - \frac{1}{4}\pi) = \frac{1}{2}\sqrt{3}$

8. $\tan(3x - \pi) = 1$

9. $\sin(\frac{1}{3}x - \frac{1}{12}\pi) = -\frac{1}{2}$

10. $\sin(\frac{1}{2}x + \frac{1}{8}\pi) = -1$

Solve the following trigonometric equations over one period.

11. $2 \sin x + 1 = 0$
12. $\sin 2x + 1 = 0$

13. $\cos 3x = 1$
14. $\tan 2x + 1 = 0$

15. $\cos^2 x + 2 \cos x + 1 = 0$
16. $\tan^2 x - 1 = 0$

17. $2 \sin^2 x = \sin x$
18. $\sec^2 2x = 1$

19. $\sec^2 x + 1 = 0$
20. $\cos^2 x = 2$

21. $\cos x = \sin x$
22. $2 \sec x \tan x + \sec^2 x = 0$

23. $\sec^2 x - 2 = \tan^2 x$
24. $4 \sin^2 x - 1 = 0$

25. $2 \cos^2 x - \sin x = 1$
26. $2 \sec x + 4 = 0$

27. $\sin^2 x - 2 \sin x + 1 = 0$
28. $\cot^2 x - 5 \cot x + 4 = 0$

29. $\tan^2 x - \tan x = 0$
30. $\cos 2x + \sin 2x = 0$

31. $\sin x \tan^2 x = \sin x$
32. $\cos x + 2 \sin^2 x = 1$

33. $\tan x + \sec x = 1$
34. $\tan x + \cot x = \sec x \csc x$

35. $\cos x + 1 = \sin x$
36. $2 \tan x - \sec^2 x = 0$

37. $\csc^5 x - 4 \csc x = 0$

6.3   TRIGONOMETRIC IDENTITIES

A *trigonometric identity* is a trigonometric equation whose solution set is the set of all permissible values of the independent variable. Thus, every trigonometric identity is a (conditional) equation, but every equation is not an identity.

EXAMPLE 6.15

The equation $\sin \theta - \cos \theta = 0$ is not an identity since the solution set is $\{\frac{1}{4}\pi + n\pi\}$. The equation $\tan^2 x + 1 = \sec^2 x$ is an identity since it is true for all x except $x = \frac{1}{2}\pi + n\pi$. These values are not in the domain of either the secant or tangent function.

To show a given trigonometric equation to be an identity, we may proceed in one of the three following methods:

(1) by a series of manipulations using other known identities to transform one side of the equation into the form of the other side;

(2) by a series of manipulations using other known identities to transform the left-hand side and the right-hand side into forms that are precisely the same;

(3) by considering the identity to be a conditional equation and

then showing that the solution set is the entire set of permissible values of the unknown.

It is incorrect to attempt to establish an identity by beginning with the assumption that it *is* an identity. Sometimes the manipulations that are performed make it seem as though that is the procedure. For example, in using methods (1) or (2) do not use operations (such as transposing) that are valid for conditional equations.

The purpose of verifying rather esoteric identities is to reinforce our knowledge of the more fundamental ones and to give us additional manipulative skill with trigonometric expressions. In a book such as this, we will attempt to keep our ultimate purpose in rather clear perspective. Hence, the identities we prove will, hopefully, be considered "reasonable."

While there is no general approach besides the three mentioned, you may find it desirable to express the trigonometric functions in terms of sines and cosines only. This will often enable you to see the manipulations which are necessary to verify a given identity.

EXAMPLE 6.16

Verify the identity $\cot x + \tan x = \csc x \sec x$.

Solution: Using method (1), we express the left-hand side in terms of sines and cosines. Thus,

$$\cot x + \tan x = \frac{\cos x}{\sin x} + \frac{\sin x}{\cos x}$$

$$= \frac{\cos^2 x + \sin^2 x}{\sin x \cos x}$$

$$= \frac{1}{\sin x \cos x}$$

$$= \csc x \sec x.$$

Therefore, we have shown that $\cot x + \tan x = \csc x \sec x$.

EXAMPLE 6.17

Show that $\sin \theta (\csc \theta - \sin \theta) = \cos^2 \theta$ is an identity.

Solution: Here the most expedient approach is to expand the left-hand side. Thus,

$$\sin \theta (\csc \theta - \sin \theta) = \sin \theta \csc \theta - \sin^2 \theta$$

$$= \sin \theta \frac{1}{\sin \theta} - \sin^2 \theta$$

$$= 1 - \sin^2 \theta$$

$$= \cos^2 \theta.$$

EXAMPLE 6.18

Verify the identity

$$\frac{\cos x \cot x}{\cot x - \cos x} = \frac{\cot x + \cos x}{\cos x \cot x}.$$

Solution: In this case we use method (2) to prove the identity. Expressing the left-hand side in terms of sines and cosines we have

$$\frac{\cos x \cot x}{\cot x - \cos x} = \frac{\cos x \dfrac{\cos x}{\sin x}}{\dfrac{\cos x}{\sin x} - \cos x}$$

$$= \frac{\dfrac{\cos^2 x}{\sin x}}{\dfrac{\cos x - \cos x \sin x}{\sin x}}$$

$$= \frac{\cos^2 x}{\sin x} \cdot \frac{\sin x}{\cos x (1 - \sin x)}$$

$$= \frac{\cos x}{1 - \sin x}.$$

We now manipulate the right-hand side to agree with this expression, thus,

$$\frac{\cot x + \cos x}{\cos x \cot x} = \frac{\dfrac{\cos x}{\sin x} + \cos x}{\cos x \dfrac{\cos x}{\sin x}}$$

$$= \frac{\dfrac{\cos x + \cos x \sin x}{\sin x}}{\dfrac{\cos^2 x}{\sin x}}$$

$$= \frac{1 + \sin x}{\cos x}.$$

Recognizing that

$$(1 + \sin x)(1 - \sin x) = 1 - \sin^2 x = \cos^2 x,$$

we multiply both numerator and denominator by $1 - \sin x$, to get

$$\frac{1 + \sin x}{\cos x} \cdot \frac{1 - \sin x}{1 - \sin x} = \frac{1 - \sin^2 x}{\cos x (1 - \sin x)}$$

$$= \frac{\cos^2 x}{\cos x (1 - \sin x)} = \frac{\cos x}{1 - \sin x}.$$

Since we have transformed both sides into the same expression, the identity is proved.

EXAMPLE 6.19

Verify the previous identity by using method (3).

Solution: We consider the equation

$$\frac{\cos x \cot x}{\cot x - \cos x} = \frac{\cot x + \cos x}{\cos x \cot x}.$$

"Cross multiplying," we obtain

$$\cos^2 x \cot^2 x = \cot^2 x - \cos^2 x.$$

Dividing both sides by $\cos^2 x$:

$$\cot^2 x = \frac{1}{\sin^2 x} - 1$$

$$= \csc^2 x - 1 = \cot^2 x.$$

The solution set to this last equation is $S = \{x \mid x \text{ a real number} \neq n\pi\}$. The set of permissible values of the original expression is the set $D = \{x \mid x \text{ a real number} \neq n\pi/2\}$. Since $D \subseteq S$, the equation is an identity.

EXAMPLE 6.20

Show that the expression $\log(\csc x - \cot x)$ is identically equal to $-\log(\csc x + \cot x)$.

Solution: By an elementary property of logarithms

$$-\log(\csc x + \cot x) = \log(\csc x + \cot x)^{-1}$$

$$= \log \frac{1}{\csc x + \cot x}.$$

Multiplying numerator and denominator of the term inside the logarithm by $\csc x - \cot x$, we have

$$-\log(\csc x + \cot x) = \log \frac{\csc x - \cot x}{\csc^2 x - \cot^2 x}.$$

Since the denominator is identically 1, the verification is completed.

EXERCISES FOR SECTION 6.3

Determine which of the following equations are identities. If it is not an identity, find the solution set on $0 \le x \le 2\pi$.

1. $(\cos x - \sin x)(\cos x + \sin x) = 2\cos^2 x - 1$

2. $\sin x \sec x = \tan x$

3. $\cos x = \cot x$

4. $1 - \cot x = \cot x \tan x - \cot x$

5. $1 - \dfrac{2}{\sec^2 x} = \sin^2 x - \cos^2 x$

6. $\cos x + 1 = \sin x$

7. $\dfrac{\cos x}{1 - \sin x} = \dfrac{1 + \sin x}{\cos x}$

8. $\sin x \cot x \tan^2 x = \sec x - \sin x \cot x$

9. $\sin x \tan x + \cos x = \sec x$

10. $\sin x \tan^2 x = \sin x$

Verify the following identities:

11. $\sin^2 x (1 + \cot^2 x) = 1$

12. $\csc x - \sin x = \cot x \cos x$

13. $(\sin^2 x - 1)(\cot^2 x + 1) = 1 - \csc^2 x$

14. $\dfrac{2 + \sec x}{\csc x} - 2 \sin x = \tan x$

15. $\dfrac{\sin x}{1 - \cos x} = \csc x + \cot x$

16. $\dfrac{\cot x + 1}{\cot x - 1} = -\dfrac{\tan x + 1}{\tan x - 1}$

17. $\dfrac{1 + \sec x}{\sin x + \tan x} = \csc x$

18. $\dfrac{1 - \sin x}{1 + \sin x} = (\sec x - \tan x)^2$

19. $(\sin^2 x + \cos^2 x)^4 = 1$

20. $\dfrac{\tan x + \cot x}{\tan x - \cot x} = \dfrac{\sec^2 x}{\tan^2 x - 1}$

21. $\dfrac{\sin x}{\csc x (1 + \cot^2 x)} = \sin^4 x$

22. $1 - \tan^4 x = 2 \sec^2 x - \sec^4 x$

23. $\tan x + \cot x = \sec x \csc x$

24. $(\cot x + \csc x)^2 = \dfrac{1 + \cos x}{1 - \cos x}$

25. $\sin^2 x (\csc^2 x - 1) = \cos^2 x$

26. $\sec x \csc x - 2 \cos x \csc x = \tan x - \cot x$

27. Show that $\log(\sec x - \cot x) = -\log(\sec x + \cot x)$

6.4   PARAMETRIC EQUATIONS

A convenient way to define the locus* of a point in the plane is by using two equations, one for x and one for y in terms of some variable, say t.

*The locus of a point in the plane is the path taken by the point in satisfying a given condition, such as a mathematical formula.

Thus, two functions of t determine the location of the set of points,

$$x = f(t),$$
$$y = g(t).$$

As t varies, the point describes a curve in the plane. The equations are called *parametric equations* of the curve; the variable t is called the *parameter*.

The determination of the locus of the point described by parametric equations is usually rather awkward, and we may find it useful to *eliminate the parameter* to obtain an equation in x and y. If the parameter functions f and g contain trigonometric terms, as they do in some very typical cases, then the use of trigonometric identities is frequently helpful in this procedure. There is no general technique to describe how to eliminate the parameter, so we will be satisfied with a few examples.

EXAMPLE 6.21

Sketch the curve in the x-y plane described parametrically by $x = 2 \sin t$, $y = 3 \cos t$

Solution: Since $\frac{1}{2}x = \sin t$ and $\frac{1}{3}y = \cos t$, we may square both of these equations and add the corresponding sides to obtain

$$(\tfrac{1}{2}x)^2 + (\tfrac{1}{3}y)^2 = \sin^2 t + \cos^2 t = 1.$$

This happens to be an ellipse and is sketched in Figure 6.5.

FIGURE 6.5

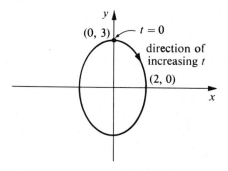

Note that the parametric representation gives a sense of direction to the curve since you can think of the point beginning at the point $(0, 3)$ when $t = 0$ and going around the curve in a clockwise sense as t increases. The point completes one revolution of the ellipse every 2π units. A curve with "direction," such as the one in this example, is said to be *oriented*.

EXAMPLE 6.22

Sketch the graph of the curve described by $x = \sin t$, $y = \sin t$.

Solution: The elimination of the parameter is a simple matter of noticing that $y = x$. The graph of $y = x$ is shown in Figure 6.6 as the line that splits the first and third quadrants.

FIGURE 6.6

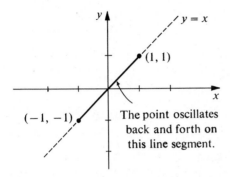

However, by the nature of the parametric equations, the values of x and y are limited between 1 and -1. Thus the point moves on the line $y = x$, but it oscillates between the points $(1, 1)$ and $(-1, -1)$.

The previous example should carry with it a general word of caution: when eliminating the parameter be careful that the process of elimination does not tend to include more points (or less) than the parametric equations themselves give.

EXAMPLE 6.23

Eliminate t from the parametric equations

$x = a + b \sec t,$
$y = c + d \tan t,$

where a, b, c, and d are positive constants.

Solution: We rewrite the two equations as

$$\frac{x - a}{b} = \sec t,$$

$$\frac{y - c}{d} = \tan t.$$

Squaring and subtracting,

$$\left(\frac{x - a}{b} \right)^2 - \left(\frac{y - c}{d} \right)^2 = 1.$$

This is the equation of a hyperbola. It is studied in more detail in analytic geometry.

EXERCISES FOR SECTION 6.4

Eliminate t from the following parametric equations to obtain one equation in x and y.

1. $x = \sin t, y = \cos t$

2. $x = 1 + \sin t, y = 1 + \cos t$

3. $x = -\cos t, y = \sin t$

4. $x = \sec t + 1, y = \tan t - 1$

5. $x = a \cos t, y = a \sin^2 t$

6. $x = \cos t, y = \sin t \cos t$

7. $x = \cos t, y = \cos t$

8. $x = \sin^2 t, y = 1$

9. $x = \cos^2 t, y = \cos^2 t$

10. $x = 2 \sin t + \cos t, y = 2 \cos t - \sin t$

6.5   GRAPHICAL SOLUTIONS OF TRIGONOMETRIC EQUATIONS

Equations containing a mixture of trigonometric and other functions may be quite difficult to solve by analytic methods. A graphical analysis will usually yield at least an approximation to the roots and will often give helpful information even when a problem can be solved analytically.

EXAMPLE 6.24

Graphically solve the equation $x = \sin \frac{1}{2}\pi x$.

FIGURE 6.7

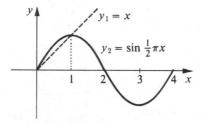

Solution: The functions $y_1 = x$ and $y_2 = \sin x$ are sketched in Figure 6.7. Since both functions are odd, the graph is drawn for positive values of x only. The solution set to the equation is the set of x coordinates of the points of intersection of the two curves. The figure shows that the values are $x = 0$ and $x = 1$; hence by the symmetry of the graph, the solution set is $\{-1, 0, 1\}$.

EXAMPLE 6.25

Graphically solve the equation $x \tan x = 1$.

FIGURE 6.8

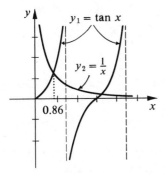

Solution: We write equation in the form $\tan x = 1/x$ and then graph the two functions $y_1 = \tan x$ and $y_2 = 1/x$, as is shown in Figure 6.8. As in the previous example, we may, without loss of generality, sketch only the part of the graphs for $x \geq 0$. The figure shows that there are infinitely many solutions of which the first positive one is approximately 0.86.

6.6   TRIGONOMETRIC INEQUALITIES

A *trigonometric inequality* is any conditional statement of inequality involving trigonometric expressions. The solution set is defined, analogous to those defined for trigonometric equations, as the set of values for which the conditional statement is true. Other related terminology is defined to be consistent with that which is used for trigonometric equations. Note that the term "permissible operation" is slightly more restrictive when used with inequalities in that multiplication or division of both sides is permitted only by positive expressions. Multiplication of both sides by a negative quantity results in a reversal of the inequality.

Aside from the very basic kinds of inequalities such as $\sin x < 1$, $\cos x > 0$, etc., most trigonometric inequalities are best solved by some combination of the graphical with the analytical.

EXAMPLE 6.26

Solve the inequality, $\sin x > \cos x$.

Solution: In Figure 6.9, both the sine and cosine functions are sketched. The points of intersection occur at the real numbers which can be written in the form $\frac{1}{4}\pi + n\pi$. The graph shows that the sine function is greater than

FIGURE 6.9

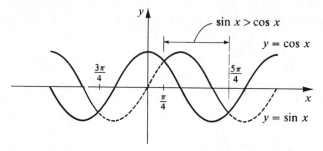

the cosine function over those intervals for which the left-hand end point is given by an odd integer. In Figure 6.9, the solution set for one period is shown as the set $\{x \mid \frac{1}{4}\pi < x < \frac{5}{4}\pi\}$.

Inequalities which are not strictly trigonometric but, which include other functions, are also best analyzed graphically.

EXAMPLE 6.27

Solve the inequality $x > \cos x$.

FIGURE 6.10

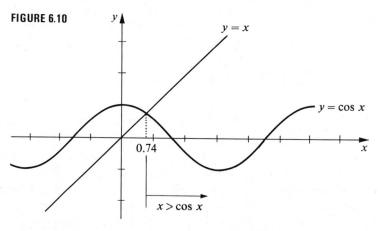

Solution: From Figure 6.10, we see that the point where $x = \cos x$ is approximately $x = 0.74$. Hence, from the graph, the solution set is

$\{x \mid x > 0.74\}$.

EXERCISES FOR SECTIONS 6.5 AND 6.6

Use graphical methods to approximate at least some of the solutions to the following equations on $(0, 2\pi)$.

1. $x = \sin x$

2. $x = \sin 2x$

3. $x \sin x = 1$

4. $x = \tan x$

5. $x = \cos x$

6. $x^2 = \cos 2\pi x$

7. $x^2 - \tan x = 0$

8. $\sin x = \cos x$

9. $\tan x = \cos x$

10. $\tan x = \sin x$

Solve the following trigonometric inequalities.

11. $\sec x > \csc x$

12. $x > \sin x$

13. $x > \sin 2\pi x$

14. $x \sin x > 1$

15. $|\sin x| < |\cos x|$

16. $\sec^2 x < 1$

7

COMPOSITE
ANGLE
IDENTITIES

7.1 THE LINEARITY PROPERTY

In mathematics, functions which obey the laws

$$f(x + y) = f(x) + f(y) \text{ and } f(ax) = af(x)$$

are said to have the *linearity property*. You may fail to see the importance of this property until you have to work with functions that do not have it. Beginning students tend to think that all functions have the linearity property, but this is far from the case, as the next two examples illustrate.

EXAMPLE 7.1

Show that the square root function does not have the linearity property.

Solution: Here we show that $\sqrt{x + y} \neq \sqrt{x} + \sqrt{y}$. Letting $x = 9$ and $y = 16$, we have

$$\sqrt{x + y} = \sqrt{9 + 16} = \sqrt{25} = 5.$$

But,

$$\sqrt{x} + \sqrt{y} = \sqrt{9} + \sqrt{16} = 3 + 4 = 7.$$

Since $5 \neq 7$, we conclude that $\sqrt{x + y} \neq \sqrt{x} + \sqrt{y}$, and, therefore, $\sqrt{x + y}$ does not have the linearity property.

EXAMPLE 7.2

Show that the cosine function does not have the linearity property.

Solution: We will show that $\cos(x + y) \neq \cos x + \cos y$. To this end, we let $x = \frac{1}{3}\pi$ and $y = \frac{1}{6}\pi$. Then,

$$\cos(x + y) = \cos(\tfrac{1}{3}\pi + \tfrac{1}{6}\pi) = \cos \tfrac{1}{2}\pi = 0.$$

But,

$$\cos x + \cos y = \cos \tfrac{1}{3}\pi + \sin \tfrac{1}{6}\pi = \tfrac{1}{2} + \tfrac{1}{2} \neq 0.$$

Therefore, we have shown that the cosine function does not have the linearity property.

The implication of Example 7.2 is that none of the trigonometric functions have the linearity property, which is indeed the case. The purpose of this chapter is to show precisely which formulas the trigonometric functions of sums and differences of angles *do* obey. The formulas will be derived from the viewpoint of trigonometric functions of angles, with the understanding that they are also valid when the domain is the set of real numbers. The most basic of these so-called addition formulas is the formula for $\cos(A - B)$. This formula is derived in the next section.

167

7.2   THE COSINE OF THE DIFFERENCE OF TWO ANGLES

The formula for $\cos(A - B)$ is so basic that it is the only one of the sum and difference formulas which must be derived directly from the definitions of the trigonometric functions.

Let A and B represent angles in standard position superimposed on a circle of radius 1. Figure 7.1a is a picture of the general situation. The terminal side of A intersects the unit circle in the point $(x_A, y_A) = (\cos A, \sin A)$.

FIGURE 7.1

(a)

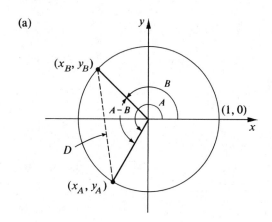

(b)

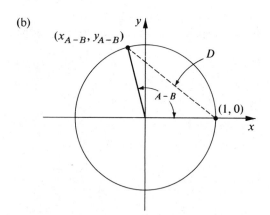

Similarly, the terminal side of B intersects the circle at $(x_B, y_B) = (\cos B, \sin B)$. The distance D between these two points is given by

$$
\begin{aligned}
D^2 &= (x_A - x_B)^2 + (y_A - y_B)^2 \\
&= (\cos A - \cos B)^2 + (\sin A - \sin B)^2 \\
&= (\cos^2 A - 2 \cos A \cos B + \cos^2 B) \\
&\quad + (\sin^2 A - 2 \sin A \sin B + \sin^2 B).
\end{aligned}
$$

Using the fact that $\cos^2 A + \sin^2 A = 1$ and $\cos^2 B + \sin^2 B = 1$, we have

$$D^2 = 2(1 - \cos A \cos B - \sin A \sin B).$$

Now rotate the angle $A - B$ until it is in standard position as shown in Figure 7.1b. The coordinates of the point of intersection of the terminal side of the angle $A - B$ and the unit circle are

$$(x_{A-B}, y_{A-B}) = [\cos(A - B), \sin(A - B)].$$

D is now the distance connecting $(1, 0)$ to this point. Using the distance formula;

$$\begin{aligned} D^2 &= (x_{A-B} - 1)^2 + (y_{A-B})^2 \\ &= (\cos(A - B) - 1)^2 + \sin^2(A - B) \\ &= \cos^2(A - B) - 2\cos(A - B) + 1 + \sin^2(A - B). \end{aligned}$$

Since $\cos^2(A - B) + \sin^2(A - B) = 1$, we can write D^2 as

$$D^2 = 2(1 - \cos(A - B))$$

Equating this result to the first expression we derived for D^2, we have

(7.1) $\cos(A - B) = \cos A \cos B + \sin A \sin B.$

This is our fundamental formula.

Formula 7.1 was derived under the conditions that $A > B$ and that A and B are between 0 and 2π. However, since

$$\cos(A - B) = \cos(B - A) = \cos(A - B + 2n\pi),$$

it follows that the formula is perfectly general. Since it is true for all angles A and B and, consequently for all real numbers, it is an *identity*.

The principal use of this formula is to derive other important relations. However, it can also be used to obtain the value of the cosine function at a particular angle (or real number) if that angle can be expressed as the difference of two angles for which the exact value of the cosine is known.

EXAMPLE 7.3

Without the use of tables, find the exact value of $\cos \frac{1}{12}\pi$.

Solution: First notice that $\frac{1}{12}\pi = \frac{1}{3}\pi - \frac{1}{4}\pi$. Hence,

$$\begin{aligned} \cos \tfrac{1}{12}\pi &= \cos(\tfrac{1}{3}\pi - \tfrac{1}{4}\pi) \\ &= \cos \tfrac{1}{3}\pi \cos \tfrac{1}{4}\pi + \sin \tfrac{1}{3}\pi \sin \tfrac{1}{4}\pi \\ &= \frac{1}{2}\left(\frac{\sqrt{2}}{2}\right) + \left(\frac{\sqrt{3}}{2}\right)\left(\frac{\sqrt{2}}{2}\right) \\ &= \frac{\sqrt{2} + \sqrt{6}}{4}. \end{aligned}$$

If, in formula 7.1, we replace B by $-B$, we obtain

$$\cos(A - (-B)) = \cos A \cos(-B) - \sin A \sin(-B).$$

Since the cosine function is even, $\cos(-B) = \cos B$; since the sine function is odd, $\sin(-B) = -\sin B$. Hence.

(7.2) $\cos(A + B) = \cos A \cos B - \sin A \sin B.$

EXAMPLE 7.4

Find the exact value of $\cos 75°$.

Solution: Since $75° = 30° + 45°$,

$\cos 75° = \cos(30° + 45°)$

$ = \cos 30° \cos 45° - \sin 30° \sin 45°$

$ = \dfrac{\sqrt{3}}{2} \cdot \dfrac{\sqrt{2}}{2} - \dfrac{1}{2} \cdot \dfrac{\sqrt{2}}{2}$

$ = \dfrac{\sqrt{6} - \sqrt{2}}{4}.$

EXAMPLE 7.5

Find the value of $\cos(A - B)$ given that $\sin A = 3/5$ in QII and $\tan B = 1/2$ in QI.

FIGURE 7.2

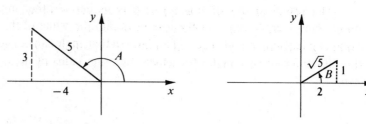

Solution: From Figure 7.2, we see that $\cos A = -4/5$, $\sin B = 1/\sqrt{5}$, and $\cos B = 2/\sqrt{5}$. Hence,

$\cos(A - B) = \cos A \cos B + \sin A \sin B$

$ = \left(-\dfrac{4}{5}\right)\left(\dfrac{2}{\sqrt{5}}\right) + \left(\dfrac{3}{5}\right)\left(\dfrac{1}{\sqrt{5}}\right)$

$ = -\dfrac{5}{5\sqrt{5}} = -\dfrac{\sqrt{5}}{5}$

In certain applied problems, we encounter functions of the form $c_1 \cos Bx + c_2 \sin Bx$. In analyzing the properties of this function, it is easy to see that it is periodic with a period of $2\pi/B$; however, in its present form, it is not easy to recognize the amplitude and phase shift of the oscillation. To obtain these properties, as well as the period, we make use of the identity

$$c_1 \cos Bx + c_2 \sin Bx = A \cos (Bx - C),$$

where $A = \sqrt{c_1^2 + c_2^2}$ and $\tan C = c_2/c_1$.

To verify this identity we note that by Equation 7.2, we have

$$A \cos(Bx - C) = A \cos C \cos Bx + A \sin C \sin Bx.$$

Therefore,

$$c_1 \cos Bx + c_2 \sin Bx = A \cos C \cos Bx + A \sin C \sin Bx,$$

if and only if, $c_1 = A \cos C$ and $c_2 = A \sin C$. Squaring c_1 and c_2 and adding, we get

$$c_1^2 + c_2^2 = A^2\cos^2 C + A^2\sin^2 C = A^2(\cos^2 C + \sin^2 C),$$

or

$$A = \sqrt{c_1^2 + c_2^2}.$$

Also, the ratio of c_2 to c_1 yields

$$\frac{c_2}{c_1} = \frac{A \sin C}{A \cos C} = \tan C.$$

EXAMPLE 7.6

Express $f(x) = \sin x + \cos x$ as a cosine function and sketch.

Solution: Using the above formulas, we have that

$$f(x) = A \cos(x - C) \text{ where } A = \sqrt{1^2 + 1^2} = \sqrt{2} \text{ and } \tan C = 1.$$

Many values of C may be chosen to satisfy $\tan C = 1$ such as $\frac{1}{4}\pi$, $\frac{3}{4}\pi$, $\frac{7}{4}\pi$, etc. Any of these will be satisfactory, but generally we choose

FIGURE 7.3

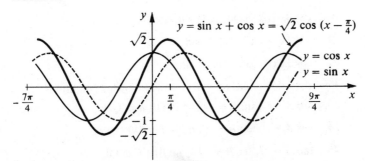

$$y = \sin x + \cos x = \sqrt{2} \cos \left(x - \tfrac{\pi}{4}\right)$$
$$y = \cos x$$
$$y = \sin x$$

a value between $-\frac{1}{2}\pi$ and $\frac{1}{2}\pi$. Hence, we let $C = \frac{1}{4}\pi$. Therefore,

$$f(x) = \sqrt{2}\cos(x - \tfrac{1}{4}\pi).$$

This is a function with amplitude $\sqrt{2}$, period 2π and phase shift $\frac{1}{4}\pi$. The graph is shown in Figure 7.3 along with the graphs of the sine and cosine functions.

EXERCISES FOR SECTIONS 7.1 AND 7.2

1. Show that $\sin(x + y) \neq \sin x + \sin y$. (Let $x = \frac{1}{3}\pi$ and $y = \frac{1}{6}\pi$.)

2. Show that $\tan(x + y) \neq \tan x + \tan y$. (Let $x = \frac{1}{3}\pi$ and $y = \frac{1}{6}\pi$.)

3. Show that $\sin 2x \neq 2\sin x$. (Let $x = \frac{1}{4}\pi$.)

4. Show that $\cos 2x \neq 2\cos x$. (Let $x = \frac{1}{4}\pi$.)

5. Show that $\tan 2x \neq 2\tan x$. (Let $x = \frac{1}{4}\pi$.)

Find the *exact* values of the following trigonometric functions.

6. $\cos 105°$ 7. $\cos\frac{1}{12}\pi$ 8. $\cos\frac{11}{12}\pi$ 9. $\cos 195°$

10. $\cos 345°$

Use Equation 7.1 to show that the following are true.

11. $\cos(\pi - \theta) = -\cos\theta$ 12. $\cos(\frac{1}{2}\pi - \theta) = \sin\theta$

13. $\cos(\frac{1}{2}\pi + \theta) = -\sin\theta$

14. Using Equation 7.1, give a proof that the cosine is an even function.

Verify the following identities.

15. $\cos(\frac{1}{3}\pi - x) = \dfrac{\cos x + \sqrt{3}\sin x}{2}$

16. $\cos(\frac{1}{4}\pi + \theta) = \dfrac{\cos\theta - \sin\theta}{\sqrt{2}}$

17. $\cos(\frac{3}{2}\pi + x) = \sin x$

18. $\cos(x + y)\cos(x - y) = \cos^2 x - \sin^2 y$

19. $\cos(x + y) + \cos(x - y) = 2\cos x \cos y$

Reduce to a single term.

20. $\cos 2x \cos 3x + \sin 2x \sin 3x$.

21. $\cos 7x \cos x - \sin 7x \sin x$.

22. $\cos\frac{1}{6}x \cos\frac{5}{6}x - \sin\frac{1}{6}x \sin\frac{5}{6}x$

Find the value of $\cos(A + B)$ for the following conditions.

23. $\cos A = \frac{1}{3}$, $\sin B = -\frac{1}{2}$, A in QI, B in QIV

24. $\cos A = \frac{3}{5}$, $\tan B = \frac{12}{5}$, both A and B acute.

25. $\tan A = \frac{24}{7}$, $\sec B = \frac{5}{3}$, A in QIII, B in QI.

26. $\sin A = \frac{1}{4}$, $\cos B = \frac{1}{2}$, both A and B in QI.

Let A and B both be positive acute angles.

27.   Find $\cos A$ if $\cos(A + B) = \frac{5}{6}$ and $\sin B = \frac{1}{3}$.

28.   Find $\cos A$ if $\cos(A - B) = \frac{3}{4}$ and $\cos B = \frac{2}{3}$.

Graph the following functions. What is the amplitude and phase shift of each?

29. $f(x) = \cos x - \sin x$

30. $f(x) = 2\cos x + 2\sin x$

31. $f(x) = \cos 2x + \sqrt{3}\sin 2x$

32. $f(x) = -\cos 2x + \sqrt{3}\sin 2x$

7.3   OTHER ADDITION FORMULAS

From the formula for the cosine of the difference, it is easy to establish that

(7.3) $\cos(\frac{1}{2}\pi - \theta) = \sin \theta$ and $\sin(\frac{1}{2}\pi - \theta) = \cos \theta.$

Note that this is a general statement of the identity relating cofunctions of complementary angles. In Chapter 2 this formula was derived with the condition that the two angles were acute. We now see that this is a general formula, true for all values of the argument.

EXAMPLE 7.7

$\cos(-10°) = \cos(90° - 100°) = \sin 100°,$

$\sin(\frac{5}{6}\pi) = \sin(\frac{1}{2}\pi - (-\frac{1}{3}\pi)) = \cos(-\frac{1}{3}\pi) = \cos \frac{1}{3}\pi.$

You know that the fundamental Pythagorean relationship is that $\sin^2 x + \cos^2 x = 1$. A formula involving *two* numbers x and y which looks quite similar is also true if x and y have a sum of $\frac{1}{2}\pi$.

EXAMPLE 7.8

If x and y are complementary numbers (that is their sum is $\frac{1}{2}\pi$), show that $\sin^2 x + \sin^2 y = 1$.

Solution: Since $x + y = \frac{1}{2}\pi$, $y = \frac{1}{2}\pi - x$. Therefore, $\sin y = \sin(\frac{1}{2}\pi - x) = \cos x$. Hence, from the Pythagorean relation,

$\sin^2 x + \cos^2 x = 1,$

we have, using $\sin y = \cos x$,

$\sin^2 x + \sin^2 y = 1.$

By letting $\theta = A + B$ in Equation 7.3, we can write,

$$\sin(A + B) = \cos(\tfrac{1}{2}\pi - (A + B))$$
$$= \cos((\tfrac{1}{2}\pi - A) - B)$$
$$= \cos(\tfrac{1}{2}\pi - A)\cos B + \sin(\tfrac{1}{2}\pi - A)\sin B.$$

(7.4) $\sin(A + B) = \sin A \cos B + \cos A \sin B.$

Similarly, if $\theta = A - B$, we have

$$\sin(A - B) = \sin A \cos(-B) + \cos A \sin(-B),$$

and, since the cosine is an even function and the sine function is odd, this becomes

(7.5) $\sin(A - B) = \sin A \cos B - \cos A \sin B.$

EXAMPLE 7.9

Find the exact value of $\sin(\tfrac{1}{12}\pi)$.

Solution: Since $\tfrac{1}{12}\pi = \tfrac{1}{3}\pi - \tfrac{1}{4}\pi$, we have that

$$\sin(\tfrac{1}{12}\pi) = \sin(\tfrac{1}{3}\pi)\cos(\tfrac{1}{4}\pi) - \cos(\tfrac{1}{3}\pi)\sin(\tfrac{1}{4}\pi)$$
$$= \frac{\sqrt{3}}{2}\frac{\sqrt{2}}{2} - \frac{1}{2}\frac{\sqrt{2}}{2}$$
$$= \frac{1}{4}(\sqrt{6} - \sqrt{2}).$$

EXAMPLE 7.10

Show that $\sin x + \cos x = \sqrt{2}\sin(x + \tfrac{1}{4}\pi)$

Solution: If $\sin x + \cos x = A\sin(x + C) = A\sin x \cos C + A\cos x \sin C$, then $A \cos C = 1$ and $A \sin C = 1$. Squaring these two equations and adding the results, we get

$$A^2\cos^2 C + A^2\sin^2 C = 1^2 + 1^2 = 2$$

or $A = \sqrt{2}.$

Also, $\dfrac{A \sin C}{A \cos C} = \dfrac{1}{1}$

so, $\tan C = 1$

and $C = \tfrac{1}{4}\pi.$

Therefore,

$$\sin x + \cos x = \sqrt{2}\sin(x + \tfrac{1}{4}\pi)$$

The sketch of this function is precisely that given in Figure 7.3. Can you verify this?

Sum and difference formulas for the tangent follow directly from those for the sine and cosine.

$$\tan(A + B) = \frac{\sin(A + B)}{\cos(A + B)}$$

$$= \frac{\sin A \cos B + \cos A \sin B}{\cos A \cos B - \sin A \sin B}.$$

Now divide both the numerator and denominator by $\cos A \cos B$:

$$\tan(A + B) = \frac{\dfrac{\sin A \cos B}{\cos A \cos B} + \dfrac{\cos A \sin B}{\cos A \cos B}}{\dfrac{\cos A \cos B}{\cos A \cos B} - \dfrac{\sin A \sin B}{\cos A \cos B}}.$$

Simplifying, we get

(7.6) $$\tan(A + B) = \frac{\tan A + \tan B}{1 - \tan A \tan B}.$$

Similarly,

(7.7) $$\tan(A - B) = \frac{\tan A - \tan B}{1 + \tan A \tan B}.$$

In summary, we have the following sum and difference formulas which have been derived:

$$\sin(A \pm B) = \sin A \cos B \pm \cos A \sin B,$$
$$\cos(A \pm B) = \cos A \cos B \mp \sin A \sin B,$$
$$\tan(A \pm B) = \frac{\tan A \pm \tan B}{1 \mp \tan A \tan B}.$$

By convention, the symbols $\pm$ and $\mp$ used in the same formula mean to use the topmost signs together and the bottommost signs together.

EXERCISES FOR SECTION 7.3

Find the exact value of the following.

1. $\sin(\frac{5}{12}\pi)$ 2. $\tan 15°$ 3. $\sin(\frac{7}{12}\pi)$

4. $\sin(345°)$ 5. $\cot(\frac{5}{12}\pi)$

Verify the following identities.

6. $\sin(A + \frac{1}{4}\pi) = \frac{\sqrt{2}}{2}(\sin A + \cos A)$

7. $\tan(A + \frac{1}{2}\pi) = -\cot A$

8. $\tan(A + \frac{1}{4}\pi) = \dfrac{1 + \tan A}{1 - \tan A}$

9. $\cot(A + B) = \dfrac{\cot A \cot B - 1}{\cot A + \cot B}$

10. $\dfrac{\sin(A + B)}{\sin(A - B)} = \dfrac{\tan A + \tan B}{\tan A - \tan B}$

11. $\sin(A + B)\sin(A - B) = \sin^2 A - \sin^2 B$

12. $\sin(A + B) + \sin(A - B) = 2\sin A \cos B$

13. $\tan A + \tan B = \dfrac{\sin(A + B)}{\cos A \cos B}$

Reduce to a single term.

14. $\sin 2x \cos 3x + \sin 3x \cos 2x$ 15. $\dfrac{\tan 3x - \tan 2x}{1 + \tan 3x \tan 2x}$

16. $\sin \tfrac{1}{3}x \cos \tfrac{2}{3}x + \sin \tfrac{2}{3}x \cos \tfrac{1}{3}x$ 17. $\dfrac{\tan(x + y) + \tan z}{1 - \tan(x + y)\tan z}$

Find the values of $\sin(A + B)$ and $\tan(A + B)$ if:

18. $\sin A = \tfrac{3}{5}$, $\cos B = \tfrac{4}{5}$, both A and B in QI.

19. $\tan A = -\tfrac{7}{24}$, $\tan B = \tfrac{5}{12}$, A in QII, B in QIII.

20. $\cos A = \tfrac{1}{3}$, $\cos B = -\tfrac{1}{3}$, A in QIV, B in QIII.

Express as a sine function with a phase shift and sketch.

21. $\sin 2x + \cos 2x$ 22. $\cos x$

23. $\sqrt{3}\sin \pi x + \cos \pi x$ 24. $7\sin 2x - 24\cos 2x$

7.4   MULTIPLE AND HALF ANGLE FORMULAS

In the two previous sections, we have been primarily interested in expanding trigonometric functions whose arguments were $A \pm B$. Now we will derive formulas for functions of $2A$ and $\tfrac{1}{2}A$. If A represents an angle, the formulas are called the double and half angle formulas, respectively.

The double angle formulas are easily proved by choosing $B = A$ in the formulas for the sum of two angles. Thus,

$$\begin{aligned} \sin 2A &= \sin(A + A) \\ &= \sin A \cos A + \sin A \cos A, \end{aligned}$$

(7.8) $\sin 2A = 2\sin A \cos A$

and

$$\begin{aligned} \cos 2A &= \cos(A + A) \\ &= \cos A \cos A - \sin A \sin A, \end{aligned}$$

(7.9) $\cos 2A = \cos^2 A - \sin^2 A.$

176   By use of the Pythagorean relationship, this last formula may also be expressed in the equivalent forms

(7.9a) $\cos 2A = 2 \cos^2 A - 1$

and

(7.9b) $\cos 2A = 1 - 2 \sin^2 A$.

Similarly,

$$\tan 2A = \frac{\tan A + \tan A}{1 - \tan A \tan A}.$$

(7.10) $\tan 2A = \dfrac{2 \tan A}{1 - \tan^2 A}$.

EXAMPLE 7.11

Find $\sin 2A$ if $\sin A = \frac{1}{3}$ and A is in QII.

FIGURE 7.4

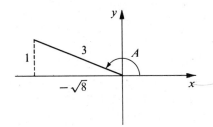

Solution: Since $\sin A = \frac{1}{3}$, we have from Figure 7.4 that $\cos A = -\frac{1}{3}\sqrt{8}$ and hence,

$$\sin 2A = 2 \sin A \cos A$$

$$= 2\left(\frac{1}{3}\right)\left(\frac{-\sqrt{8}}{3}\right) = \frac{-2\sqrt{8}}{9}.$$

Note that $\sin 2A \neq \frac{2}{3}$!

EXAMPLE 7.12

Sketch the graph of $y = \sin x \cos x$. Where does the maximum value of this function occur?

Solution: Initially you may think that you must graph this function by "point plotting", but, by multiplying and dividing the right-hand side by 2, you obtain,

$$y = \frac{2 \sin x \cos x}{2} = \frac{1}{2} \sin 2x.$$

Thus, the graph of this function is a sine wave with amplitude $\frac{1}{2}$ and period π.

Its maximum value of $\frac{1}{2}$ occurs at $x = \frac{1}{4}\pi + 2n\pi$. (See Figure 7.5.)

FIGURE 7.5

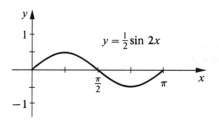

The half-angle formulas are direct consequences of the formulas for the cosine of a double angle. Since

$$\cos 2A = 2 \cos^2 A - 1,$$

we have, upon solving for $\cos A$,

$$\cos A = \pm\sqrt{\frac{1 + \cos 2A}{2}}.$$

Using the formula $\cos 2A = 1 - 2 \sin^2 A$ and solving for $\sin A$,

$$\sin A = \pm\sqrt{\frac{1 - \cos 2A}{2}}.$$

By letting $A = \frac{1}{2}x$ in both of these formulas, we have

(7.11) $\cos \frac{1}{2}x = \pm\sqrt{(1 + \cos x)/2}$,

and

(7.12) $\sin \frac{1}{2}x = \pm\sqrt{(1 - \cos x)/2}$.

To get the formula for $\tan \frac{1}{2}x$, we write

$$\tan \frac{1}{2}x = \frac{\sin \frac{1}{2}x}{\cos \frac{1}{2}x}$$

$$= \frac{\sqrt{(1 - \cos x)/2}}{\sqrt{(1 + \cos x)/2}}$$

$$= \sqrt{(1 - \cos x)/(1 + \cos x)}.$$

Multiplying numerator and denominator by this expression by $(1 + \cos x)$, we get

$$\tan \tfrac{1}{2}x = \sqrt{(1 - \cos^2 x)/(1 + \cos x)^2}$$
$$= \sqrt{\sin^2 x/(1 + \cos x)^2}.$$

Therefore,

(7.13) $\tan \tfrac{1}{2}x = \dfrac{\sin x}{1 + \cos x}.$

EXAMPLE 7.13

If $\tan \theta = -\tfrac{4}{3}$ and $-\tfrac{1}{2}\pi < \theta < 0$, find $\sin \tfrac{1}{2}\theta$ and $\cos \tfrac{1}{2}\theta$.

FIGURE 7.6

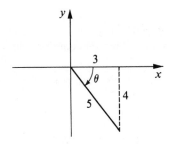

Solution: Figure 7.6 shows the angle θ in standard position. From this, $\cos \theta = \tfrac{3}{5}$, and hence,

$$\sin \tfrac{1}{2}\theta = -\sqrt{\frac{1 - (3/5)}{2}} = -\frac{\sqrt{5}}{5},$$

(The minus sign is chosen because $\sin \tfrac{1}{2}\theta$ is negative on the indicated range). Similarly,

$$\cos \tfrac{1}{2}\theta = \sqrt{\frac{1 + (3/5)}{2}} = \sqrt{4/5} = \frac{2\sqrt{5}}{5}.$$

EXAMPLE 7.14

Find an expression for $\sin 3\theta$ in terms of $\sin \theta$.

Solution:

$$\begin{aligned}
\sin 3\theta &= \sin(2\theta + \theta) \\
&= \sin 2\theta \cos \theta + \sin \theta \cos 2\theta \\
&= 2 \sin \theta \cos^2 \theta + \sin \theta (1 - 2 \sin^2 \theta) \\
&= 2 \sin \theta (1 - \sin^2 \theta) + \sin \theta (1 - 2 \sin^2 \theta) \\
&= 3 \sin \theta - 4 \sin^3 \theta.
\end{aligned}$$

EXAMPLE 7.15

Solve the equation $\cos 2x = \cos x$ on the interval $0 \leq x \leq 2\pi$.

Solution: We first use the identity for $\cos 2x$ to transform the equation into one involving $\cos x$.

$2 \cos^2 x - 1 = \cos x$.

Transferring $\cos x$ to the left-hand side,

$2 \cos^2 x - \cos x - 1 = 0$.

Factoring:

$(2 \cos x + 1)(\cos x - 1) = 0$.

From this we have the two separate equations

$2 \cos x + 1 = 0$ and $\cos x = 1$.

The solution set to the first of these on $0 \leq x \leq 2\pi$ is $x = \frac{2}{3}\pi$ and $\frac{4}{3}\pi$ and, to the second one, is $x = 0$ and $x = 2\pi$. Hence, the complete solution set is

$\{0, \frac{2}{3}\pi, \frac{4}{3}\pi, 2\pi\}$.

EXAMPLE 7.16

If $\sin 2\theta = \frac{1}{3}$, find $\sin \theta$ and $\cos \theta$.

Solution: Since

$\sin 2\theta = \frac{1}{3}$,

$\cos 2\theta = \sqrt{8}/3$,

and

$\tan \theta = \dfrac{\sin 2\theta}{1 + \cos 2\theta}$,

we obtain,

$\tan \theta = \dfrac{1/3}{1 + \sqrt{8}/3} = \dfrac{1}{3 + \sqrt{8}}$.

Hence,

$\sin \theta = \dfrac{1}{\sqrt{18 + 6\sqrt{8}}}$,

$\cos \theta = \dfrac{3 + \sqrt{8}}{\sqrt{18 + 6\sqrt{8}}}$.

Express each of the following functions as a single trigonometric term.

1. $2 \sin 3x \cos 3x$

2. $6 \sin \frac{1}{2}x \cos \frac{1}{2}x$

3. $\sin^2 4x - \cos^2 4x$

4. $4 \sin^2 x \cos^2 x$

5. $\dfrac{2 \tan \frac{1}{6}x}{1 - \tan^2 \frac{1}{6}x}$

6. $\dfrac{\sin 6x}{1 + \cos 6x}$

7. Sketch the graph of the function $f(x) = \sin 2x \cos 2x$. What is the maximum value of the function? Where does it occur?

8. Sketch the graph of the two functions $f(x) = \cos^2 x - \sin^2 x$ and $g(x) = \cos^2 x + \sin^2 x$. In each case tell what the maximum values are.

9. Sketch the graph of the function $f(x) = \sec x \csc x$. Does this function have a maximum? Where is this function undefined?

10. Sketch the graph of the function $f(x) = (2 \tan x)/(1 + \tan^2 x)$. What is the maximum value of this function? What is the period?

11. Sketch the graph of the function $f(x) = \tan x + \cot x$. Where is this function undefined? What is the period?

12. Sketch the graph of the function $f(x) = \cot x - \tan x$. What are the zeros of this function? Is it bounded or unbounded? What is the period?

Find $\sin 2A$, $\cos 2A$, and $\tan 2A$ given that:

13. $\sin A = \frac{3}{5}$, A in QI

14. $\cos A = -\frac{12}{13}$, A in QIII

15. $\tan A = \frac{7}{24}$, A in QIII

16. $\sec A = -\frac{13}{5}$, A in QII

Determine the exact values of the following.

17. $\sin \frac{1}{8}\pi$

18. $\cos \frac{5}{8}\pi$

19. $\tan 157.5°$

20. $\sin 67.5°$

21. $\cos \frac{1}{12}\pi$

Verify the following identities.

22. $(\sin x + \cos x)^2 = 1 + \sin 2x$

23. $\cos 3x = 4 \cos^3 x - 3 \cos x$

24. $\sin 4x = 4 \cos x \sin x(1 - 2 \sin^2 x)$

25. $\tan x + \cot x = 2 \csc 2x$

26. $\cos 4x = 8 \cos^4 x - 8 \cos^2 x + 1$

27. $\cot^2 \frac{1}{2}x = \dfrac{\sec x + 1}{\sec x - 1}$

28. $\cos^4 x = \frac{3}{8} + \frac{1}{2}\cos 2x + \frac{1}{8}\cos 4x$

Find the indicated functional value.

29. Find $\tan \theta$ if $\sin 2\theta = \frac{5}{13}$.

30. Find $\sin \theta$ if $\sin 2\theta = \frac{3}{5}$.

31. Find $\cos \theta$ if $\cos 2\theta = \frac{24}{25}$.

Solve the following equations for those numbers which belong to the interval $0 \le x \le 2\pi$.

32. $\sin 2x = \sin x$ 33. $\sin x = \cos x$

34. $\sin 2x \sin x + \cos x = 0$ 35. $\tan 2x = \tan x$

36. $\cos x - \sin 2x = 0$ 37. $\sin 2x + \cos 2x = 0$

38. $\sin 2x - 2 \cos x + \sin x - 1 = 0$

39. $2(\sin^2 2x - \cos^2 2x) = 1$

40. $\sin 2x \cos x - \frac{1}{2} \sin 3x = \frac{1}{2} \sin x$

Simplify the following expressions.

41. $(\sin x + \cos x)^2 - \sin 2x$ 42. $\dfrac{\sin 4x}{1 - \cos 4x}$

43. $\sec^4 x - \tan^4 x - 2 \tan^2 x$ 44. $\dfrac{\sin 2x}{\sin x} - \dfrac{\cos 2x}{\cos x}$

45. $\cos 2x + \sin 2x \tan x$

7.5   SUMS AND DIFFERENCES OF SINES AND COSINES

Sometimes you will want to factor a sum of sines and cosines into a product. A scheme, based on the addition formulas, is shown below.

EXAMPLE 7.17

Factor $\sin 7x + \sin 3x$.

Solution: We write

$$\sin 7x + \sin 3x = \sin(5x + 2x) + \sin(5x - 2x)$$
$$= \sin 5x \cos 2x + \sin 2x \cos 5x$$
$$+ \sin 5x \cos 2x - \sin 2x \cos 5x$$
$$= 2 \sin 5x \cos 2x.$$

The method, illustrated in the preceding example, is called the *average angle method.* In the general case, we can proceed

$$\sin A + \sin B = \sin \left(\frac{A + B}{2} + \frac{A - B}{2} \right) + \sin \left(\frac{A + B}{2} - \frac{A - B}{2} \right)$$

$$= \sin \frac{A + B}{2} \cos \frac{A - B}{2} + \cos \frac{A + B}{2} \sin \frac{A - B}{2}$$

$$+ \sin \frac{A + B}{2} \cos \frac{A - B}{2} - \cos \frac{A + B}{2} \sin \frac{A - B}{2}.$$

$$(7.14) \quad \sin A + \sin B = 2 \sin \frac{A + B}{2} \cos \frac{A - B}{2}.$$

The following formulas are derived analogously. If you followed the technique, above, you will not have to memorize them.

$$(7.15) \quad \sin A - \sin B = 2 \cos \frac{A + B}{2} \sin \frac{A - B}{2}$$

$$(7.16) \quad \cos A + \cos B = 2 \cos \frac{A + B}{2} \cos \frac{A - B}{2}$$

$$(7.17) \quad \cos A - \cos B = -2 \sin \frac{A + B}{2} \sin \frac{A - B}{2}$$

EXAMPLE 7.18

The difference quotient of a function is defined to be

$$\Delta f = \frac{f(x + \Delta x) - f(x)}{\Delta x}.$$

Find the difference quotient for the sine function.

Solution: We first compute $\sin(x + \Delta x) - \sin x$.

$$\sin(x + \Delta x) - \sin x = 2 \cos \frac{(x + \Delta x) + x}{2} \sin \frac{(x + \Delta x) - x}{2}$$

$$= 2 \sin \frac{\Delta x}{2} \cos \frac{2x + \Delta x}{2}.$$

Thus, the difference quotient for the sine function is

$$\frac{\sin(\Delta x/2)}{\Delta x/2} \cos \frac{2x + \Delta x}{2}.$$

7.6   PRODUCT FORMULAS

Our objective in this section is to find formulas to express products of trigonometric functions as sums of trigonometric functions. The derivations are made from the formulas for the sine and cosine of the sum and difference. If we add the formulas for $\sin(A + B)$ and $\sin(A - B)$ we obtain,

$$(7.18) \quad \sin A \cos B = \tfrac{1}{2}\{\sin(A + B) + \sin(A - B)\}.$$

Upon subtracting $\sin(A - B)$ from $\sin(A + B)$ and simplifying:

$$(7.19) \quad \cos A \sin B = \tfrac{1}{2}\{\sin(A + B) - \sin(A - B)\}.$$

183

In like manner, by first adding and then subtracting the formulas for $\cos(A + B)$ and $\cos(A - B)$, we obtain:

(7.20) $\cos A \cos B = \frac{1}{2}\{\cos(A + B) + \cos(A - B)\},$

(7.21) $\sin A \sin B = \frac{1}{2}\{\cos(A - B) - \cos(A + B)\}.$

EXAMPLE 7.19

Express $\sin mx \cos nx$ as a sum of functions.

Solution: Using Equation 7.18 with $A = mx$ and $B = nx$, we have

$\sin mx \cos nx = \frac{1}{2}\{\sin(mx + nx) + \sin(mx - nx)\}$

$= \frac{1}{2}\{\sin(m + n)x + \sin(m - n)x\}.$

EXAMPLE 7.20

In the analysis of some types of harmonic motion the governing equation is $y(t) = A(\cos \omega t - \cos \omega_0 t)$ where the difference of ω and ω_0 is considered to be very small. Make a sketch of the graph of this function.

Solution: By using Equation 7.21, we write

$$y(t) = 2A \sin \frac{\omega_0 - \omega}{2} t \sin \frac{\omega_0 + \omega}{2} t.$$

If ω is close to ω_0, the resultant oscillation can be interpreted to have a frequency close to $\omega_0/2\pi$ (and of course close to $\omega/2\pi$) with variable

FIGURE 7.7

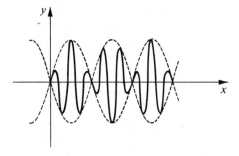

amplitude given by

$$2A \sin \frac{\omega_0 - \omega}{2} t,$$

which fluctuates with frequency $(\omega - \omega_0)/\pi$.
Oscillations of this type are called *beats*. (See Figure 7.7.)

Express each of the following as a product.

1. $\sin 3\theta + \sin \theta$

2. $\cos 3\alpha - \cos 8\alpha$

3. $\sin 8x + \sin 2x$

4. $\sin \frac{1}{2}x - \sin \frac{1}{4}x$

5. $\cos 50° - \cos 30°$

6. $\sin \frac{3}{4}\pi - \sin \frac{1}{4}\pi$

7. $\sin \frac{3}{4} - \sin \frac{1}{4}$

Express each of the following as a sum or difference.

8. $\sin 3x \cos x$

9. $\cos x \sin \frac{1}{2}x$

10. $\cos \frac{1}{3}\pi \sin \frac{2}{3}\pi$

11. $\cos 6x \cos 2x$

12. $\sin \frac{1}{4}\pi \sin \frac{1}{12}\pi$

Verify the following identities.

13. $\dfrac{\sin x + \sin y}{\cos x + \cos y} = \tan \frac{1}{2}(x + y)$

14. $\dfrac{\sin x + \sin y}{\sin x - \sin y} = \dfrac{\tan \frac{1}{2}(x + y)}{\tan \frac{1}{2}(x - y)}$

15. $\dfrac{\cos 3x + \cos x}{\sin 3x + \sin x} = \cot 2x$

16. $\cos 7x + \cos 5x + 2 \cos x \cos 2x = 4 \cos 4x \cos 2x \cos x$

17. $\dfrac{\sin 2x + \sin 2y}{\cos 2x + \cos 2y} = \tan(x + y)$

18. $\dfrac{\sin 9x - \sin 5x}{\sin 14x} = \dfrac{\sin 2x}{\sin 7x}$

19. Find the difference quotient for $\cos x$.

Solve the following equations on $0 \leq x \leq \pi$.

20. $\sin 3x + \sin 5x = 0$

21. $\sin x - \sin 5x = 0$

22. $\cos 3x - \cos x = 0$

23. $\cos 2x - \cos 3x = 0$

24. Let $f(x) = \sin(2x + 1) + \sin(2x - 1)$. Make a sketch of the graph of the function. What is the period and amplitude?

25. Let $f(x) = \cos(3x + 1) + \cos(3x - 1)$. Make a sketch of the graph of this function and give the period and amplitude.

26. Make a sketch of the graph of the function $f(x) = \cos 99x - \cos 101x$.

8

INVERSE
FUNCTIONS

A *relation* is a very general type of association or pairing of two quantities usually called variables—one being the *independent* variable and the other the *dependent* variable. Traditionally, we write the independent variable followed by the dependent variable, so that such pairings are said to be "*ordered.*" For instance, when we write the pairing (2, 5), it is understood that the value of the independent variable is 2 and that of the dependent variable is 5. You have already seen this idea in graphing a function where the x coordinate of the point is given first, followed by the y coordinate.

Relations are usually described in one or more of the following ways:

(1)   by a set of ordered pairs, such as $\{(2, 1), (-3, 2), (0, 5)\}$;
(2)   by an equation, such as $x^2 + y^2 - 1 = 0$ or $y - \sin x = 0$;
(3)   by a graph, such as those shown in Figure 8.1.

FIGURE 8.1

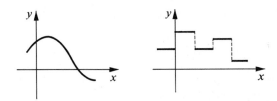

Given any relation R, we can obtain another one by merely interchanging the numbers in each of the ordered pairs. A relation obtained in this manner is called the *inverse* of the given relation and is denoted by R^{-1}. (The $^{-1}$ notation does not represent a negative exponent; it is simply a symbol for the inverse relation.)

Suppose we are given the relation

$$R = \{(2, 1), (-3, 2), (0, 5)\}.$$

Then, the inverse relation is

$$R^{-1} = \{(1, 2), (2, -3), (5, 0)\}.$$

Notice that we have simply interchanged the first and second element in each ordered pair. R and R^{-1} are represented graphically in Figure 8.2 along with the line $y = x$. Inspection of this figure reveals that the graph of R^{-1} is the mirror reflection of R in the line $y = x$. This will *always* be the case when a relation and its inverse are plotted on the same coordinate axes.

Next, consider the equations $y = 2x + 4$ and $x = 2y + 4$. We solve the second equation for y in terms of x to get $y = \frac{1}{2}x - 2$. By plotting $y = 2x + 4$ and $y = \frac{1}{2}x - 2$ on the same set of coordinates as shown in

FIGURE 8.2

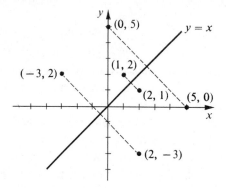

Figure 8.3, we see that their graphs are mirror images in the line $y = x$. Therefore, $x = 2y + 4$ is the inverse of $y = 2x + 4$. Notice that the equation defining the inverse of a given relation is obtained by interchanging the x and y in the equation which defines the relation.

FIGURE 8.3

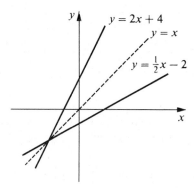

EXAMPLE 8.1

Given the relation R defined by $y = x + 1$, find R^{-1}.

Solution: By interchanging the x and y variables, the equation

$$x = y + 1$$

defines R^{-1}. Since it is customary to solve for the dependent variable, we may write R^{-1} as

$$y = x - 1.$$

The graph of R and R^{-1} are shown in Figure 8.4 where once again we notice that they are mirror images about the line $y = x$.

FIGURE 8.4

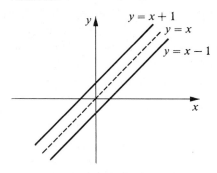

EXAMPLE 8.2

Given $R = \{(x, y)|F(x, y) = 0\}$, find R^{-1}.

Solution: The inverse in this case can be written

$R^{-1} = \{(y, x)|F(x, y) = 0\}$.

More typically, the ordered pairs are displayed with the variable x as the "first" number and the variable y as the "second," which is denoted by

$R^{-1} = \{(x, y)|F(y, x) = 0\}$.

Thus, we see that the same basic equation relates the two variables, but with the domain and range interchanged.

The concept of a *function* has been used throughout this book and is one of the really important ideas in mathematics. You may recall that a function is a special kind of relation in which each value of the first variable uniquely determines at most one value of the second. We interpret a function graphically by saying that a relation is a function if, and only if, any vertical line meets the graph of the relation in at most one point. For instance, the graphs in Figure 8.5a and 8.5b represent functions but 8.5c does not.

FIGURE 8.5

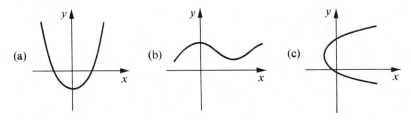

(a)   (b)   (c)

The inverse of a function may or may not be a function. As for any relation, an inverse relation is called a function if a vertical line intersects its graph in at most one point. Since a function and its inverse are mirror images of one another in the line $y = x$, you can tell directly from the graph of the function whether or not its inverse is a function. If the graph of a function intersects a horizontal line in, at most, one point, its inverse is a function; otherwise, it is not. Figure 8.6a shows a function whose inverse is also a function, and Figure 8.6b shows one whose inverse is not a function.

FIGURE 8.6

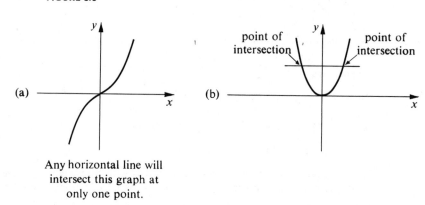

(a)

(b)

point of intersection

point of intersection

Any horizontal line will intersect this graph at only one point.

Functions whose inverse relations are also functions are called *one-to-one* functions because, for each value of x, there is at most one value of y; conversely, for each y, there is at most one value of x. More specifically, *a function f is one-to-one if $f(a) = f(b)$ implies $a = b$.* Thus, the function

$$f = \{(2, 3), (4, 7), (6, 3)\}$$

is not a one-to-one function because $f(2) = 3 = f(6)$, but $2 \neq 6$.

Graphically, a one-to-one function is one for which both horizontal and vertical lines intersect its graph in at most one point. In Figure 8.6 the first function is one-to-one, the second is not.

Generally, if a relation is a function, we will use $y = f(x)$ to describe it. In this case, the inverse of the function f is written f^{-1}.

EXAMPLE 8.3

The function $f(x) = x + 1$ has an inverse function given by the rule $f^{-1}(x) = x - 1$.

EXAMPLE 8.4

The function $y = \sin x$ does not have an inverse function since the graph of the sine function is such that a horizontal line will cross its graph in more than one point—indeed, infinitely many points.

EXERCISES FOR SECTION 8.1

1. In Exercises *a–h*, indicate which are functions and which are relations.

   a. $\{(2, 6), (3, 5), (0, 4)\}$ b. $\{(-1, 2), (2, 3), (6, -1)\}$

   c. $\{(3, 7), (5, 9), (-3, 9), (3, 2)\}$ d. $\{(1, 2), (2, 1)\}$

   e. $y = 3x + 2$ f. $y = x^2$

   g. $y = \pm\sqrt{x}$ h. $y = x^3$

2. In Exercises 1, find the inverse relations and indicate which are functions.

3. Draw the graph of each relation and its inverse in Exercises 1. (Remember, functions are special kinds of relations.)

4. Which of the functions in Exercises 1 are one-to-one?

5. Suppose f and f^{-1} are defined by identical formulas, what can you say about the graph of f?

6. Are the trigonometric functions one-to-one functions?

8.2   INVERSE TRIGONOMETRIC FUNCTIONS

In many applications it is highly desirable to work with one-to-one functions since, given any x, there is a uniquely determined value of y; conversely, given a y, there is a unique value of x which is paired with it. As you can see by examining their graphs, none of the six trigonometric functions are one-to-one. Therefore, none of the trigonometric functions have an inverse, a fact that causes difficulty in certain applications. To circumvent this difficulty, we limit the domain of each trigonometric function to a set of values, called *principal values*, for which it is one-to-one. Thus, at least for the principal values, each of the trigonometric functions will have an inverse. The principal values for each of the six trigonometric functions is indicated in Table 8.1.

TABLE 8.1   Table of Principal Values of the Trigonometric Functions

$\sin x, \quad -\frac{1}{2}\pi \leq x \leq \frac{1}{2}\pi$	$\cot x, \quad 0 < x < \pi$
$\cos x, \quad 0 \leq x \leq \pi$	$\csc x, \quad -\frac{1}{2}\pi \leq x \leq \frac{1}{2}\pi, x \neq 0$
$\tan x, \quad -\frac{1}{2}\pi < x < \frac{1}{2}\pi$	$\sec x, \quad 0 \leq x \leq \pi, x \neq \frac{1}{2}\pi$

    Figure 8.7 shows a sketch of each of the six trigonometric functions limited to the principal values. Some authors choose to actually rename the functions when the domain is so limited by calling them the (capitalized) Trigonometric functions. With that convention, the graphs shown in Figure 8.7 would be of the Sine, Cosine, Tangent, etc.

191

FIGURE 8.7   Principal values of the trigonometric functions

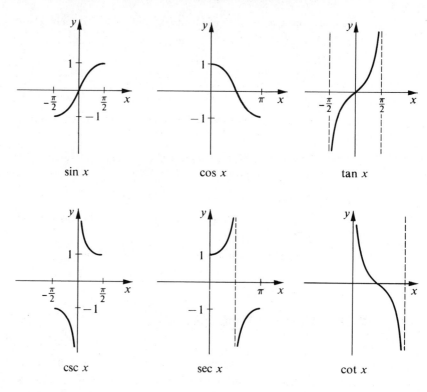

sin x

cos x

tan x

csc x

sec x

cot x

EXAMPLE 8.5

Find the principal value of x for which (a) $\cos x = -\frac{1}{2}$ and (b) $\sin x = -\frac{1}{2}$.

FIGURE 8.8

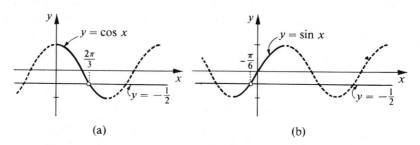

(a)

(b)

Solution: Figure 8.8a shows the cosine function, and 8.8b shows the sine function intersecting the line $y = -\frac{1}{2}$. In each case, the interval of principal values is made heavier so that you can see that only one value of x on that interval satisfies the equation. Thus, the principal value of x for which $\cos x = -\frac{1}{2}$ is $x = \frac{2}{3}\pi$. The principal value of x for which $\sin x = -\frac{1}{2}$ is for $x = -\frac{1}{6}\pi$.

We are now in a position to define functions inverse to the six trigonometric functions on the intervals of principal values. Actually, you need not continually affirm that a particular trigonometric function is limited to its principal values because the only way that its inverse can exist (as a function) is by such a limitation.

The inverse for $y = \sin x$ (where x is limited to the principal values of the sine function) is found by interchanging x and y to get $x = \sin y$ and then solving for y. We cannot algebraically solve $x = \sin y$ for y, but we know that a solution should state that "y is a number or angle whose sine is x". The word "arcsin" is traditionally used to convey this idea, and, therefore, the inverse to $x = \sin y$ is written $y = \arcsin x$.* This notation is particularly descriptive since you can think of it as meaning "the arc length of the unit circle whose sine is x." Thus, $\arcsin \frac{1}{2}$ is the arc or angle whose sine is $\frac{1}{2}$; that is, $\frac{1}{6}\pi$. Note that only one value for the angle is obtained, and this *must* be chosen from the set of principal values.

The definition of each of the six inverse trigonometric functions proceeds in a similar manner. The domain of each function is limited to its principal values so that a one-to-one function is obtained, thereby, making an inverse function possible.

DEFINITION 8.1

The Inverse Trigonometric Functions

$y = \arcsin x$ means $x = \sin y$, $\frac{1}{2}\pi \leq y \leq \frac{1}{2}\pi$

$y = \arccos x$ means $x = \cos y$, $0 \leq y \leq \pi$

$y = \arctan x$ means $x = \tan y$, $\frac{1}{2}\pi < y < \frac{1}{2}\pi$

$y = \text{arccot } x$ means $x = \cot y$, $0 < y < \pi$

$y = \text{arcsec } x$ means $x = \sec y$, $0 \leq y \leq \pi$, $y \neq \frac{1}{2}\pi$

$y = \text{arccsc } x$ means $x = \csc y$, $\frac{1}{2}\pi \leq y \leq \frac{1}{2}\pi$, $y \neq 0$

EXAMPLE 8.6

Find $\arccos \left(\frac{1}{3}\right)$.

Solution: We let $y = \arccos \left(\frac{1}{3}\right)$. Then,

$\frac{1}{3} = \cos y$,   where $0 \leq y \leq \pi$.

By use of Table B, we find that $y = 1.23$.

---

*Another notation that is used for the inverse to $y = \sin x$ is $y = \sin^{-1} x$. (read: "the inverse sine of x"). This notation is somewhat confusing since it suggests taking the reciprocal of $\sin x$. For this reason, we will use arcsin to designate the inverse sine function.

EXAMPLE 8.7

Find arctan (-1) and arccot (-1).

Solution: Let $y = $ arctan (-1) and $u = $ arccot (-1). Then,

$$-1 = \tan y, \quad -\tfrac{1}{2}\pi < y < \tfrac{1}{2}\pi,$$

and

$$-1 = \cot u, \quad 0 < u < \pi.$$

Thus,

$$y = -\tfrac{1}{4}\pi \quad \text{and} \quad u = \tfrac{3}{4}\pi.$$

Since the tangent and cotangent are reciprocal functions, you might have expected that the arctan (-1) and arccot (-1) yield the same value. This example shows the necessity of adhering strictly to the definitions of the inverse functions, giving close attention to the principal values.

EXAMPLE 8.8

Find $\sin(\arccos \tfrac{1}{2})$.

Solution: We first let $\theta = $ arccos $\tfrac{1}{2}$. Then, θ is the angle as shown in Figure 8.9 from which it is easy to see that

$$\sin(\arccos \tfrac{1}{2}) = \sin \theta = \sqrt{3}/2.$$

FIGURE 8.9

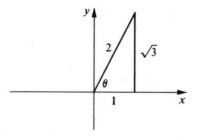

EXAMPLE 8.9

Find $\cos(\arcsin x)$.

Solution: If we let $\theta = $ arcsin x, then we wish to find $\cos \theta$. The expression $\theta = $ arcsin x can also be written $x = \sin \theta$ and $\cos \theta = \pm\sqrt{1 - \sin^2 \theta}$.

Therefore,

$$\cos \theta = \pm\sqrt{1 - \sin^2 \theta} = \pm\sqrt{1 - x^2}$$

or

$$\cos(\arcsin x) = \pm\sqrt{1 - x^2}.$$

In passing, we note that

$$\sin(\arcsin x) = x,$$
$$\cos(\arccos x) = x,$$

and so forth, for all six trigonometric functions. This result is a direct consequence of the inverse nature of the functions involved. Also *if x is limited to the principal values* of the function,

$$\arcsin(\sin x) = x,$$
$$\arccos(\cos x) = x,$$

and so forth.

In closing this section, we want to point out that, while the choice of principal values is a matter of convention, there are some important reasons why these particular values are so chosen. For example, the reason for defining the principal values of cos x to be $0 \leq x \leq \pi$ is so that

$$\arccos x = \tfrac{1}{2}\pi - \arcsin x,$$

a relation expressing the fact that the angle whose cosine is x is the complement of the angle whose sine is x. Thus, once the principal values of the sine function are chosen to be between $-\tfrac{1}{2}\pi$ and $\tfrac{1}{2}\pi$, this complementary relation will automatically mean that

$$0 \leq \arccos x \leq \pi.$$

It should be noted, however, that not all writers agree on the specific choices for principal values. For example, the principal values of the secant function is often chosen to be between 0 and $\tfrac{1}{2}\pi$ when it is positive and between $-\pi$ and $-\tfrac{1}{2}\pi$ when it is negative. This latter method has the advantage of simplifying some rather important formulas of calculus but has the disadvantage of failing to satisfy the relation

$$\text{arcsec } x = \arccos \frac{1}{x} \text{ when } x < 0.$$

For your purposes, you should be aware that the choices of principal values, while not being dictated by whim, are a matter of convention.

EXERCISES FOR SECTION 8.2

Find the exact value of each of the following:

1. $\arcsin \tfrac{1}{2}$ 2. $\arcsin 1$ 3. $\arctan 1$

4. $\operatorname{arccot}(-\sqrt{3})$ 5. $\operatorname{arccot} 0$ 6. $\operatorname{arcsec} 1$

7. $\arctan \sqrt{3}$ 8. $\arccos(-1)$ 9. $\sin(\arcsin 1)$

10. $\sec(\arcsin \frac{1}{2})$ 11. $\sin(\arctan 2)$ 12. $\sec(\arccos \frac{1}{3})$

13. $\cos(\arcsin \frac{1}{4})$ 14. $\tan(\operatorname{arcsec} x)$ 15. $\sin(\arccos x^2)$

16. $\tan(\arcsin x)$ 17. $\cos(\arcsin(x - 4))$

18. Show that the inverse sine function does not have the linearity property by showing that $\arcsin 2x \neq 2 \arcsin x$.

19. Show that the inverse cosine function does not have the linearity property by showing that $\arccos x + \arccos y \neq \arccos(x + y)$.

20. Make a table listing the domain and range of each of the six inverse trigonometric functions.

What function is inverse to:

21. $\arcsin x$ 22. $\arccos 3x$

23. $3 \arccos x$ 24. $\arcsin \sqrt{1 + x}$

Sketch the graph of:

25. $\arcsin(\sin x)$ 26. $\arcsin(\cos x)$

Simplify:

27. $\sin(2 \arcsin x)$ 28. $\cos(\arccos x + \arcsin y)$

29. $\sin(\arcsin x + \arcsin y)$

30. A picture u feet high is placed on a wall with its base v feet above the level of the observer's eye. If the observer stands x feet from the wall, show that the angle of vision α subtended by the picture is given by

$$\alpha = \operatorname{arccot} \frac{x}{u + v} - \operatorname{arccot} \frac{x}{v}.$$

8.3   GRAPHS OF THE INVERSE TRIGONOMETRIC FUNCTIONS

The graphs of the six inverse trigonometric functions are found by direct appeal to the definition and by a knowledge of the graphs of the trigonometric functions. For example: $y = \arcsin x$ if, and only if, $x = \sin y$ where $-\frac{1}{2}\pi \leq y \leq \frac{1}{2}\pi$. It follows that $y = \arcsin x$ looks like a piece of the relation $x = \sin y$. In Figure 8.10, we see such a graph.

The other parts of Figure 8.10 show the graphs of the remaining inverse functions. In each case, you can think of the graph of the original function wrapped around the y axis and then consider the portion which corresponds to the principal values.

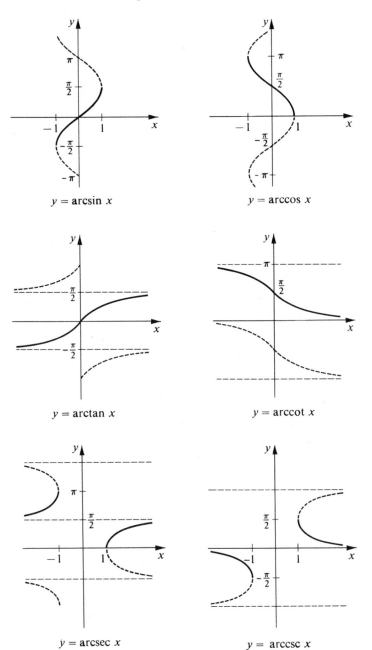

$y = \arcsin x$

$y = \arccos x$

$y = \arctan x$

$y = \mathrm{arccot}\, x$

$y = \mathrm{arcsec}\, x$

$y = \mathrm{arccsc}\, x$

EXAMPLE 8.10

Sketch the graph of arccos $2x$.

Solution: First, we let $y = \arccos 2x$. Then by definition of an inverse, we have $2x = \cos y$ or $x = \frac{1}{2}\cos y$ which has a period of 2π and an amplitude of $\frac{1}{2}$. Sketching this cosine wave around the y axis from 0 to π, we have the graph of $y = $ arccos $2x$. (See Figure 8.11.)

FIGURE 8.11

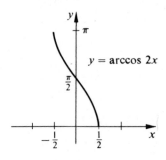

$y = $ arccos $2x$

EXAMPLE 8.11

Sketch the graph of 2 arccos x.

Solution: Let $y = 2$ arccos x. Then dividing by 2, we get

$\frac{1}{2}y = $ arccos x.

Hence, by definition,

$x = \cos \frac{1}{2}y$.

This cosine wave has an amplitude of one and a period of 4π. The principal values in this case are $0 \le \frac{1}{2}y \le \pi$ or $0 \le y \le 2\pi$. (See Figure 8.12.)

FIGURE 8.12

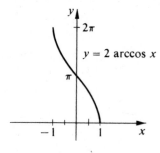

$y = 2$ arccos x

EXERCISES FOR SECTION 8.3

Sketch the graph of each of the following functions:

1. arcsin $2x$ 2. arccos $2x$ 3. 2 arccos $\frac{1}{2}x$

4. $\frac{1}{2}$ arcsin $\frac{1}{2}x$ 5. arctan $3x$ 6. arctan $x + \frac{1}{2}\pi$

Certain equations and identities involve the use of the inverse trigonometric functions. We will exhibit the techniques of solving equations and identities of this type in the following examples. You should note that the common thread through the examples is to take some trigonometric function of both sides of the equality.

EXAMPLE 8.12

Solve the equation:

$$\arctan x = \arcsin \tfrac{4}{5} + \arccos \tfrac{-3}{5}.$$

Solution: We take the tangent of both sides to obtain

$$\tan(\arctan x) = \tan(\arcsin \tfrac{4}{5} + \arccos \tfrac{-3}{5}).$$

Note that the tangent of the sum of the right-hand side is *not* the sum of the tangent of the individual terms since the tangent function does not obey the linearity property. We let $\alpha = \arcsin \tfrac{4}{5}$ and $\beta = \arccos \tfrac{-3}{5}$. These angles are displayed in Figure 8.13.

FIGURE 8.13

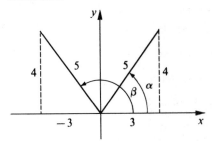

Thus,

$$x = \tan(\alpha + \beta)$$
$$= \frac{\tan \alpha + \tan \beta}{1 - \tan \alpha \tan \beta}.$$

From Figure 8.13, it is now a simple matter to determine that $\tan \alpha = \tfrac{4}{3}$ and that $\tan \beta = -\tfrac{4}{3}$ from which

$$x = \frac{\tfrac{4}{3} - \tfrac{4}{3}}{1 + \tfrac{4}{3} \cdot \tfrac{4}{3}} = 0.$$

EXAMPLE 8.13

Verify the identity $2 \arccos x = \arccos(2x^2 - 1)$.

Solution: We take the cosine of the left-hand side to obtain

$$\cos(2 \arccos x).$$

By letting $\theta = \arccos x$, we have

$$\cos(2 \arccos x) = \cos 2\theta = \cos^2\theta - \sin^2\theta.$$

From Figure 8.14, we read off the values of $\cos \theta$ to be x and $\sin \theta$ to be $\sqrt{1 - x^2}$. Hence,

$$\cos(2 \arccos x) = x^2 - (1 - x^2) = 2x^2 - 1,$$

which is what we wanted to show.

FIGURE 8.14

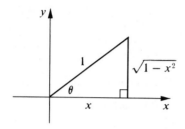

EXERCISES FOR SECTION 8.4

Solve the following equations:

1. $\arccos x = \arccos \frac{4}{5} - \arcsin \frac{3}{5}$

2. $\arctan x = \text{arccot } 3 + \text{arccsc } \sqrt{5}$

3. $\arcsin x = \arctan \frac{5}{7} + \arctan \frac{1}{6}$

4. $\arcsin x = \arcsin \frac{5}{13} + \arccos \frac{4}{5}$

5. $\arccos x = \arctan 1 + \arctan \frac{1}{2}$

6. $\arcsin x = \arcsin 1 - \arcsin(-1)$

Verify the following identities:

7. $2 \arcsin x = \arccos(1 - 2x^2)$

8. $\cos(\arcsin x + \arccos y) = y\sqrt{1 - x^2} - x\sqrt{1 - y^2}$

9. $\cos 2(\arccos y) = 2y^2 - 1$

10. $\arcsin \theta = \arctan \dfrac{\theta}{\sqrt{1 - \theta^2}}$

11. $3 \arcsin \theta = \arcsin(3\theta - 4\theta^3)$

12. $\arctan x + \arctan y = \arctan \dfrac{x + y}{1 - xy}$

13. $2 \arctan x = \arctan \dfrac{2x}{1 - x^2}$

14. $\tan(\arctan x + \arctan 1) = \dfrac{1 + x}{1 - x}$

9

LOGARITHMS

9.1   DEFINITION

In this chapter you will learn something of the usefulness of logarithms in making computations in trigonometry. You may easily omit the chapter if you are satisfied that you will always have computing machines available, or if "slide rule accuracy" is sufficient.

We begin with a statement of the definition of the logarithm and its relation to the exponent.

DEFINITION 9.1

The logarithm of a positive number x to the base $b (\neq 1)$ is the power to which b must be raised to give x. That is,

$y = \log_b x$ if, and only if, $x = b^y$.

The equation $y = \log_b x$ is read, "y is the logarithm of x to the base b." The following examples illustrate this definition.

EXAMPLE 9.1

(a) $\log_2 8 = 3$, since $2^3 = 8$

(b) $\log_3 \frac{1}{9} = -2$, since $3^{-2} = \frac{1}{9}$

(c) $\log_{10} 10{,}000 = 4$, since $10^4 = 10{,}000$

EXAMPLE 9.2

Find the base a if $\log_a 16 = 4$.

Solution: Since $2^4 = 16$, we conclude that the desired base is $a = 2$.

EXAMPLE 9.3

Find the number x if $\log_3 x = -3$.

Solution: Since $3^{-3} = \frac{1}{27}$, we conclude that $x = \frac{1}{27}$.

EXERCISES FOR SECTION 9.1

Write a logarithmic equation equivalent to the given exponential equation.

1. $x = 2^3$ 2. $y = 3^8$ 3. $M = 5^{-3}$

4. $N = 10^{-2}$ 5. $L = 7^2$

Find the base of the logarithm function such that:

6. $\log_b 8 = 1$ 7. $\log_b 4 = 2$ 8. $\log_b (1/4) = -2$

9. $\log_b 100 = 2$ 10. $\log_b (1/3) = -1$

Solve the following equations for the unknown.

11. $\log_{10} x = 4$ 12. $\log_5 N = 2$ 13. $\log_x 10 = 1$

14. $\log_x 25 = 2$ 15. $\log_x 64 = 3$ 16. $\log_{16} x = 2$

17. $\log_{27} x = \frac{2}{3}$ 18. $\log_2 \frac{1}{8} = x$ 19. $\log_3 9 = x$

20. $\log_{10} 10^7 = x$ 21. $\log_b b^a = x$ 22. $\log_b x = b$

23. $\log_x 2 = \frac{1}{3}$ 24. $\log_x 0.0001 = -2$ 25. $\log_x 6 = \frac{1}{2}$

26. $\log_6 x = 0$ 27. $6^{\log 6^x} = 6$ 28. $x^{\log_x x} = 3$

29. Let $f(x) = \log_3 x$. Find $f(9), f(\frac{1}{27}), f(81)$.

30. Let $f(x) = \log_2 x$. By example, show that:

     a. $f(x + y) \neq f(x) + f(y)$ b. $f(ax) \neq af(x)$

31. A power supply has a power output in watts approximated by the equation

$$P = 64(2)^{-3t}$$

where t is in days. How many days does it take for the power supply to reduce to a power output of 1 watt?

32. A certain radioactive material decays exponentially by the equation

$$A(t) = A_0 2^{-t/5}.$$

Find the half-life of the material.

9.2   BASIC PROPERTIES OF THE LOGARITHM

Logarithmic expressions must often be rearranged or simplified. These simplifications are accomplished by three basic Rules of Logarithms which correspond precisely to the three fundamental rules for exponents and are necessary consequences of them.

RULE 1

$\mathbf{Log_a}\ \mathbf{MN} = \mathbf{log_a}\ \mathbf{M} + \mathbf{log_a}\ \mathbf{N}$

Proof: Let $u = \log_a M$ and $v = \log_a N$. Then,

$a^u = M$ and $a^v = N$,

from which

$MN = a^u a^v = a^{u+v}.$

Expressing, again, in terms of logarithms:

$$\log_a MN = u + v = \log_a M + \log_a N.$$

RULE 2

$\log_a M^c = c \log_a M$, where c is any real number.

Proof: Let $u = \log_a M$. Then,

$$a^u = M \quad \text{and} \quad (a^u)^c = a^{uc} = M^c.$$

In terms of logarithms, this may be expressed as

$$\log M^c = uc = c \log_a M.$$

RULE 3

$\log_a (M/N) = \log_a M - \log_a N$

Proof: $M/N = M(N)^{-1}$. Now apply the previous two rules.

In words, Rule 1 says "the logarithm of a product is equal to the sum of the logarithms of the individual terms" while Rule 3 says "the logarithm of a quotient is the difference of the logarithms of the individual terms." Examine these rules carefully and notice where they do *not* apply. For example, *there is no rule for simplifying expressions of the form* $\log(x + y)$ or $\log(x - y)$.

EXAMPLE 9.4

$$\log_2 8 \cdot 64 \cdot 128 = \log_2 8 + \log_2 64 + \log_2 128$$
$$= 3 + 6 + 7 = 16.$$

EXAMPLE 9.5

$$\log x - \log x^2 + \log(x^2 + 1) - \log(x^2 - 1) + \log(x - 1)$$
$$= \log \frac{x(x^2 + 1)(x - 1)}{x^2(x^2 - 1)}$$
$$= \log \frac{x^2 + 1}{x(x + 1)}.$$

EXERCISES FOR SECTION 9.2

Given that $\log_{10} 2 = 0.3010$, $\log_{10} 3 = 0.4771$, and $\log_{10} 7 = 0.8451$, find the following.

1. $\log_{10} \frac{3}{2}$

2. $\log_{10} 4$

3. $\log_{10} 12$

4. $\log_{10}30$ 5. $\log_{10}90$ 6. $\log_{10}\sqrt{2}$

7. $\log_{10}\sqrt[3]{3}$ 8. $\log_{10}21^{1/3}$ 9. $\log_{10}2400$

10. $\log_{10}.00018$

Simplify the following expressions.

11. $\log_2 x^2 - \log_2 x$ 12. $\log_2(x^2 - 1) - \log_2(x - 1)$

13. $\log_3 x + \log_3(1/x)$ 14. $\log_6(\sec x + \tan x)^{-1}$

15. Let $\log_e I = (-Rt/L) + \log_e I_0$. Show that $I = I_0 e^{-Rt/L}$.

16. If y is directly proportional to x^p, what relation exists between $\log y$ and $\log x$.

Solve the following for the unknown.

17. $\log_2(x + 3) = -1$ 18. $\log_2(x - 1) > 1$

19. $\log_3(x + 1) > 2$ 20. $\log_2(2 - x) < -1$

21. $\log_{10}(2x - 1) < 3$ 22. $0 < \log_b x < 1$

23. $2 < \log_2 x < 3$ 24. $\log_2\sqrt{x} < 3$

25. Compare the functions $f(x) = \log_b x^2$ and $g(x) = 2\log_b x$. In what way are they the same? In what way different?

26. Let $f(x) = \log_a x$ and $g(x) = \log_{1/a} x$. Show that $g(x) = f(1/x)$.

27. If $\log_a x = 2$, find $\log_{1/a} x$ and $\log_a(1/x)$.

28. Compare the graphs of the functions $f(x) = \log_2 2x$, $g(x) = \log_2 x$, $h(x) = \log_2\sqrt{x}$ and $m(x) = \log_2 x^2$.

29. Given the graph of $y = \log x$, is there a convenient way to obtain the graph of:
     a. $\log x^p$?   b. $\log px$?   c. $\log(x + p)$?   d. $\log(x/p)$?

30. If $f(x) = \log_b x$, is $f(x + y) = f(x) + f(y)$?

9.3   COMMON LOGARITHMS

Historically, logarithms to the base 10 have been used most frequently—especially in simplifying numerical computation. These logarithms have come to be known as *common logarithms*. We customarily omit the numerical subscript when discussing common logarithms. Thus, in this book, $\log x$ means $\log_{10} x$.

Table C in the Appendix is a listing of common logarithms of numbers between 1 and 10 in steps of 0.01. This table is a "four place" table which means that it gives values accurate to four decimal places. To find the logarithm of a number between 1 and 10, locate the first two digits of the number in the left column. The columns at the top are headed by the third digit of the number. Thus, to find the logarithm of 5.31, look down the left-hand column until you come to 5.3. Then move over to the column headed by 1 to find that log 5.31 = 0.7251.

To find the number whose logarithm is given, we use Table C "in reverse." Such a procedure is often called finding *antilogarithms*. Thus, since log 2 = 0.3010, antilog 0.3010 = 2.

Table C lists logarithms for numbers *m* such that $1 \leq m \leq 10$. The corresponding range values are $0 \leq \log m \leq 1$; that is, all the values in the table are fractions between 0 and 1.

To find the logarithm of any number we use the fact that any positive number *M* may be written as the product of a number *m* (where *m* is between 1 and 10) and 10^c (where *c* is an integer). That is,

$$M = m \cdot 10^c, \qquad 1 \leq m < 10.$$

A number so written is said to be in *scientific form*. Several examples are given in the next example.

EXAMPLE 9.6

$$53.1 = 5.31 \times 10^1$$
$$0.00531 = 5.31 \times 10^{-3}$$
$$5310000 = 5.31 \times 10^6$$

By using the scientific form of a number *M*, we can write

$$\log M = \log(m \cdot 10^c).$$

Using Rule 1 for logarithms, we get

$$\log M = \log 10^c + \log m.$$

Finally, using Rule 2,

$$\log M = c \log 10 + \log m$$
$$= c + \log m.$$

This is the *standard* or uniform way to express logarithms—as the sum of an integer and a positive number between 0 and 1. The quantity log *m* is called the *mantissa* of log *M* and is always a number between 0 and 1. The quantity *c* is called the *characteristic* of log *M* and is always an integer.

EXAMPLE 9.7

Find (a) log 5.31 (b) log 5,310,000 (c) log 0.00531.

Solution:

(a) Since $53.1 = 5.31 \times 10^1$, we have

$$\log 53.1 = 1 + \log 5.31 = 1 + 0.7251 = 1.7251.$$

(b) Since $5,310,000 = 5.31 \times 10^6$, we have

$\log 5,310,000 = 6 + \log 5.31 = 6 + 0.7251 = 6.7251.$

(c) Since $0.00531 = 5.31 \times 10^{-3}$, we have

$\log 0.00531 = -3 + \log 5.31 = -3 + 0.7251.$

We usually do not combine a negative characteristic with the mantissa because this tends to obscure both the mantissa and the characteristic; hence, it would be difficult to recover them when finding antilogarithms. Sometimes, we express the negative characteristic as a positive number minus ten. Thus, since $-3 = 7 - 10$, we can write

$\log 0.00531 = -3 + 0.7251 = 7.7251 - 10.$

EXAMPLE 9.8

(a) Antilog $(2.4099) = 2.57 \times 10^2 = 257$
(b) Antilog $(7.4099 - 10) = 2.57 \times 10^{-3} = 0.00257$
(c) Antilog $(-6.5901) = $ antilog $(-7 + 0.4099) = 2.57 \times 10^{-7}$

Notice that in (c) it was necessary to initially express the number as the sum of a number between 0 and 1 and an integer before consulting a table of logarithms. Note, for example, that -6.5901 is not equal to $-6 + 0.5901$, but rather $-7 + 0.4099$.

EXAMPLE 9.9

Find the value of $10^{-4.0970}$.

Solution: Let $N = 10^{-4.0970}$, then

$\log N = -4.0970 = -5 + 0.9030 = 5.9030 - 10.$

Since, antilog $0.9030 \approx 8,$

$N = 8 \times 10^{-5} = 0.00008.$

EXAMPLE 9.10

Solve for x: $10^x = 4000.$

Solution: The necessary power of 10 is nothing more than log 4000. But $4000 = 4 \times 10^3$. Hence,

$x = \log 4000 = 3 + \log 4 = 3 + 0.6021 = 3.6021.$

EXERCISES FOR SECTION 9.3

Evaluate each of the following:

1. a. log 5.41   b. log 5410   c. log 0.00541

2. a.   log 1.25   b.   log 125   c.   log 0.125

3. a.   log 9.03   b.   log 0.000903   c.   log 903,000

4. a.   log 8.89   b.   log 88.9   c.   log 0.0889

5. a.   log (5.25)(3.65)   b.   log (5.25/3.65)

6. a.   log (8.03)(7.54)   b.   log (8.03/7.54)

7. a.   log (0.255)(85.6)   b.   log (0.255/85.6)

8. a.   log (0.295)(3.11)   b.   log (0.295/3.11)

9. a.   log (258)(3670)   b.   log (258/3670)

10. a.   log (1110)(56300)   b.   log (1110/56300)

11. a.   antilog 3.2601   b.   antilog 0.2601
     c.   antilog 8.2601 $-$ 10

12. a.   antilog 0.9258   b.   antilog 5.9258
     c.   antilog 9.9258 $-$ 10

13. a.   antilog 1.1818   b.   antilog 3.1818 $-$ 10
     c.   antilog 6.1818

14. a.   antilog 2.8692   b.   antilog 7.8692
     c.   antilog 3.8692 $-$ 10

15. a.   antilog 0.6053   b.   antilog -2.3947
     c.   antilog -0.3947

Solve for x:

16. $10^x = 20$ 17. $10^x = 25$ 18. $10^x = (1.54)(674)$

19. $10^x = \sqrt{20}$ 20. $10^{x+2} = 17^4$ 21. $10^{x-1} = 5^{10}$

9.4   INTERPOLATION

Table C does not include the logarithm of every number between 1 and 10, only those in steps of 0.01. To approximate logarithms of numbers written with one more digit accuracy, you may proceed in a variety of ways. Perhaps the most common is the linear interpolation method based on proportional parts introduced in Section 2.5. This type of estimation assumes that for a small increase in the number, the increase in the logarithm is proportional. Rather than completely describe the process (which is detailed in 2.5), we will be content with a few examples.

EXAMPLE 9.11

Use linear interpolation to approximate log 2573.

Solution: Since $2573 = 2.573 \times 10^3$, the characteristic is 3. The mantissa lies between the mantissa for 2.570 and 2.580. From Table C, the entries for 2.570 and 2.580 are found to be 0.4099 and 0.4116, respectively.

Number	Mantissa
$10\begin{bmatrix} 3\begin{bmatrix}2.570 \\ 2.573\end{bmatrix} \\ 2.580\end{bmatrix}$	$\begin{bmatrix}\begin{bmatrix}.4099 \\ ....\end{bmatrix}c \\ .4116\end{bmatrix}17$

We can establish the following proportion

$$\frac{c}{17} = \frac{3}{10}$$

or

$$c = \frac{3}{10}(17) = 5.1 \approx 5.$$

The required mantissa of log 2.573 is then $0.4099 + 0.0005 = 0.4104$. Therefore, log 2573 = 3.4104.

Note that in the preceding example we rounded off the number c to four digits after the decimal point. Otherwise, it would seem that interpolation was increasing the accuracy of the table which, of course, is impossible.

EXAMPLE 9.12

Find antilog of 2.4059.

Solution: Since the mantissa is 0.4059 and the characteristic is 2, we must find the number corresponding to the mantissa 0.4059 and then multiply by 10^2. Using Table C, we arrange the work as follows:

Number	Mantissa
$10\begin{bmatrix} n\begin{bmatrix}2.540 \\ ....\end{bmatrix} \\ 2.550\end{bmatrix}$	$\begin{bmatrix}\begin{bmatrix}.4048 \\ .4059\end{bmatrix}11 \\ .4065\end{bmatrix}17$

$$\frac{n}{10} = \frac{11}{17},$$

$$n = \frac{11}{17}(10) = 6.4 \approx 6.$$

Therefore, the desired number is $2.546 \times 10^2 = 254.6$.

EXERCISES FOR SECTION 9.4

Use the method of linear interpolation to approximate the common logarithm of each of the following numbers.

1. 2.361   2. 5842   3. .009573   4. 3.142   5. 2.718

6. 49,990   7. 642,300   8. 5.011   9. 1,005   10. 62.45

Find the number x to 4 significant digits by using linear interpolation.

11. $\log x = 2.1110$ 12. $\log x = 8.1284 - 10$

13. $\log x = 7.814$ 14. $\log x = 3.4141$

15. $\log x = 7.7228 - 10$ 16. $\log x = \frac{1}{2}$

17. $\log x = 0.25$ 18. $\log x = \frac{1}{3}$

19. $\log x = \pi$ 20. $\log x = -\pi$

Find the number x. (The number e is approximately equal to 2.718.)

21. $10^x = e$ 22. $10^x = \pi$ 23. $10^x = e^2$ 24. $10^x = 0.1441$

25. $10^x = \sqrt{2.169}$

Write as an approximate decimal.

26. $\sqrt[4]{20}$ 27. 10^π 28. π^e 29. $\sqrt{10}$ 30. $10^{0.4368}$

31.   Using $\log 3 = 0.4771$ and $\log 4 = 0.6020$, approximate $\log 3.5$ by linear interpolation and compare to the value in Table C.

32.   Use the fact that $\sqrt{4} = 2$ and $\sqrt{9} = 3$ and linear interpolation to approximate $\sqrt{7}$. Is the approximation high or low?

33.   Let $f(x) = 2x - 3$. Use the values of $f(2)$ and $f(3)$ along with linear interpolation to approximate $f(2.5)$. How accurate is your result.

9.5   COMPUTATIONS WITH LOGARITHMS

With the advent of high speed mechanical and electronic computing devices, the use of common logarithms for computational purposes has been relegated to a minor role. Even so, basic logarithmic computation remains important. Further, the arithmetic of logarithmic computation should increase your appreciation for some of the background theory. We choose not to explore all the "short cuts" and conventions related to logarithmic computation; a few examples should suffice.

Some of the following examples could as easily have been worked by conventional arithmetic, but the aim here is to illustrate and not to be too concerned with whether the use of logarithms is the preferred technique.

EXAMPLE 9.13

Use logarithms to evaluate

$$M = \frac{2158 \times 0.512}{0.00042}.$$

Solution: We find $\log M$ and use the rules of logarithms to write:

$\log M = \log 2158 + \log 0.0512 - \log 0.00042$

$\log 2158$ is found by interpolation to be 3.3341

log 0.512 is found directly to be $-1 + 0.7093$
log 0.00042 is found directly to be $-4 + 0.6232$

Hence,

$\log M = 3.3341 + (-1 + 0.7093) - (-4 + 0.6232)$
$= 3 + 0.3341 - 1 + 0.7093 + 4 - 0.6232.$

Adding the characteristics, yields

$\log M = 6 + (0.3341 + 0.7093 - 0.6232)$
$= 6 + 0.4202$
$= 6.4202.$

By interpolation, antilog $0.4202 = 2.631$, and hence,

$M = 2.631 \times 10^6.$

EXAMPLE 9.14

Use logarithms to approximate $(25.4)^{1/4}$.

Solution: Let $M = (25.4)^{1/4}$. Then $\log M = \log(25.4)^{1/4} = (1/4)\log 25.4$. From Table C, $\log 25.4 = 1.4048$ and hence,

$\log M = 0.3512,$
$M = \text{antilog } 0.3512.$

By interpolation

$M = 2.245.$

EXAMPLE 9.15

Find the power to which 3 must be raised to give 5.

Solution: We are looking for a number x such that

$3^x = 5.$

Taking the common logarithm of both sides, we have

$\log 3^x = \log 5,$

or, using Rule 2 for logarithms,

$x \log 3 = \log 5,$

$x = \dfrac{\log 5}{\log 3}$

$= \dfrac{0.6990}{0.4771}.$

$\log x = \log \dfrac{0.6990}{0.4771} = \log 0.6990 - \log 0.4771$

$= (9.8445 - 10) - (9.6786 - 10) = 0.1659,$

$x = \text{antilog } 0.1659 = 1.465.$

EXAMPLE 9.16

An approximate rule for atmospheric pressure at altitudes less than 50 miles can be shown to be

$$P = 14.7(0.5)^{h/3.25}$$

where P is in psi when h is altitude in miles. What altitude is just above 99 percent of the atmosphere?

Solution: Because density and pressure are proportional, the desired altitude is the point at which the pressure is 1 percent of standard atmospheric pressure. Hence

$$(0.01)(14.7) = 14.7(\tfrac{1}{2})^{h/3.25},$$
$$0.01 = (\tfrac{1}{2})^{h/3.25}.$$

Taking the logarithm of both sides, we obtain,

$$\log 0.01 = \frac{h}{3.25} \log \tfrac{1}{2}.$$

Solving for h, we have

$$h = \frac{(3.25)(\log 0.01)}{\log \tfrac{1}{2}}$$
$$= \frac{(3.25)(-2)}{-0.3010}$$
$$= 21.6 \text{ miles.}$$

EXERCISES FOR SECTION 9.5

Use logarithms to approximate each of the following computations to three significant digits.

1. $(65.7)(0.00411)$

2. $\dfrac{365 \times 1.423}{120 \times 0.00133}$

3. $2563^{1/3}$

4. $\dfrac{(0.39)(23.7)}{0.00505}$

5. $\sqrt[5]{8}$

6. $(0.16)^3$

7. $3.1^{3.1}$

8. $\dfrac{21.2 + 46.3}{\sqrt{5}}$

9. $\dfrac{123.8 + 95.3}{543.2}$

10. $\dfrac{76.1 + \log(8 \times 10^{40})}{\log 5.3}$

11. $\dfrac{-52.3 \times 64}{\log 3.83}$

12. $10^{-4.213}$

13. $2^{-1.431}$

14. $3^{1.212}$

15. $(\sqrt{2})^{\sqrt{2}}$

Solve for x:

16. $10^x = \pi$ 17. $2^x = \pi$ 18. $2^x = 3$

19. $3^x = \dfrac{201}{314}$ 20. $10^x = 5.555$

↗ 21.   The period T, in seconds, of a simple pendulum of length L, in feet, is given by $T = 2\pi\sqrt{L/32.2}$. Approximate the period of a pendulum which is a yard long.

↗ 22.   The difference in intensity level of two sounds with intensities I and I_0 is defined to $10 \log (I/I_0)$ decibels. Find the intensity level in decibels of the sound produced by an electric motor which is 175.6 times greater than I_0.

9.6   LOGARITHMS OF TRIGONOMETRIC FUNCTIONS

Table D in the Appendix is a table of the logarithms of the trigonometric values for angles from $0°$ to $90°$ in $10'$ intervals. For convenience in arranging the table, the -10 part of the characteristic has been omitted. Thus, you must add -10 to the tabulated entry. Further, when finding antilogarithms from this table, you must always express the number in this standard form.

As with the other trigonometric tables, the table is arranged so that if an angle is listed to the left, the corresponding trigonometric values are to be read from the headings at the top of the page; the headings at the bottom correspond to the angles listed to the right.

EXAMPLE 9.17

Find: (a) log sin $32°10'$ (b) log csc $32°10'$

Solution:

(a)   From Table D: log sin $32°10' = 9.7262 - 10$.
(b)   From the same table: log csc $32°10' = 10.2738 - 10 = 0.2738$.
Note that log sin $32°10' +$ log csc $32°10' = 0$. Can you explain why?

EXAMPLE 9.18

Use linear interpolation and Table D to find log tan $33°26'$.

Solution: We arrange the work as follows:

θ	log tan θ
$\begin{array}{c}10'\begin{bmatrix}33°30'\\6'\begin{bmatrix}33°26'\\33°20'\end{bmatrix}\end{bmatrix}\end{array}$	$\begin{array}{c}\left.\begin{array}{c}9.8208 - 10\\ ?\\9.8180 - 10\end{array}\right]h\quad.0028\end{array}$

$h = \frac{6}{10}(.0028) = 0.0017$.

Therefore, log $33°26' \approx 9.8197 - 10$.

EXAMPLE 9.19

Find θ if log sin $\theta = -0.4557$.

Solution: We first write -0.4557 as $9.5443 - 10$. Then, from Table D, we have,

$\theta = 20°30'$

EXAMPLE 9.20

Find θ if log sin $\theta = 9.9200 - 10$.

Solution: There is no value in Table D which will give an exact value for θ so interpolation must be used.

θ	log sin θ
$10'\begin{bmatrix} 56°20' \\ h\begin{bmatrix} ? \\ 56°10' \end{bmatrix}\end{bmatrix}$	$\begin{bmatrix} 9.9203 - 10 \\ 9.9200 - 10 \\ 9.9194 - 10\end{bmatrix}.0006\end{bmatrix}.0009$

$$h = \frac{.0006}{.0009}(10') = \frac{2}{3}(10') \approx 7'$$

Thus, $\theta = 56°17'$

EXERCISES FOR SECTION 9.6

Find the following, using Table D and linear interpolation when necessary.

1. log sin 25°
2. log cos 50°
3. log tan 45°
4. log sin 95°10'
5. log cos 58°20'
6. log csc 80°15'
7. log sec 40°12'
8. log cot 26°52'
9. log cot 3°15'
10. log cos 18°24'

Find the value of θ, if θ is a positive acute angle.

11. log sin $\theta = 9.5375 - 10$
12. log csc $\theta = 0.0000$
13. log tan $\theta = 0.0762$
14. log sec $\theta = 0.0814$
15. log cos $\theta = 9.9186 - 10$
16. log cos $\theta = -0.0113$
17. log tan $\theta = -2.5363$
18. log cot $\theta = 0.2690$
19. log cos $\theta = 9.8400 - 10$
20. log sin $\theta = 9.3600 - 10$

The term "logarithmic solution" refers to the technique of using logarithms to perform the necessary multiplications and divisions when finding the unknown parts of a triangle. Historically, the rise of logarithms is intertwined with that of trigonometry since difficult trigonometric problems were solvable only with the computational elegance of logarithms. In this and the next section, we use examples to describe the method.

EXAMPLE 9.21

Use logarithms to solve for the unknown parts of the right triangle ABC where $a = 54.2$ and $A = 64°50'$.

FIGURE 9.1

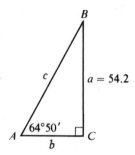

Solution: In Figure 9.1, a representative triangle is drawn. We know that the unknown parts are given by the formulas

$$B = 90° - A, \qquad b = a \cot A, \qquad c = a \csc A.$$

Since $A = 64°50'$, $B = 90° - A = 90° - 64°50' = 25°10'$. We use logarithms to compute b:

$$b = a \cot A$$
$$b = 54.2 \cot 64°50'$$
$$\log b = \log 54.2 + \log \cot 64°50'$$
$$= 1.7340 + (9.6720 - 10)$$
$$\log b = 1.4060$$
$$b = \text{antilog } 1.4060 = 25.47$$

Similarly,

$$c = a \csc A$$
$$c = 54.2 \csc 64°50'$$
$$\log c = \log 54.2 + \log \csc 64°50'$$
$$= 1.7340 + (10.0433 - 10)$$
$$\log c = 1.7773$$
$$c = \text{antilog } 1.7773 = 59.88$$

EXAMPLE 9.22

Use logarithms (where possible) to solve for the unknown parts of a triangle ABC if $a = 205.3$ and $b = 124.8$.

FIGURE 9.2

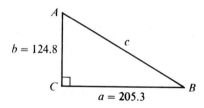

Solution: A sketch of the triangle is shown in Figure 9.2. We have

$$\tan A = \frac{205.3}{124.8}, \quad c = 205.3 \csc A, \quad B = 90° - A.$$

From the first of these relations

$$\begin{aligned}\log \tan A &= \log 205.3 - \log 124.8 \\ &= 2.3124 - 2.0962 \\ &= 0.2162 \\ &= 10.2162 - 10.\end{aligned}$$

Now we use Table D to get,

$$A = 58°42'.$$

To solve for c we write,

$$\begin{aligned}\log c &= \log 205.3 + \log \csc 58°42' \\ &= 2.3124 + 0.0683 \\ &= 2.3807.\end{aligned}$$

Hence,

$$c = 240.3.$$

Lastly,

$$\begin{aligned}B &= 90° - 58°42' \\ &= 31°18'.\end{aligned}$$

EXERCISES FOR SECTION 9.7

Use Tables C and D to solve for the unknown parts of the following right triangles.

1. $a = 8.33,$ $A = 38°10'$ 2. $b = 4.37,$ $A = 51°$

3. $b = 53.4,$ $B = 22°15'$ 4. $a = 108,$ $b = 504$

5. $a = 43$, $c = 74$ 6. $A = 17°40'$, $c = 250$

7. $A = 60°30'$, $a = 966.4$ 8. $a = 422.5$, $b = 674.7$

9. $B = 28°18'$, $a = 1053$ 10. $B = 43°47'$, $c = 162.8$

9.8   LOGARITHMIC SOLUTION OF OBLIQUE TRIANGLES

The following examples show how logarithms are used to solve some typical oblique triangles.

EXAMPLE 9.23

Solve the triangle ABC where $a = 44.7$, $B = 76°$ and $C = 38°$.

FIGURE 9.3

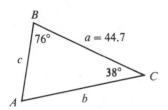

Solution: See Figure 9.3. Angle A is found from the relation

$A = 180° - 76° - 38° = 66°$.

The remaining sides are found using the Law of Sines.

$$\frac{\sin 66°}{44.7} = \frac{\sin 76°}{b} = \frac{\sin 38°}{c}.$$

In terms of logarithms, this gives

$\log b = \log 44.7 + \log \sin 76° + \log \csc 66°$,

and

$\log c = \log 44.7 + \log \sin 38° + \log \csc 66°$.

Using Tables C and D,

$\log b = 1.6503 + 9.9869 - 10 + 0.0393 = 1.6765$,
$\log c = 1.6503 + 9.7893 - 10 + 0.0393 = 1.4789$.

Thus, $b = 47.48$, $c = 30.12$.

In the next example, we exhibit the use of the Law of Cosines in a logarithmic solution.

EXAMPLE 9.24

Solve the triangle ABC given that $a = 60.3$, $c = 86.4$ and $B = 84°20'$.

FIGURE 9.4

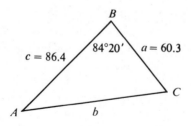

Solution: See Figure 9.4. From the Law of Cosines,

$$b^2 = a^2 + c^2 - 2ac \cos B,$$

$$\cos A = \frac{b^2 + c^2 - a^2}{2bc},$$

$$\cos C = \frac{a^2 + b^2 - c^2}{2ab}.$$

We first make some preliminary computations.

$$\log a^2 = \log (60.3)^2 = 2 \log 60.3 = 2(1.7803) = 3.5606,$$
$$\log c^2 = \log (86.4)^2 = 2 \log 86.4 = 2(1.9365) = 3.8730.$$

$$\begin{aligned}
\log 2ac \cos B &= \log 2 + \log 60.3 + \log 86.4 + \log \cos 84°20' \\
&= .3010 + 1.7803 + 1.9365 + 8.9945 - 10 \\
&= 3.0123.
\end{aligned}$$

Therefore, $a^2 = 3635$, $c^2 = 7465$, $2ac \cos B = 1029$, from which

$$b^2 = a^2 + c^2 - 2ac \cos B = 3635 + 7465 - 1029 = 10071.$$

Hence,

$$\log b^2 = \log 10071 = 4.0030,$$
$$\log b = 2.0015.$$

Take the antilogarithm,

$$b = 100.3.$$

To find the angle A, we use the logarithmic formula,

$$\begin{aligned}
\log \cos A &= \log (b^2 + c^2 - a^2) - \log 2 - \log b - \log c \\
&= \log 13900 - \log 2 - \log b - \log c \\
&= 4.1430 - 0.3010 - 2.0015 - 1.9365 \\
&= -0.0960 = 9.9040 - 10.
\end{aligned}$$

Using Table D,

$$A = 36°42'.$$

The angle C is then computed by

$$C = 180° - (A + B)$$
$$= 180° - 121°2'$$
$$= 58°58'.$$

EXAMPLE 9.25

Solve the triangle ABC given that $a = 35.2$, $b = 58.4$ and $c = 48.7$.

Solution: To find the unknown parts, we first use the Law of Cosines to find the largest of the three angles. This avoids any ambiguity when the Law of Sines is used to compute the other two angles. We make some preliminary computations to allow the determination of the logarithm of $a^2 + c^2 - b^2$.

$$\log a^2 = 2 \log a = 2 \log 35.2 = 2(1.5465) = 3.0930$$
$$\log b^2 = 2 \log b = 2 \log 58.4 = 2(1.7664) = 3.5328$$
$$\log c^2 = 2 \log c = 2 \log 48.7 = 2(1.6875) = 3.3750$$

Therefore, $a^2 = 1239$, $b^2 = 3410$, $c^2 = 2371$, and $a^2 + c^2 - b^2 = 200$. Hence, using the logarithmic form of the Law of Cosines to find the angle B,

$$\log \cos B = \log 200 - \log 2 - \log a - \log c$$
$$= 2.3010 - 0.3010 - 1.5465 - 1.6875$$
$$= -1.2340 = 8.7660 - 10.$$

From Table D, $B = 86°39'$.

The logarithmic form of the Law of Sines in terms of $\log \sin A$ is:

$$\log \sin A = \log a + \log \sin B - \log b$$
$$= 1.5468 + 9.9993 - 10 - 1.7664$$
$$= 9.7797 - 10,$$
$$A = 37°1'.$$

Similarly,

$$\log \sin C = \log c + \log \sin B - \log b$$
$$= 1.6875 + 9.9993 - 10 - 1.7664$$
$$= 9.9204 - 10,$$
$$C = 56°22'.$$

EXERCISES FOR SECTION 9.8

Solve for the unknown parts of the following triangles. If no triangle can be formed by the given parts, then indicate this fact.

1. $A = 37°20'$, $B = 68°30'$, $a = 273$

2. $B = 119°40'$, $C = 31°30'$, $b = 0.0808$

3. $A = 53°33'$, $C = 92°26'$, $c = 0.9847$

4. $b = 1906, A = 55°44', C = 81°29'$

5. $a = 59.49, B = 50°52', C = 28°37'$

6. $b = 0.216, c = 0.267, B = 74°15'$

7. $a = 3.00, b = 4.00, c = 2.00$

8. $a = 120, b = 145, C = 94°25'$

9. $a = 20, b = 30, c = 20$

10. $A = 33°20', a = 12.3, b = 25.6$

10

COMPLEX
NUMBERS

10.1   THE NEED FOR COMPLEX NUMBERS

We sometimes think of numbers as the invention of the human mind because they may be developed on the basis of obtaining solutions to certain types of equations. For example, beginning with the set of positive integers (counting numbers), the negative integers were invented in order to be able to solve an equation like $x + 7 = 4$. Likewise, the set of rational numbers was invented so that linear equations such as $2x = 3$ would have a solution. In order to solve $x^2 = 2$, it was necessary to invent the irrational numbers $\pm\sqrt{2}$. The irrational numbers together with the rational numbers comprise the set of real numbers.

For most applications, the set of real numbers is sufficient, but there are instances in which this set is inadequate. For instance, in solving the equation $x^2 + 1 = 0$, we obtain the root $x = \sqrt{-1}$. Since the square of every real number is nonnegative, it is apparent that $\sqrt{-1}$ is not a real number. If we use i to represent $\sqrt{-1}$, then i is a number that has the property that $i^2 = -1$. With this understanding, we can write the roots of $x^2 + 1 = 0$ as $x = \pm i$. The number i is called a *pure imaginary** number and, in general, is the square root of -1. Thus,

$$\sqrt{-4} = \pm 2i,$$
$$\sqrt{-7} = \pm i\sqrt{7}.$$

Numbers of the form bi, where b is a real number, make up the set of imaginary numbers.

EXAMPLE 10.1

Solve the equation $x^2 + 9 = 0$.

Solution:

$$x^2 + 9 = 0$$
$$x^2 = -9$$
$$x = \pm\sqrt{-9} = \pm 3i$$

In solving the equation $x^2 - 2x + 5 = 0$, we find the solution to be $x = 1 \pm\sqrt{-4}$. Using the concept of an imaginary number, this can be written $x = 1 \pm 2i$. Thus, we have a number that is a combination of a real number and an imaginary number; such numbers are called *complex* numbers. For convenience, we make the following definition:

---

*The word "imaginary" is, in a sense, an unfortunate choice of words since it may lead you to believe that they have a more "ficticious" character than the so-called "real" numbers.

A complex number z is any number of the form $z = a + bi$, where a and b are real numbers and $i = \sqrt{-1}$.

The real number a is called the *real part* of z while the real number b is called the imaginary part of z. By convention, if $b = 1$, the number is written $a + i$. Further, if $b = 0$, the imaginary part is customarily omitted and the number is said to be pure real. If $a = 0$ and $b \neq 0$, the real part is omitted and the number is said to be pure imaginary.

Two complex numbers are equal if, and only if, their real parts are equal and their imaginary parts are equal. Thus, $a + bi$ and $c + di$ are equal if, and only if, $a = c$ and $b = d$.

Combinations of complex numbers may be assumed to obey the ordinary algebraic rules for real numbers. Thus the sum, difference, product, and quotient of two complex numbers are found in the same manner as the sum, difference, product, and quotient of two real binomials—bearing in mind that $i^2 = -1$.

EXAMPLE 10.2

Find the sum and difference of $3 + 5i$ and $-9 + 2i$.

Solution:

(a) $(3 + 5i) + (-9 + 2i) = (3 - 9) + (5 + 2)i = -6 + 7i$

(b) $(3 + 5i) - (-9 + 2i) = (3 + 9) + (5 - 2)i = 12 + 3i$

EXAMPLE 10.3

Find the product $(3 - 2i)(4 + i)$.

Solution:

$$
\begin{aligned}
(3 - 2i)(4 + i) &= 12 + 3i - 8i - 2i^2 \\
&= 12 - 5i + 2 \\
&= 14 - 5i
\end{aligned}
$$

The number $a - bi$ is called the *conjugate* of $a + bi$. To find the quotient of the two complex numbers, we use the following scheme: *multiply numerator and denominator of the given quotient by the conjugate of the denominator*. The technique is illustrated in the next example.

EXAMPLE 10.4

Find the quotient $\dfrac{2 + 3i}{4 - 5i}$.

Solution:

$$\frac{2 + 3i}{4 - 5i} = \frac{(2 + 3i)(4 + 5i)}{(4 - 5i)(4 + 5i)}$$

$$= \frac{8 + (12 + 10)i + 15i^2}{16 - 25i^2}$$

$$= \frac{-7 + 22i}{16 + 25}$$

$$= \frac{-7 + 22i}{41}$$

EXERCISES FOR SECTION 10.1

Perform each of the indicated operations expressing all answers in the form $a + bi$.

1. $(3 + 2i) + (4 + 3i)$
2. $(6 + 3i) + (5 - i)$
3. $(5 - 2i) + (-7 + 5i)$
4. $(-1 + i) + (2 - i)$
5. $(1 + i) + (3 - i)$
6. $7 - (5 + 3i)$
7. $(3 + 5i) - 4i$
8. $(3 + 2i) + (3 - 2i)$
9. $(2 + 3i)(4 + 5i)$
10. $(7 + 2i)(-1 - i)$
11. $(5 - i)(5 + i)$
12. $(6 - 3i)(6 + 3i)$
13. $(4 + \sqrt{3}i)^2$
14. $(5 - 2i)^2$
15. $6i(4 - 3i)$
16. $3i(-2 - i)$
17. $\dfrac{3 + 2i}{1 + i}$
18. $\dfrac{4i}{2 + i}$
19. $\dfrac{3}{2 - 3i}$
20. $\dfrac{7 - 2i}{6 - 5i}$
21. $\dfrac{1}{5i}$
22. $\dfrac{-3 + i}{-2 - i}$
23. $\dfrac{-1 - 3i}{4 - \sqrt{2}i}$
24. $\dfrac{i}{2 + \sqrt{5}i}$

25. Show that the sum of a complex number and its conjugate is a real number.

26. Show that the product of a complex number and its conjugate is a real number.

10.2   GRAPHICAL REPRESENTATION OF COMPLEX NUMBERS

Since complex numbers are ordered pairs of real numbers, some two-dimensional configuration is necessary to represent them graphically. The Cartesian coordinate system is often used for this purpose; in which case, it is called the *complex plane*. The x-axis is used to represent the real part of the complex number, and the y-axis to represent the imaginary part. Hence, they are called the real and imaginary axes respectively. Thus, the complex number $x + iy$ is represented by the point whose coordinates are (x, y) as shown in Figure 10.1. For this reason, the complex number $z = x + iy$ is said to be written in *rectangular form*.

FIGURE 10.1

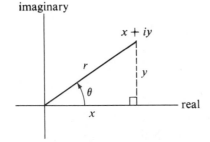

It is often convenient to think of a complex number $x + iy$ as representing a vector. With reference to Figure 10.1, the complex number $x + iy$ can be represented by the vector drawn from the origin to the point $x + iy$ with coordinates (x, y).

EXAMPLE 10.5

Represent $5 + 3i$, $-2 + 4i$, $-1 - 3i$, and $5 - i$ in the complex plane. (See Figure 10.2).

FIGURE 10.2

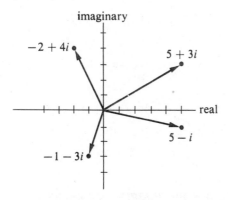

It is instructional to show the graphical representation of the sum of two complex numbers. Recalling that the sum of $a + bi$ and $c + di$ is given by

$$(a + bi) + (c + di) = (a + c) + (b + d)i,$$

we have represented $a + bi$, $c + di$, and $(a + c) + (b + d)i$ in Figure 10.3. The result can be seen to be the same as if we had applied the parallelogram law to the vectors representing $a + bi$ and $c + di$. Note that $c + di$ is subtracted from $a + bi$ by plotting $a + bi$ and $-c - di$, and then using the parallelogram law.

FIGURE 10.3   Addition of complex numbers

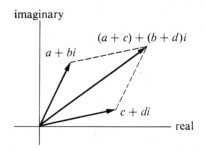

EXERCISES FOR SECTION 10.2

Perform the indicated operations graphically and check the results algebraically.

1. $(4 + i) + (3 + 5i)$
2. $(3 + 2i) + (1 - 3i)$
3. $(4 + 3i) + (-2 + i)$
4. $(-5 - 7i) + (-1 + 3i)$
5. $(2 - 4i) + (-3 + i)$
6. $i + (3 + 4i)$
7. $(5 + 3i) - 6$
8. $(3 + 2i) + (3 - 2i)$
9. $(5 - 3i) + (5 + 3i)$
10. $(6 + 4i) - 2i$
11. $(1 + 3i) - (2 - 5i)$
12. $(2 - i) - i$
13. $(2 + \sqrt{3}i) - (-1 - i)$
14. $(\sqrt{5} - i) - (\sqrt{5} + 3i)$
15. $(-3 + 2i) - (-3 - 2i)$
16. $(10 - 3i) - (10 + 3i)$

10.3   POLAR REPRESENTATION OF COMPLEX NUMBERS

In discussing graphical representations of complex numbers, we indicated the convenience of thinking of a complex number in terms of a vector drawn from the origin to the point in the plane. This conceptual use of vectors to represent complex numbers suggests an alternate method for

FIGURE 10.4   Polar form

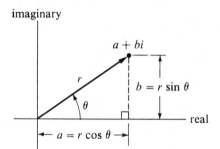

describing complex numbers. Referring to Figure 10.4, we see that the complex number $a + bi$ can also be located in the plane by giving the length of the vector and the angle that the vector makes with the positive real axis. Also, from Figure 10.4, we observe that $a = r \cos \theta$ and $b = r \sin \theta$. Therefore,

$$(10.1) \quad z = a + bi = r(\cos \theta + i \sin \theta).$$

The right-hand side of this equation is called the *trigonometric* or *polar* form of the complex number $a + bi$. The quantity $(\cos \theta + i \sin \theta)$ is sometimes written *cis* θ, in which case, we write

$$(10.2) \quad z = r \ cis \ \theta$$

as the polar form of the complex number z. The number r is called the *modulus* or magnitude of the complex number z and is given by

$$r = \sqrt{a^2 + b^2}.$$

The angle θ is called the *argument* of the complex number. Since $\tan \theta = b/a$ in Figure 10.4, it follows that θ is an angle whose tangent is b/a; that is,

$$\theta = \arctan \frac{b}{a}.$$

Note that a given complex number has many arguments, all differing by multiples of 2π. Sometimes we limit the argument to some interval of length 2π and thus obtain a *principal value*. In this book, unless we say otherwise, the principal values will be between $-\pi$ and π; that is, between $-180°$ and $180°$.

EXAMPLE 10.6

Represent $z = 1 + \sqrt{3}i$ in polar form. (See Figure 10.5.)

Solution: Since

$$r = \sqrt{1^2 + (\sqrt{3})^2} = \sqrt{4} = 2$$

227

FIGURE 10.5

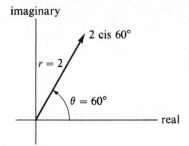

imaginary

2 cis 60°

$r = 2$

$\theta = 60°$

real

and

$$\theta = \arctan \sqrt{3} = 60°,$$

we have

$$1 + \sqrt{3}i = 2(\cos 60° + i \sin 60°) = 2 \text{ cis } 60°.$$

EXAMPLE 10.7

Express $z = 6(\cos 120° + i \sin 120°)$ in rectangular form. (See Figure 10.6.)

FIGURE 10.6

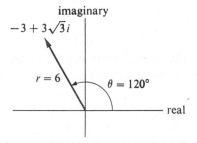

imaginary

$-3 + 3\sqrt{3}i$

$r = 6$ $\theta = 120°$

real

Solution: Using the fact that $a = r \cos \theta$ and $b = r \sin \theta$, we have

$$a = 6 \cos 120° = 6(-\frac{1}{2}) = -3,$$

$$b = 6 \sin 120° = 6\left(\frac{\sqrt{3}}{2}\right) = 3\sqrt{3}.$$

Therefore,

$$z = a + bi = -3 + 3\sqrt{3}i.$$

The polar form of complex numbers makes it easy to give a geometric interpretation to the product of two complex numbers. Thus, if $z_1 = r_1 \text{ cis } \theta_1$

and $z_2 = r_2 \operatorname{cis} \theta_2$, the product $z_1 z_2$ may be written

$$z_1 z_2 = r_1(\cos \theta_1 + i \sin \theta_1) \cdot r_2(\cos \theta_2 + i \sin \theta_2)$$
$$= r_1 r_2 [\cos \theta_1 \cos \theta_2 + i \cos \theta_1 \sin \theta_2$$
$$+ i \sin \theta_1 \cos \theta_2 + i^2 \sin \theta_1 \sin \theta_2]$$
$$= r_1 r_2 [(\cos \theta_1 \cos \theta_2 - \sin \theta_1 \sin \theta_2)$$
$$+ i(\cos \theta_1 \sin \theta_2 + \sin \theta_1 \cos \theta_2)].$$

Now, by using the identities for the sine and cosine of the sum of two angles, we have

$$(10.3) \quad z_1 z_2 = r_1 r_2 [\cos(\theta_1 + \theta_2) + i \sin(\theta_1 + \theta_2)] = r_1 r_2 \operatorname{cis}(\theta_1 + \theta_2).$$

Therefore, the modulus of the product of two complex numbers is the product of the individual moduli and the argument of the product is the sum of the individual arguments. Graphically, multiplication of z_1 by z_2 results in a rotation of the vector through z_1 by an angle equal to the argument of z_2 and an expansion or contraction of the modulus depending on whether $|z_2| > 1$ or $|z_2| < 1$. (See Figure 10.7.)

FIGURE 10.7 Multiplication of complex numbers

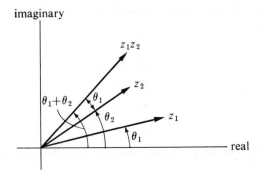

EXAMPLE 10.8

Multiply $z_1 = -1 + \sqrt{3}i$ and $z_2 = 1 + i$, using the polar form of each.

Solution: Computing the modulus and argument of each complex number yields

$$r_1 = \sqrt{(-1)^2 + (\sqrt{3})^2} = 2, \qquad \theta_1 = \arctan \frac{\sqrt{3}}{-1} = 120°$$

$$r_2 = \sqrt{1^2 + 1^2} = \sqrt{2}, \qquad \theta_2 = \arctan \frac{1}{1} = 45°.$$

Therefore,

$$z_1 z_2 = (2 \operatorname{cis} 120°)(\sqrt{2} \operatorname{cis} 45°) = 2\sqrt{2} \operatorname{cis}(120° + 45°)$$
$$= 2\sqrt{2} \operatorname{cis} 165°.$$

In the same manner as in the above discussion, we may show that if $z_1 = r_1 \text{ cis } \theta_1$ and $z_2 = r_2 \text{ cis } \theta_2$, then

(10.4) $\dfrac{z_1}{z_2} = \dfrac{r_1}{r_2} \cos(\theta_1 - \theta_2) + i \sin(\theta_1 - \theta_2) = \dfrac{r_1}{r_2} \text{ cis}(\theta_1 - \theta_2).$

In words, the modulus of the quotient of two complex numbers is the quotient of the individual moduli, and the argument is the difference of the individual arguments.

EXAMPLE 10.9

Divide $z_1 = 2 \text{ cis } 120°$ by $z_2 = \sqrt{2} \text{ cis } 45°$.

Solution:

$$\frac{z_1}{z_2} = \frac{2 \text{ cis } 120°}{\sqrt{2} \text{ cis } 45°} = \frac{2}{\sqrt{2}} \text{ cis}(120° - 45°) = \sqrt{2} \text{ cis } 75°$$

EXERCISES FOR SECTION 10.3

Plot each of the following complex numbers and then express it in polar form.

1. $1 - \sqrt{3}\, i$ 2. $3 + 4i$

3. $\sqrt{5} + 2i$ 4. $\sqrt{3} - i$

5.   9   6. $5i$

7. $3 - 4i$ 8. $-1 + i$

9. $5 - 6i$ 10. $-3 - 4i$

Plot each of the following complex numbers and then express it in rectangular form.

11. $2 \text{ cis } 30°$ 12. $4 \text{ cis } 60°$

13. $5 \text{ cis } 135°$ 14. $10 \text{ cis } 90°$

15. $\sqrt{3} \text{ cis } 210°$ 16. $\sqrt{5} \text{ cis } 180°$

17. $3 \text{ cis } 300°$ 18. $7 \text{ cis } 0°$

19. $10 \text{ cis } 20°$ 20. $2 \text{ cis } 100°$

Perform the indicated operations. If the complex numbers are not already in polar form, put them in that form before proceeding.

21. $(4 \text{ cis } 30°)(3 \text{ cis } 60°)$ 22. $(2 \text{ cis } 120°)(\sqrt{5} \text{ cis } 180°)$

23. $(\sqrt{2} \text{ cis } 90°)(\sqrt{2} \text{ cis } 240°)$ 24. $(5 \text{ cis } 180°)(3 \text{ cis } 90°)$

25. $(10 \text{ cis } 35°)(2 \text{ cis } 100°)$ 26. $(3 \text{ cis } 45°)(2 \text{ cis } 120°)$

27. $(3 + 4i)(\sqrt{3} - i)$ 28. $3i(2 - i)$

29. $\dfrac{10 \text{ cis } 30°}{2 \text{ cis } 90°}$ 30. $\dfrac{5 \text{ cis } 29°}{3 \text{ cis } 4°}$

31. $\dfrac{4 \text{ cis } 26°40'}{2 \text{ cis } 19°10'}$

32. $\dfrac{12 \text{ cis } 100°}{3 \text{ cis } 23°}$

33. $\dfrac{1 - i}{\sqrt{3} + i}$

34. $\dfrac{\sqrt{3} + i}{\sqrt{3} - i}$

35. $\dfrac{4i}{-1 + i}$

36. $\dfrac{5}{1 + i}$

37. Prove *Euler's Identities*:

$$\cos \theta = \frac{1}{2} \left[\text{cis } \theta + \text{cis}(-\theta) \right],$$

$$\sin \theta = \frac{1}{2i} \left[\text{cis } \theta - \text{cis}(-\theta) \right].$$

10.4 DEMOIVRE'S THEOREM

The square of the complex number $z = r \text{ cis } \theta$ is given by

$$z^2 = (r \text{ cis } \theta)(r \text{ cis } \theta)$$
$$= r^2 \text{ cis } 2\theta.$$

Likewise,

$$z^3 = z^2 \cdot z = (r^2 \text{ cis } 2\theta) \cdot (r \text{ cis } \theta)$$
$$= r^3 \text{ cis } 3\theta.$$

We expect the pattern exhibited for r^2 and r^3 to apply as well to r^4, r^5, r^6, etc. As a matter of fact if $z = r \text{ cis } \theta$, then

(10.5) $z^n = r^n \text{ cis } n\theta$

This result is known as *DeMoivre's Theorem*. The theorem is true for all real values of n, a fact that we shall accept without proof.

EXAMPLE 10.10

Use DeMoivre's Theorem to find $(-2 + 2i)^4$.

Solution: Here we have

$$r = \sqrt{2^2 + (-2)^2} = \sqrt{8}, \qquad \theta = 135°.$$

Therefore,

$$(-2 + 2i)^4 = \sqrt{8} \, (\cos 135° + i \sin 135°)^4$$
$$= (\sqrt{8})^4 \left[\cos 4(135°) + i \sin 4(135°) \right]$$
$$= 64 \left[\cos 540° + i \sin 540° \right]$$
$$= 64 \left[\cos 180° + i \sin 180° \right]$$
$$= -64.$$

In the system of real numbers, there is no square root of -1, no fourth root of -81, and so on. However, if we use complex numbers, we can find the nth root of any number by using DeMoivre's Theorem.

Recalling that DeMoivre's Theorem is valid for all real n, it is possible to evaluate $[r \text{ cis } \theta]^{1/n}$ as

$$(10.6) \quad [r \text{ cis } \theta]^{1/n} = r^{1/n} \text{ cis } \frac{\theta}{n} = \sqrt[n]{r} \text{ cis } \frac{\theta}{n}.$$

Since $\cos \theta$ and $\sin \theta$ are periodic functions with a period of 360°, we can write $\cos \theta = \cos(\theta + k \cdot 360°)$ and $\sin \theta = \sin(\theta + k \cdot 360°)$ where k is an integer. Hence,

$$(10.7) \quad [r \text{ cis } \theta]^{1/n} = \sqrt[n]{r} \text{ cis } \left(\frac{\theta + k \cdot 360°}{n} \right).$$

For a given number n, the right side of this equation takes on n distinct values corresponding to $k = 0, 1, 2, \ldots, n - 1$. For $k > n - 1$, the result is merely a duplication of the first n values.

EXAMPLE 10.11

Find the square roots of $4i$.

Solution: We first express $4i$ in polar form using:

$$r = \sqrt{0^2 + 4^2} = 4 \text{ and } \theta = 90°.$$

Thus,

$4i = 4 \text{ cis } 90°$

and, the square roots of $4i$ are given by

$$2 \text{ cis } \left(\frac{90° + k \cdot 360°}{2} \right).$$

Therefore, we have for $k = 0$,

$2 \text{ cis } 45° = \sqrt{2} + \sqrt{2}i,$

FIGURE 10.8

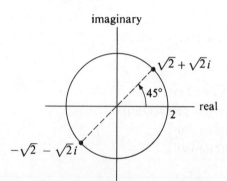

and for $k = 1$,

$$2 \text{ cis } 225° = -\sqrt{2} - \sqrt{2}\,i.$$

It is convenient and informative to plot these values in the complex plane as shown in Figure 10.8. Notice that both roots are located on a circle of radius 2, but 180° apart.

EXAMPLE 10.12

Find the three cube roots of unity.

Solution: In polar form, the number 1 may be written $1 \text{ cis } 0°$. Thus,

$$\sqrt[3]{1 \text{ cis } 0°} = 1 \text{ cis } \left(\frac{0° + k \cdot 360°}{3}\right).$$

For $k = 0$,

$$1 \text{ cis } 0° = 1.$$

For $k = 1$,

$$1 \text{ cis } 120° = \frac{-1 + \sqrt{3}\,i}{2}.$$

For $k = 2$,

$$1 \text{ cis } 240° = \frac{-1 - \sqrt{3}\,i}{2}.$$

These roots are displayed in Figure 10.9. Notice that they are located on a circle of radius 1 at equally spaced intervals of 120°.

FIGURE 10.9

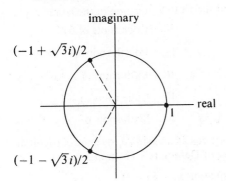

EXAMPLE 10.13

Find the fourth roots of $-1 + \sqrt{3}\,i$.

Solution: Writing $-1 + \sqrt{3}\,i$ in polar form, we have

$$-1 + \sqrt{3}\,i = 2 \text{ cis } 120°.$$

Therefore,

$$[-1 + \sqrt{3}\,i]^{1/4} = \sqrt[4]{2} \text{ cis } \frac{120° + k \cdot 360°}{4}.$$

The four roots correspond to $k = 0, 1, 2, 3$; that is,

for $k = 0$, $\sqrt[4]{2} \text{ cis } 30° = \sqrt[4]{2}\left(\frac{\sqrt{3}}{2} + \frac{1}{2}i\right),$

for $k = 1$, $\sqrt[4]{2} \text{ cis } 120° = \sqrt[4]{2}\left(-\frac{1}{2} + \frac{\sqrt{3}}{2}i\right),$

for $k = 2$, $\sqrt[4]{2} \text{ cis } 210° = \sqrt[4]{2}\left(-\frac{\sqrt{3}}{2} - \frac{1}{2}i\right),$

for $k = 3$, $\sqrt[4]{2} \text{ cis } 300° = \sqrt[4]{2}\left(\frac{1}{2} - \frac{\sqrt{3}}{2}i\right).$

EXERCISES FOR SECTION 10.4

Use DeMoivre's Theorem to evaluate each of the following powers. Leave the answer in polar form.

1. $(-1 + \sqrt{3}i)^3$ 2. $(1 + i)^4$

3. $(\sqrt{3} \text{ cis } 60°)^4$ 4. $(\sqrt{3} - i)^6$

5. $(-2 + 2i)^5$ 6. $(-1 + 3i)^3$

7. $(-\sqrt{3} + i)^7$ 8. $(2 \text{ cis } 20°)^5$

9. $(2 + 5i)^4$ 10. $(3 + 2i)^{10}$

Find the indicated roots and sketch their location in the complex plane.

11. Fifth roots of 1   12. Cube roots of 64

13. Fourth roots of i 14. Fourth roots of -16.

15. Square roots of $1 + i$ 16. Fifth roots of $\sqrt{3} + i$

17. Sixth roots of $-\sqrt{3} + i$ 18. Cube roots of $-1 + i$

19. Fourth roots of $-1 + \sqrt{3}\,i$ 20. Sixth roots of $-i$

21. Obtain an expression for $\cos 2\theta$ and $\sin 2\theta$ in terms of trigonometric functions of θ by making use of DeMoivre's Theorem.

22. Find all roots of the equation $x^4 + 81 = 0$.

23. Find all roots of $x^3 + 64 = 0$.

APPENDIX A

TABLES

TABLE A   Values of the Trigonometric Functions for Degrees

x	$\sin x$	$\cos x$	$\tan x$	$\cot x$	$\sec x$	$\csc x$	
0° 0′	.00000	1.0000	.00000		1.0000		90° 0′
10′	.00291	1.0000	.00291	343.77	1.0000	343.78	50′
20′	.00582	1.0000	.00582	171.88	1.0000	171.89	40′
30′	.00873	1.0000	.00873	114.59	1.0000	114.59	30′
40′	.01164	.9999	.01164	85.940	1.0001	85.946	20′
50′	.01454	.9999	.01455	68.750	1.0001	68.757	10′
1° 0′	.01745	.9998	.01746	57.290	1.0002	57.299	89° 0′
10′	.02036	.9998	.02036	49.104	1.0002	49.114	50′
20′	.02327	.9997	.02328	42.964	1.0003	42.976	40′
30′	.02618	.9997	.02619	38.188	1.0003	38.202	30′
40′	.02908	.9996	.02910	34.368	1.0004	34.382	20′
50′	.03199	.9995	.03201	31.242	1.0005	31.258	10′
2° 0′	.03490	.9994	.03492	28.6363	1.0006	28.654	88° 0′
10′	.03781	.9993	.03783	26.4316	1.0007	26.451	50′
20′	.04071	.9992	.04075	24.5418	1.0008	24.562	40′
30′	.04362	.9990	.04366	22.9038	1.0010	22.926	30′
40′	.04653	.9989	.04658	21.4704	1.0011	21.494	20′
50′	.04943	.9988	.04949	20.2056	1.0012	20.230	10′
3° 0′	.05234	.9986	.05241	19.0811	1.0014	19.107	87° 0′
10′	.05524	.9985	.05533	18.0750	1.0015	18.103	50′
20′	.05814	.9983	.05824	17.1693	1.0017	17.198	40′
30′	.06105	.9981	.06116	16.3499	1.0019	16.380	30′
40′	.06395	.9980	.06408	15.6048	1.0021	15.637	20′
50′	.06685	.9978	.06700	14.9244	1.0022	14.958	10′
4° 0′	.06976	.9976	.06993	14.3007	1.0024	14.336	86° 0′
10′	.07266	.9974	.07285	13.7267	1.0027	13.763	50′
20′	.07556	.9971	.07578	13.1969	1.0029	13.235	40′
30′	.07846	.9969	.07870	12.7062	1.0031	12.746	30′
40′	.08136	.9967	.08163	12.2505	1.0033	12.291	20′
50′	.08426	.9964	.08456	11.8262	1.0036	11.868	10′
5° 0′	.08716	.9962	.08749	11.4301	1.0038	11.474	85° 0′
10′	.09005	.9959	.09042	11.0594	1.0041	11.105	50′
20′	.09295	.9957	.09335	10.7119	1.0044	10.758	40′
30′	.09585	.9954	.09629	10.3854	1.0046	10.433	30′
40′	.09874	.9951	.09923	10.0780	1.0049	10.128	20′
50′	.10164	.9948	.10216	9.7882	1.0052	9.839	10′
6° 0′	.10453	.9945	.10510	9.5144	1.0055	9.5668	84° 0′
	$\cos x$	$\sin x$	$\cot x$	$\tan x$	$\csc x$	$\sec x$	x

TABLE A Trigonometric Functions for Degrees (continued)

x	sin x	cos x	tan x	cot x	sec x	csc x	
6° 0'	.1045	.9945	.10510	9.5144	1.0055	9.5668	84° 0'
10'	.1074	.9942	.10805	9.2553	1.0058	9.3092	50'
20'	.1103	.9939	.11099	9.0098	1.0061	9.0652	40'
30'	.1132	.9936	.11394	8.7769	1.0065	8.8337	30'
40'	.1161	.9932	.11688	8.5555	1.0068	8.6138	20'
50'	.1190	.9929	.11983	8.3450	1.0072	8.4647	10'
7° 0'	.1219	.9925	.12278	8.1443	1.0075	8.2055	83° 0'
10'	.1248	.9922	.12574	7.9530	1.0079	8.0157	50'
20'	.1276	.9918	.12869	7.7704	1.0083	7.8344	40'
30'	.1305	.9914	.13165	7.5958	1.0086	7.6613	30'
40'	.1334	.9911	.1346	7.4287	1.0090	7.4957	20'
50'	.1363	.9907	.1376	7.2687	1.0094	7.3372	10'
8° 0'	.1392	.9903	.1405	7.1154	1.0098	7.1853	82° 0'
10'	.1421	.9899	.1435	6.9682	1.0102	7.0396	50'
20'	.1449	.9894	.1465	6.8269	1.0107	6.8998	40'
30'	.1478	.9890	.1495	6.6912	1.0111	6.7655	30'
40'	.1507	.9886	.1524	6.5606	1.0116	6.6363	20'
50'	.1536	.9881	.1554	6.4348	1.0120	6.5121	10'
9° 0'	.1564	.9877	.1584	6.3138	1.0125	6.3925	81° 0'
10'	.1593	.9872	.1614	6.1970	1.0129	6.2772	50'
20'	.1622	.9868	.1644	6.0844	1.0134	6.1661	40'
30'	.1650	.9863	.1673	5.9758	1.0139	6.0589	30'
40'	.1679	.9858	.1703	5.8708	1.0144	5.9554	20'
50'	.1708	.9853	.1733	5.7694	1.0149	5.8554	10'
10° 0'	.1736	.9848	.1763	5.6713	1.0154	5.7588	80° 0'
10'	.1765	.9843	.1793	5.5764	1.0160	5.6653	50'
20'	.1794	.9838	.1823	5.4845	1.0165	5.5749	40'
30'	.1822	.9833	.1853	5.3955	1.0170	5.4874	30'
40'	.1851	.9827	.1883	5.3093	1.0176	5.4026	20'
50'	.1880	.9822	.1914	5.2257	1.0182	5.3205	10'
11° 0'	.1908	.9816	.1944	5.1446	1.0187	5.2408	79° 0'
10'	.1937	.9811	.1974	5.0658	1.0193	5.1636	50'
20'	.1965	.9805	.2004	4.9894	1.0199	5.0886	40'
30'	.1994	.9799	.2035	4.9152	1.0205	5.0159	30'
40'	.2022	.9793	.2065	4.8430	1.0211	4.9452	20'
50'	.2051	.9787	.2095	4.7729	1.0217	4.8765	10'
12° 0'	.2079	.9781	.2126	4.7046	1.0223	4.8097	78° 0'
	cos x	sin x	cot x	tan x	csc x	sec x	x

TABLE A   Trigonometric Functions for Degrees (continued)

x	sin x	cos x	tan x	cot x	sec x	csc x	
12° 0′	.2079	.9781	.2126	4.7046	1.0223	4.8097	78° 0′
10′	.2108	.9775	.2156	4.6382	1.0230	4.7448	50′
20′	.2136	.9769	.2186	4.5736	1.0236	4.6817	40′
30′	.2164	.9763	.2217	4.5107	1.0243	4.6202	30′
40′	.2193	.9757	.2247	4.4494	1.0249	4.5604	20′
50′	.2221	.9750	.2278	4.3897	1.0256	4.5022	10′
13° 0′	.2250	.9744	.2309	4.3315	1.0263	4.4454	77° 0′
10′	.2278	.9737	.2339	4.2747	1.0270	4.3901	50′
20′	.2306	.9730	.2370	4.2193	1.0277	4.3362	40′
30′	.2334	.9724	.2401	4.1653	1.0284	4.2837	30′
40′	.2363	.9717	.2432	4.1126	1.0291	4.2324	20′
50′	.2391	.9710	.2462	4.0611	1.0299	4.1824	10′
14° 0′	.2419	.9703	.2493	4.0108	1.0306	4.1336	76° 0′
10′	.2447	.9696	.2524	3.9617	1.0314	4.0859	50′
20′	.2476	.9689	.2555	3.9136	1.0321	4.0394	40′
30′	.2504	.9681	.2586	3.8667	1.0329	3.9939	30′
40′	.2532	.9674	.2617	3.8208	1.0337	3.9495	20′
50′	.2560	.9667	.2648	3.7760	1.0345	3.9061	10′
15° 0′	.2588	.9659	.2679	3.7321	1.0353	3.8637	75° 0′
10′	.2616	.9652	.2711	3.6891	1.0361	3.8222	50′
20′	.2644	.9644	.2742	3.6470	1.0369	3.7817	40′
30′	.2672	.9636	.2773	3.6059	1.0377	3.7420	30′
40′	.2700	.9628	.2805	3.5656	1.0386	3.7032	20′
50′	.2728	.9621	.2836	3.5261	1.0394	3.6652	10′
16° 0′	.2756	.9613	.2867	3.4874	1.0403	3.6280	74° 0′
10′	.2784	.9605	.2899	3.4495	1.0412	3.5915	50′
20′	.2812	.9596	.2931	3.4124	1.0421	3.5559	40′
30′	.2840	.9588	.2962	3.3759	1.0430	3.5209	30′
40′	.2868	.9580	.2994	3.3402	1.0439	3.4867	20′
50′	.2896	.9572	.3026	3.3052	1.0448	3.4532	10′
17° 0′	.2924	.9563	.3057	3.2709	1.0457	3.4203	73° 0′
10′	.2952	.9555	.3089	3.2371	1.0466	3.3881	50′
20′	.2979	.9546	.3121	3.2041	1.0476	3.3565	40′
30′	.3007	.9537	.3153	3.1716	1.0485	3.3255	30′
40′	.3035	.9528	.3185	3.1397	1.0495	3.2951	20′
50′	.3062	.9520	.3217	3.1084	1.0505	3.2653	10′
18° 0′	.3090	.9511	.3249	3.0777	1.0515	3.2361	72° 0′
	cos x	sin x	cot x	tan x	csc x	sec x	x

TABLE A   Trigonometric Functions for Degrees (continued)

x	$\sin x$	$\cos x$	$\tan x$	$\cot x$	$\sec x$	$\csc x$	
18° 0'	.3090	.9511	.3249	3.0777	1.0515	3.2361	72° 0'
10'	.3118	.9502	.3281	3.0475	1.0525	3.2074	50'
20'	.3145	.9492	.3314	3.0178	1.0535	3.1792	40'
30'	.3173	.9483	.3346	2.9887	1.0545	3.1516	30'
40'	.3201	.9474	.3378	2.9600	1.0555	3.1244	20'
50'	.3228	.9465	.3411	2.9319	1.0566	3.0977	10'
19° 0'	.3256	.9455	.3443	2.9042	1.0576	3.0716	71° 0'
10'	.3283	.9446	.3476	2.8770	1.0587	3.0458	50'
20'	.3311	.9436	.3508	2.8502	1.0598	3.0206	40'
30'	.3338	.9426	.3541	2.8239	1.0609	2.9957	30'
40'	.3365	.9417	.3574	2.7980	1.0620	2.9714	20'
50'	.3393	.9407	.3607	2.7725	1.0631	2.9474	10'
20° 0'	.3420	.9397	.3640	2.7475	1.0642	2.9238	70° 0'
10'	.3448	.9387	.3673	2.7228	1.0653	2.9006	50'
20'	.3475	.9377	.3706	2.6985	1.0665	2.8779	40'
30'	.3502	.9367	.3739	2.6746	1.0676	2.8555	30'
40'	.3529	.9356	.3772	2.6511	1.0688	2.8334	20'
50'	.3557	.9346	.3805	2.6279	1.0700	2.8118	10'
21° 0'	.3584	.9336	.3839	2.6051	1.0712	2.7904	69° 0'
10'	.3611	.9325	.3872	2.5826	1.0724	2.7695	50'
20'	.3638	.9315	.3906	2.5605	1.0736	2.7488	40'
30'	.3665	.9304	.3939	2.5386	1.0748	2.7285	30'
40'	.3692	.9293	.3973	2.5172	1.0760	2.7085	20'
50'	.3719	.9283	.4006	2.4960	1.0773	2.6888	10'
22° 0'	.3746	.9272	.4040	2.4751	1.0785	2.6695	68° 0'
10'	.3773	.9261	.4074	2.4545	1.0798	2.6504	50'
20'	.3800	.9250	.4108	2.4342	1.0811	2.6316	40'
30'	.3827	.9239	.4142	2.4142	1.0824	2.6131	30'
40'	.3854	.9228	.4176	2.3945	1.0837	2.5949	20'
50'	.3881	.9216	.4210	2.3750	1.0850	2.5770	10'
23° 0'	.3907	.9205	.4245	2.3559	1.0864	2.5593	67° 0'
10'	.3934	.9194	.4279	2.3369	1.0877	2.5419	50'
20'	.3961	.9182	.4314	2.3183	1.0891	2.5247	40'
30'	.3987	.9171	.4348	2.2998	1.0904	2.5078	30'
40'	4014	.9159	.4383	2.2817	1.0918	2.4912	20'
50'	.4041	.9147	.4417	2.2637	1.0932	2.4748	10'
24° 0'	.4067	.9135	.4452	2.2460	1.0946	2.4586	66° 0'
	$\cos x$	$\sin x$	$\cot x$	$\tan x$	$\csc x$	$\sec x$	x

TABLE A   Trigonometric Functions for Degrees (continued)

x	$\sin x$	$\cos x$	$\tan x$	$\cot x$	$\sec x$	$\csc x$	
24° 0′	.4067	.9135	.4452	2.2460	1.0946	2.4586	66° 0′
10′	.4094	.9124	.4487	2.2286	1.0961	2.4426	50′
20′	.4120	.9112	.4522	2.2113	1.0975	2.4269	40′
30′	.4147	.9100	.4557	2.1943	1.0990	2.4114	30′
40′	.4173	.9088	.4592	2.1775	1.1004	2.3961	20′
50′	.4200	.9075	.4628	2.1609	1.1019	2.3811	10′
25° 0′	.4226	.9063	.4663	2.1445	1.1034	2.3662	65° 0′
10′	.4253	.9051	.4699	2.1283	1.1049	2.3515	50′
20′	.4279	.9038	.4734	2.1123	1.1064	2.3371	40′
30′	.4305	.9026	.4770	2.0965	1.1079	2.3228	30′
40′	.4331	.9013	.4806	2.0809	1.1095	2.3088	20′
50′	.4358	.9001	.4841	2.0655	1.1110	2.2949	10′
26° 0′	.4384	.8988	.4877	2.0503	1.1126	2.2812	64° 0′
10′	.4410	.8975	.4913	2.0353	1.1142	2.2677	50′
20′	.4436	.8962	.4950	2.0204	1.1158	2.2543	40′
30′	.4462	.8949	.4986	2.0057	1.1174	2.2412	30′
40′	.4488	.8936	.5022	1.9912	1.1190	2.2282	20′
50′	.4514	.8923	.5059	1.9768	1.1207	2.2154	10′
27° 0′	.4540	.8910	.5095	1.9626	1.1223	2.2027	63° 0′
10′	.4566	.8897	.5132	1.9486	1.1240	2.1902	50′
20′	.4592	.8884	.5169	1.9347	1.1257	2.1779	40′
30′	.4617	.8870	.5206	1.9210	1.1274	2.1657	30′
40′	.4643	.8857	.5243	1.9074	1.1291	2.1537	20′
50′	.4669	.8843	.5280	1.8940	1.1308	2.1418	10′
28° 0′	.4695	.8829	.5317	1.8807	1.1326	2.1301	62° 0′
10′	.4720	.8816	.5354	1.8676	1.1343	2.1185	50′
20′	.4746	.8802	.5392	1.8546	1.1361	2.1070	40′
30′	.4772	.8788	.5430	1.8418	1.1379	2.0957	30′
40′	.4797	.8774	.5467	1.8291	1.1397	2.0846	20′
50′	.4823	.8760	.5505	1.8165	1.1415	2.0736	10′
29° 0′	.4848	.8746	.5543	1.8040	1.1434	2.0627	61° 0′
10′	.4874	.8732	.5581	1.7917	1.1452	2.0519	50′
20′	.4899	.8718	.5619	1.7796	1.1471	2.0413	40′
30′	.4924	.8704	.5658	1.7675	1.1490	2.0308	30′
40′	.4950	.8689	.5696	1.7556	1.1509	2.0204	20′
50′	.4975	.8675	.5735	1.7437	1.1528	2.0101	10′
30° 0′	.5000	.8660	.5774	1.7321	1.1547	2.0000	60° 0′
	$\cos x$	$\sin x$	$\cot x$	$\tan x$	$\csc x$	$\sec x$	x

x	$\sin x$	$\cos x$	$\tan x$	$\cot x$	$\sec x$	$\csc x$	
30° 0′	.5000	.8660	.5774	1.7321	1.1547	2.0000	60° 0′
10′	.5025	.8646	.5812	1.7205	1.1567	1.9900	50′
20′	.5050	.8631	.5851	1.7090	1.1586	1.9801	40′
30′	.5075	.8616	.5890	1.6977	1.1606	1.9703	30′
40′	.5100	.8601	.5930	1.6864	1.1626	1.9606	20′
50′	.5125	.8587	.5969	1.6753	1.1646	1.9511	10′
31° 0′	.5150	.8572	.6009	1.6643	1.1666	1.9416	59° 0′
10′	.5175	.8557	.6048	1.6534	1.1687	1.9323	50′
20′	.5200	.8542	.6088	1.6426	1.1708	1.9230	40′
30′	.5225	.8526	.6128	1.6319	1.1728	1.9139	30′
40′	.5250	.8511	.6168	1.6212	1.1749	1.9049	20′
50′	.5275	.8496	.6208	1.6107	1.1770	1.8959	10′
32° 0′	.5299	.8480	.6249	1.6003	1.1792	1.8871	58° 0′
10′	.5324	.8465	.6289	1.5900	1.1813	1.8783	50′
20′	.5348	.8450	.6330	1.5798	1.1835	1.8699	40′
30′	.5373	.8434	.6371	1.5697	1.1857	1.8612	30′
40′	.5398	.8418	.6412	1.5597	1.1879	1.8527	20′
50′	.5422	.8403	.6453	1.5497	1.1901	1.8444	10′
33° 0′	.5446	.8387	.6494	1.5399	1.1924	1.8361	57° 0′
10′	.5471	.8371	.6536	1.5301	1.1946	1.8279	50′
20′	.5495	.8355	.6577	1.5204	1.1969	1.8198	40′
30′	.5519	.8339	.6619	1.5108	1.1992	1.8118	30′
40′	.5544	.8323	.6661	1.5013	1.2015	1.8039	20′
50′	.5568	.8307	.6703	1.4919	1.2039	1.7960	10′
34° 0′	.5592	.8290	.6745	1.4826	1.2062	1.7883	56° 0′
10′	.5616	.8274	.6787	1.4733	1.2086	1.7806	50′
20′	.5640	.8258	.6830	1.4641	1.2110	1.7730	40′
30′	.5664	.8241	.6873	1.4550	1.2134	1.7655	30′
40′	.5688	.8225	.6916	1.4460	1.2158	1.7581	20′
50′	.5712	.8208	.6959	1.4370	1.2183	1.7507	10′
35° 0′	.5736	.8192	.7002	1.4281	1.2208	1.7435	55° 0′
10′	.5760	.8175	.7046	1.4193	1.2233	1.7362	50′
20′	.5783	.8158	.7089	1.4106	1.2258	1.7291	40′
30′	.5807	.8141	.7133	1.4019	1.2283	1.7221	30′
40′	.5831	.8124	.7177	1.3934	1.2309	1.7151	20′
50′	.5854	.8107	.7221	1.3848	1.2335	1.7082	10′
36° 0′	.5878	.8090	.7265	1.3764	1.2361	1.7013	54° 0′
	$\cos x$	$\sin x$	$\cot x$	$\tan x$	$\csc x$	$\sec x$	x

TABLE A **Trigonometric Functions for Degrees (continued)**

x	$\sin x$	$\cos x$	$\tan x$	$\cot x$	$\sec x$	$\csc x$	
36° 0′	.5878	.8090	.7265	1.3764	1.2361	1.7013	54° 0′
10′	.5901	.8073	.7310	1.3680	1.2387	1.6945	50′
20′	.5925	.8056	.7355	1.3597	1.2413	1.6878	40′
30′	.5948	.8039	.7400	1.3514	1.2440	1.6812	30′
40′	.5972	.8021	.7445	1.3432	1.2467	1.6746	20′
50′	.5995	.8004	.7490	1.3351	1.2494	1.6681	10′
37° 0′	.6018	.7986	.7536	1.3270	1.2521	1.6616	53° 0′
10′	.6041	.7969	.7581	1.3190	1.2549	1.6553	50′
20′	.6065	.7951	.7627	1.3111	1.2577	1.6489	40′
30′	.6088	.7934	.7673	1.3032	1.2605	1.6427	30′
40′	.6111	.7916	.7720	1.2954	1.2633	1.6365	20′
50′	.6134	.7898	.7766	1.2876	1.2662	1.6304	10′
38° 0′	.6157	.7880	.7813	1.2799	1.2690	1.6243	52° 0′
10′	.6180	.7862	.7860	1.2723	1.2719	1.6183	50′
20′	.6202	.7844	.7907	1.2647	1.2748	1.6123	40′
30′	.6225	.7826	.7954	1.2572	1.2779	1.6064	30′
40′	.6248	.7808	.8002	1.2497	1.2808	1.6005	20′
50′	.6271	.7790	.8050	1.2423	1.2837	1.5948	10′
39° 0′	.6293	.7771	.8098	1.2349	1.2868	1.5890	51° 0′
10′	.6316	.7753	.8146	1.2276	1.2898	1.5833	50′
20′	.6338	.7735	.8195	1.2203	1.2929	1.5777	40′
30′	.6361	.7716	.8243	1.2131	1.2960	1.5721	30′
40′	.6383	.7698	.8292	1.2059	1.2991	1.5666	20′
50′	.6406	.7679	.8342	1.1988	1.3022	1.5611	10′
40° 0′	.6428	.7660	.8391	1.1918	1.3054	1.5557	50° 0′
10′	.6450	.7642	.8441	1.1847	1.3086	1.5504	50′
20′	.6472	.7623	.8491	1.1778	1.3118	1.5450	40′
30′	.6494	.7604	.8541	1.1708	1.3151	1.5398	30′
40′	.6517	.7585	.8591	1.1640	1.3184	1.5346	20′
50′	.6539	.7566	.8642	1.1571	1.3217	1.5294	10′
41° 0′	.6561	.7547	.8693	1.1504	1.3250	1.5243	49° 0′
10′	.6583	.7528	.8744	1.1436	1.3284	1.5192	50′
20′	.6604	.7509	.8796	1.1369	1.3318	1.5142	40′
30′	.6626	.7490	.8847	1.1303	1.3352	1.5092	30′
40′	.6648	.7470	.8899	1.1237	1.3386	1.5042	20′
50′	.6670	.7451	.8952	1.1171	1.3421	1.4993	10′
42° 0′	.6691	.7431	.9004	1.1106	1.3456	1.4945	48° 0′
	$\cos x$	$\sin x$	$\cot x$	$\tan x$	$\csc x$	$\sec x$	x

TABLE A   Trigonometric Functions for Degrees (continued)

x	$\sin x$	$\cos x$	$\tan x$	$\cot x$	$\sec x$	$\csc x$	
42° 0′	.6691	.7431	.9004	1.1106	1.3456	1.4945	48° 0′
10′	.6713	.7412	.9057	1.1041	1.3492	1.4897	50′
20′	.6734	.7392	.9110	1.0977	1.3527	1.4849	40′
30′	.6756	.7373	.9163	1.0913	1.3563	1.4802	30′
40′	.6777	.7353	.9217	1.0850	1.3600	1.4755	20′
50′	.6799	.7333	.9271	1.0786	1.3636	1.4709	10′
43° 0′	.6820	.7314	.9325	1.0724	1.3673	1.4663	47° 0′
10′	.6841	.7294	.9380	1.0661	1.3711	1.4617	50′
20′	.6862	.7274	.9435	1.0599	1.3748	1.4572	40′
30′	.6884	.7254	.9490	1.0538	1.3786	1.4527	30′
40′	.6905	.7234	.9545	1.0477	1.3824	1.4483	20′
50′	.6926	.7214	.9601	1.0416	1.3863	1.4439	10′
44° 0′	.6947	.7193	.9657	1.0355	1.3902	1.4396	46° 0′
10′	.6967	.7173	.9713	1.0295	1.3941	1.4352	50′
20′	.6988	.7153	.9770	1.0235	1.3980	1.4310	40′
30′	.7009	.7133	.9827	1.0176	1.4020	1.4267	30′
40′	.7030	.7112	.9884	1.0117	1.4061	1.4225	20′
50′	.7050	.7092	.9942	1.0058	1.4101	1.4184	10′
45° 0′	.7071	.7071	1.0000	1.0000	1.4142	1.4142	45° 0′
	$\cos x$	$\sin x$	$\cot x$	$\tan x$	$\csc x$	$\sec x$	x

TABLE B   Values of the Trigonometric Functions for Radians and Real Numbers

t	sin t	cos t	tan t	cot t	sec t	csc t
.00	.0000	1.0000	.0000	.....	1.000	.....
.01	.0100	1.0000	.0100	99.997	1.000	100.00
.02	.0200	.9998	.0200	49.993	1.000	50.00
.03	.0300	.9996	.0300	33.323	1.000	33.34
.04	.0400	.9992	.0400	24.987	1.001	25.01
.05	.0500	.9988	.0500	19.983	1.001	20.01
.06	.0600	.9982	.0601	16.647	1.002	16.68
.07	.0699	.9976	.0701	14.262	1.002	14.30
.08	.0799	.9968	.0802	12.473	1.003	12.51
.09	.0899	.9960	.0902	11.081	1.004	11.13
.10	.0998	.9950	.1003	9.967	1.005	10.02
.11	.1098	.9940	.1104	9.054	1.006	9.109
.12	.1197	.9928	.1206	8.293	1.007	8.353
.13	.1296	.9916	.1307	7.649	1.009	7.714
.14	.1395	.9902	.1409	7.096	1.010	7.166
.15	.1494	.9888	.1511	6.617	1.011	6.692
.16	.1593	.9872	.1614	6.197	1.013	6.277
.17	.1692	.9856	.1717	5.826	1.015	5.911
.18	.1790	.9838	.1820	5.495	1.016	5.586
.19	.1889	.9820	.1923	5.200	1.018	5.295
.20	.1987	.9801	.2027	4.933	1.020	5.033
.21	.2085	.9780	.2131	4.692	1.022	4.797
.22	.2182	.9759	.2236	4.472	1.025	4.582
.23	.2280	.9737	.2341	4.271	1.027	4.386
.24	.2377	.9713	.2447	4.086	1.030	4.207
.25	.2474	.9689	.2553	3.916	1.032	4.042
.26	.2571	.9664	.2660	3.759	1.035	3.890
.27	.2667	.9638	.2768	3.613	1.038	3.749
.28	.2764	.9611	.2876	3.478	1.041	3.619
.29	.2860	.9582	.2984	3.351	1.044	3.497
.30	.2955	.9553	.3093	3.233	1.047	3.384
.31	.3051	.9523	.3203	3.122	1.050	3.278
.32	.3146	.9492	.3314	3.018	1.053	3.179
.33	.3240	.9460	.3425	2.920	1.057	3.086
.34	.3335	.9428	.3537	2.827	1.061	2.999
.35	.3429	.9394	.3650	2.740	1.065	2.916
.36	.3523	.9359	.3764	2.657	1.068	2.839
.37	.3616	.9323	.3879	2.578	1.073	2.765
.38	.3709	.9287	.3994	2.504	1.077	2.696
.39	.3802	.9249	.4111	2.433	1.081	2.630

TABLE B   The Trigonometric Functions for Radians and Real Numbers (continued)

t	sin t	cos t	tan t	cot t	sec t	csc t
.40	.3894	.9211	.4228	2.365	1.086	2.568
.41	.3986	.9171	.4346	2.301	1.090	2.509
.42	.4078	.9131	.4466	2.239	1.095	2.452
.43	.4169	.9090	.4586	2.180	1.100	2.399
.44	.4259	.9048	.4708	2.124	1.105	2.348
.45	.4350	.9004	.4831	2.070	1.111	2.299
.46	.4439	.8961	.4954	2.018	1.116	2.253
.47	.4529	.8916	.5080	1.969	1.122	2.208
.48	.4618	.8870	.5206	1.921	1.127	2.166
.49	.4706	.8823	.5334	1.875	1.133	2.125
.50	.4794	.8776	.5463	1.830	1.139	2.086
.51	.4882	.8727	.5594	1.788	1.146	2.048
.52	.4969	.8678	.5726	1.747	1.152	2.013
.53	.5055	.8628	.5859	1.707	1.159	1.978
.54	.5141	.8577	.5994	1.668	1.166	1.945
.55	.5227	.8525	.6131	1.631	1.173	1.913
.56	.5312	.8473	.6269	1.595	1.180	1.883
.57	.5396	.8419	.6410	1.560	1.188	1.853
.58	.5480	.8365	.6552	1.526	1.196	1.825
.59	.5564	.8309	.6696	1.494	1.203	1.797
.60	.5646	.8253	.6841	1.462	1.212	1.771
.61	.5729	.8196	.6989	1.431	1.220	1.746
.62	.5810	.8139	.7139	1.401	1.229	1.721
.63	.5891	.8080	.7291	1.372	1.238	1.697
.64	.5972	.8021	.7445	1.343	1.247	1.674
.65	.6052	.7961	.7602	1.315	1.256	1.652
.66	.6131	.7900	.7761	1.288	1.266	1.631
.67	.6210	.7838	.7923	1.262	1.276	1.610
.68	.6288	.7776	.8087	1.237	1.286	1.590
.69	.6365	.7712	.8253	1.212	1.297	1.571
.70	.6442	.7648	.8423	1.187	1.307	1.552
.71	.6518	.7584	.8595	1.163	1.319	1.534
.72	.6594	.7518	.8771	1.140	1.330	1.517
.73	.6669	.7452	.8949	1.117	1.342	1.500
.74	.6743	.7385	.9131	1.095	1.354	1.483
.75	.6816	.7317	.9316	1.073	1.367	1.467
.76	.6889	.7248	.9505	1.052	1.380	1.452
.77	.6961	.7179	.9697	1.031	1.393	1.437
.78	.7033	.7109	.9893	1.011	1.407	1.422
.79	.7104	.7038	1.009	.9908	1.421	1.408

TABLE B   The Trigonometric Functions for Radians and Real Numbers (continued)

t	sin t	cos t	tan t	cot t	sec t	csc t
.80	.7174	.6967	1.030	.9712	1.435	1.394
.81	.7243	.6895	1.050	.9520	1.450	1.381
.82	.7311	.6822	1.072	.9331	1.466	1.368
.83	.7379	.6749	1.093	.9146	1.482	1.355
.84	.7446	.6675	1.116	.8964	1.498	1.343
.85	.7513	.6600	1.138	.8785	1.515	1.331
.86	.7578	.6524	1.162	.8609	1.533	1.320
.87	.7643	.6448	1.185	.8437	1.551	1.308
.88	.7707	.6372	1.210	.8267	1.569	1.297
.89	.7771	.6294	1.235	.8100	1.589	1.287
.90	.7833	.6216	1.260	.7936	1.609	1.277
.91	.7895	.6137	1.286	.7774	1.629	1.267
.92	.7956	.6058	1.313	.7615	1.651	1.257
.93	.8016	.5978	1.341	.7458	1.673	1.247
.94	.8076	.5898	1.369	.7303	1.696	1.238
.95	.8134	.5817	1.398	.7151	1.719	1.229
.96	.8192	.5735	1.428	.7001	1.744	1.221
.97	.8249	.5653	1.459	.6853	1.769	1.212
.98	.8305	.5570	1.491	.6707	1.795	1.204
.99	8360	.5487	1.524	.6563	1.823	1.196
1.00	.8415	.5403	1.557	.6421	1.851	1.188
1.01	.8468	.5319	1.592	.6281	1.880	1.181
1.02	.8521	.5234	1.628	.6142	1.911	1.174
1.03	.8573	.5148	1.665	.6005	1.942	1.166
1.04	.8624	.5062	1.704	.5870	1.975	1.160
1.05	.8674	.4976	1.743	.5736	2.010	1.153
1.06	.8724	.4889	1.784	.5604	2.046	1.146
1.07	.8772	.4801	1.827	.5473	2.083	1.140
1.08	.8820	.4713	1.871	.5344	2.122	1.134
1.09	.8866	.4625	1.917	.5216	2.162	1.128
1.10	.8912	.4536	1.965	.5090	2.205	1.122
1.11	.8957	.4447	2.014	.4964	2.249	1.116
1.12	.9001	4357	2.066	.4840	2.295	1.111
1.13	.9044	.4267	2.120	.4718	2.344	1.106
1.14	.9086	.4176	2.176	.4596	2.395	1.101
1.15	.9128	.4085	2.234	.4475	2.448	1.096
1.16	.9168	.3993	2.296	.4356	2.504	1.091
1.17	.9208	.3902	2.360	.4237	2.563	1.086
1.18	.9246	.3809	2.427	.4120	2.625	1.082
1.19	.9284	.3717	2.498	.4003	2.691	1.077

TABLE B   The Trigonometric Functions for Radians and Real Numbers (continued)

t	$\sin t$	$\cos t$	$\tan t$	$\cot t$	$\sec t$	$\csc t$
1.20	.9320	.3624	2.572	.3888	2.760	1.073
1.21	.9356	.3530	2.650	.3773	2.833	1.069
1.22	.9391	.3436	2.733	.3659	2.910	1.065
1.23	.9425	.3342	2.820	.3546	2.992	1.061
1.24	.9458	.3248	2.912	.3434	3.079	1.057
1.25	.9490	.3153	3.010	.3323	3.171	1.054
1.26	.9521	.3058	3.113	.3212	3.270	1.050
1.27	.9551	.2963	3.224	.3102	3.375	1.047
1.28	.9580	.2867	3.341	.2993	3.488	1.044
1.29	.9608	.2771	3.467	.2884	3.609	1.041
1.30	.9636	.2675	3.602	.2776	3.738	1.038
1.31	.9662	.2579	3.747	.2669	3.878	1.035
1.32	.9687	.2482	3.903	.2562	4.029	1.032
1.33	.9711	.2385	4.072	.2456	4.193	1.030
1.34	.9735	.2288	4.256	2350	4.372	1.027
1.35	.9757	.2190	4.455	.2245	4.566	1.025
1.36	.9779	.2092	4.673	.2140	4.779	1.023
1.37	.9799	.1994	4.913	.2035	5.014	1.021
1.38	.9819	.1896	5.177	.1931	5.273	1.018
1.39	.9837	.1798	5.471	.1828	5.561	1.017
1.40	.9854	.1700	5.798	.1725	5.883	1.015
1.41	.9871	.1601	6.165	.1622	6.246	1.013
1.42	.9887	.1502	6.581	.1519	6.657	1.011
1.43	.9901	.1403	7.055	.1417	7.126	1.010
1.44	.9915	.1304	7.602	.1315	7.667	1.009
1.45	.9927	.1205	8.238	.1214	8.299	1.007
1.46	.9939	.1106	8.989	.1113	9.044	1.006
1.47	.9949	.1006	9.887	.1011	9.938	1.005
1.48	.9959	.0907	10.983	.0910	11.029	1.004
1.49	.9967	.0807	12.350	.0810	12.390	1.003
1.50	.9975	.0707	14.101	.0709	14.137	1.003
1.51	.9982	.0608	16.428	.0609	16.458	1.002
1.52	.9987	.0508	19.670	.0508	19.695	1.001
1.53	.9992	.0408	24.498	.0408	24.519	1.001
1.54	.9995	.0308	32.461	.0308	32.476	1.000
1.55	.9998	.0208	48.078	.0208	48.089	1.000
1.56	.9999	.0108	92.620	.0108	92.626	1.000
1.57	1.0000	.0008	1255.8	.0008	1255.8	1.000

TABLE C   Four-Place Logarithms of Numbers from 1 to 10

n	0	1	2	3	4	5	6	7	8	9
1.0	+0.0000	0043	0086	0128	0170	0212	0253	0294	0334	0374
1.1	.0414	0453	0492	0531	0569	0607	0645	0682	0719	0755
1.2	.0792	0828	0864	0899	0934	0969	1004	1038	1072	1106
1.3	.1139	1173	1206	1239	1271	1303	1335	1367	1399	1430
1.4	.1461	1492	1523	1553	1584	1614	1644	1673	1703	1732
1.5	.1761	1790	1818	1847	1875	1903	1931	1959	1987	2014
1.6	.2041	2068	2095	2122	2148	2175	2201	2227	2253	2279
1.7	.2304	2330	2355	2380	2405	2430	2455	2480	2504	2529
1.8	.2553	2577	2601	2625	2648	2672	2695	2718	2742	2765
1.9	.2788	2810	2833	2856	2878	2900	2923	2945	2967	2989
2.0	.3010	3032	3054	3075	3096	3118	3139	3160	3181	3201
2.1	.3222	3243	3263	3284	3304	3324	3345	3365	3385	3404
2.2	.3424	3444	3464	3483	3502	3522	3541	3560	3579	3598
2.3	.3617	3636	3655	3674	3692	3711	3729	3747	3766	3784
2.4	.3802	3820	3838	3856	3874	3892	3909	3927	3945	3962
2.5	.3979	3997	4014	4031	4048	4065	4082	4099	4116	4133
2.6	.4150	4166	4183	4200	4216	4232	4249	4265	4281	4298
2.7	.4314	4330	4346	4362	4378	4393	4409	4425	4440	4456
2.8	.4472	4487	4502	4518	4533	4548	4564	4579	4594	4609
2.9	.4624	4639	4654	4669	4683	4698	4713	4728	4742	4757
3.0	.4771	4786	4800	4814	4829	4843	4857	4871	4886	4900
3.1	.4914	4928	4942	4955	4969	4983	4997	5011	5024	5038
3.2	.5051	5065	5079	5092	5105	5119	5132	5145	5159	5172
3.3	.5185	5198	5211	5224	5237	5250	5263	5276	5289	5302
3.4	.5315	5328	5340	5353	5366	5378	5391	5403	5416	5428
3.5	.5441	5453	5465	5478	5490	5502	5514	5527	5539	5551
3.6	5563	5575	5587	5599	5611	5623	5635	5647	5658	5670
3.7	.5682	5694	5705	5717	5729	5740	5752	5763	5775	5786
3.8	5798	5809	5821	5832	5843	5855	5866	5877	5888	5899
3.9	.5911	5922	5933	5944	5955	5966	5977	5988	5999	6010
4.0	.6021	6031	6042	6053	6064	6075	6085	6096	6107	6117
4.1	.6128	6138	6149	6160	6170	6180	6191	6201	6212	6222
4.2	.6232	6243	6253	6263	6274	6284	6294	6304	6314	6325
4.3	.6335	6345	6355	6365	6375	6385	6395	6405	6415	6425
4.4	.6435	6444	6454	6464	6474	6484	6493	6503	6513	6522
4.5	.6532	6542	6551	6561	6571	6580	6590	6599	6609	6618
4.6	.6628	6637	6645	6656	6665	6675	6684	6693	6702	6712
4.7	.6721	6730	6739	6749	6758	6767	6776	6785	6794	6803
4.8	.6812	6821	6830	6839	6848	6857	6866	6875	6884	6893
4.9	.6902	6911	6920	6928	6937	6946	6955	6964	6972	6981
5.0	+.6990	6998	7007	7016	7024	7033	7042	7050	7059	7067
5.1	.7076	7084	7093	7101	7110	7118	7126	7135	7143	7152
5.2	.7160	7168	7177	7185	7193	7202	7210	7218	7226	7235
5.3	.7243	7251	7259	7267	7275	7284	7292	7300	7308	7316
5.4	.7324	7332	7340	7348	7356	7364	7372	7380	7388	7396

TABLE C   Four-Place Logarithms of Numbers from 1 to 10 (continued)

n	0	1	2	3	4	5	6	7	8	9
5.5	.7404	7412	7419	7427	7435	7443	7451	7459	7466	7474
5.6	.7482	7490	7497	7505	7513	7520	7528	7536	7543	7551
5.7	.7559	7566	7574	7582	7589	7597	7604	7612	7619	7627
5.8	.7634	7642	7649	7657	7664	7672	7679	7686	7694	7701
5.9	.7709	7716	7723	7731	7738	7745	7752	7760	7767	7774
6.0	.7782	7789	7796	7803	7810	7818	7825	7832	7839	7846
6.1	.7853	7860	7868	7875	7882	7889	7896	7903	7910	7917
6.2	.7924	7931	7938	7945	7952	7959	7966	7973	7980	7987
6.3	.7993	8000	8007	8014	8021	8028	8035	8041	8048	8055
6.4	.8062	8069	8075	8082	8089	8096	8102	8109	8116	8122
6.5	.8129	8136	8142	8149	8156	8162	8169	8176	8182	8189
6.6	.8195	8202	8209	8215	8222	8228	8235	8241	8248	8254
6.7	.8261	8267	8274	8280	8287	8293	8299	8306	8312	8319
6.8	.8325	8331	8338	8344	8351	8357	8363	8370	8376	8382
6.9	.8388	8395	8401	8407	8414	8420	8426	8432	8439	8445
7.0	.8451	8457	8463	8470	8476	8482	8488	8494	8500	8506
7.1	.8513	8519	8525	8531	8537	8543	8549	8555	8561	8567
7.2	.8573	8579	8585	8591	8597	8603	8609	8615	8621	8627
7.3	.8633	8639	8645	8651	8657	8663	8669	8675	8681	8686
7.4	.8692	8698	8704	8710	8716	8722	8727	8733	8739	8745
7.5	.8751	8756	8762	8768	8774	8779	8785	8791	8797	8802
7.6	.8808	8814	8820	8825	8831	8837	8842	8848	8854	8859
7.7	.8865	8871	8876	8882	8887	8893	8899	8904	8910	8915
7.8	.8921	8927	8932	8938	8943	8949	8954	8960	8965	8971
7.9	.8976	8982	8987	8993	8998	9004	9009	9015	9020	9025
8.0	.9031	9036	9042	9047	9053	9058	9063	9069	9074	9079
8.1	.9085	9090	9096	9101	9106	9112	9117	9122	9128	9133
8.2	.9138	9143	9149	9154	9159	9165	9170	9175	9180	9186
8.3	.9191	9196	9201	9206	9212	9217	9222	9227	9232	9238
8.4	.9243	9248	9253	9258	9263	9269	9274	9279	9284	9289
8.5	.9294	9299	9304	9309	9315	9320	9325	9330	9335	9340
8.6	.9345	9350	9355	9360	9365	9370	9375	9380	9385	9390
8.7	.9395	9400	9405	9410	9415	9420	9425	9430	9435	9440
8.8	.9445	9450	9455	9460	9465	9469	9474	9479	9484	9489
8.9	.9494	9499	9504	9509	9513	9518	9523	9528	9533	9538
9.0	.9542	9547	9552	9557	9562	9566	9571	9576	9581	9586
9.1	.9590	9595	9600	9605	9609	9614	9619	9624	9628	9633
9.2	.9638	9643	9647	9652	9657	9661	9666	9671	9675	9680
9.3	.9685	9689	9694	9699	9703	9708	9713	9717	9722	9727
9.4	.9731	9736	9741	9745	9750	9754	9759	9763	9768	9773
9.5	.9777	9782	9786	9791	9795	9800	9805	9809	9814	9818
9.6	.9823	9827	9832	9836	9841	9845	9850	9854	9859	9863
9.7	.9868	9872	9877	9881	9886	9890	9894	9899	9903	9908
9.8	.9912	9917	9921	9926	9930	9934	9939	9943	9948	9952
9.9	.9956	9961	9965	9969	9974	9978	9983	9987	9991	9996

TABLE D   Four-Place Logarithms of Trigonometric Functions--Angle x in Degrees

Attach -10 to Logarithms Obtained from this Table

x	L sin x	L cos x	L tan x	L cot x	L sec x	L csc x	
0°00′	No value	10.0000	No value	No value	10.0000	No value	90°00′
10′	7.4637	.0000	7.4637	12.5363	.0000	12.5363	50′
20′	.7648	.0000	.7648	.2352	.0000	.2352	40′
30′	7.9408	.0000	7.9409	12.0591	.0000	12.0592	30′
40′	8.0658	.0000	8.0658	11.9342	.0000	11.9342	20′
50′	.1627	10.0000	.1627	.8373	.0000	.8373	10′
1°00′	8.2419	9.9999	8.2419	11.7581	10.0001	11.7581	89°00′
10′	.3088	.9999	.3089	.6911	.0001	.6912	50′
20′	.3668	.9999	.3669	.6331	.0001	.6332	40′
30′	.4179	.9999	.4181	.5819	.0001	.5821	30′
40′	.4637	.9998	.4638	.5362	.0002	.5363	20′
50′	.5050	.9998	.5053	.4947	.0002	.4950	10′
2°00′	8.5428	9.9997	8.5431	11.4569	10.0003	11.4572	88°00′
10′	.5776	.9997	.5779	.4221	.0003	.4224	50′
20′	.6097	.9996	.6101	.3899	.0004	.3903	40′
30′	.6397	.9996	.6401	.3599	.0004	.3603	30′
40′	.6677	.9995	.6682	.3318	.0005	.3323	20′
50′	.6940	.9995	.6945	.3055	.0005	.3060	10′
3°00′	8.7188	9.9994	8.7194	11.2806	10.0006	11.2812	87°00′
10′	.7423	.9993	.7429	.2571	.0007	.2577	50′
20′	.7645	.9993	.7652	.2348	.0007	.2355	40′
30′	.7857	.9992	.7865	.2135	.0008	.2143	30′
40′	.8059	.9991	.8067	.1933	.0009	.1941	20′
50′	.8251	.9990	.8261	.1739	.0010	.1749	10′
4°00′	8.8436	9.9989	8.8446	11.1554	10.0011	11.1564	86°00′
10′	.8613	.9989	.8624	.1376	.0011	.1387	50′
20′	.8783	.9988	.8795	.1205	.0012	.1217	40′
30′	.8946	.9987	.8960	.1040	.0013	.1054	30′
40′	.9104	.9986	.9118	.0882	.0014	.0896	20′
50′	.9256	.9985	.9272	.0728	.0015	.0744	10′
5°00′	8.9403	9.9983	8.9420	11.0580	10.0017	11.0597	85°00′
10′	.9545	.9982	.9563	.0437	.0018	.0455	50′
20′	.9682	.9981	.9701	.0299	.0019	.0318	40′
30′	.9816	.9980	.9836	.0164	.0020	.0184	30′
40′	8.9945	.9979	8.9966	11.0034	.0021	11.0055	20′
50′	9.0070	.9977	9.0093	10.9907	.0023	10.9930	10′
6°00′	9.0192	9.9976	9.0216	10.9784	10.0024	10.9808	84°00′
10′	.0311	.9975	.0336	.9664	.0025	.9689	50′
20′	.0426	.9973	.0453	.9547	.0027	.9574	40′
30′	.0539	.9972	.0567	.9433	.0028	.9461	30′
40′	.0648	.9971	.0678	.9322	.0029	.9352	20′
50′	.0755	.9969	.0786	.9214	.0031	.9245	10′
7°00′	9.0859	9.9968	9.0891	10.9109	10.0032	10.9141	83°00′
	L cos x	L sin x	L cot x	L tan x	L csc x	L sec x	x

TABLE D   Four-Place Logarithms of Trigonometric Functions--Angle *x* in Degrees (continued)

Attach − 10 to Logarithms Obtained from this Table

x	L sin *x*	L cos *x*	L tan *x*	L cot *x*	L sec *x*	L csc *x*	
7°00′	9.0859	9.9968	9.0891	10.9109	10.0032	10.9141	83°00′
10′	.0961	.9966	.0995	.9005	.0034	.9039	50′
20′	.1060	.9964	.1096	.8904	.0036	.8940	40′
30′	.1157	.9963	.1194	.8806	.0037	.8843	30′
40′	.1252	.9961	.1291	.8709	.0039	.8748	20′
50′	.1345	.9959	.1385	.8615	.0041	.8655	10′
8°00′	9.1436	9.9958	9.1478	10.8522	10.0042	10.8564	82°00′
10′	.1525	.9956	.1569	.8431	.0044	.8475	50′
20′	.1612	.9954	.1658	.8342	.0046	.8388	40′
30′	.1697	.9952	.1745	.8255	.0048	.8303	30′
40′	.1781	.9950	.1831	.8169	.0050	.8219	20′
50′	.1863	.9948	.1915	.8085	.0052	.8137	10′
9°00′	9.1943	9.9946	9.1997	10.8003	10.0054	10.8057	81°00′
10′	.2022	.9944	.2078	.7922	.0056	.7978	50′
20′	.2100	.9942	.2158	.7842	.0058	.7900	40′
30′	.2176	.9940	.2236	.7764	.0060	.7824	30′
40′	.2251	.9938	.2313	.7687	.0062	.7749	20′
50′	.2324	.9936	.2389	.7611	.0064	.7676	10′
10°00′	9.2397	9.9934	9.2463	10.7537	10.0066	10.7603	80°00′
10′	.2468	.9931	.2536	.7464	.0069	.7532	50′
20′	.2538	.9929	.2609	.7391	.0071	.7462	40′
30′	.2606	.9927	.2680	.7320	.0073	.7394	30′
40′	.2674	.9924	.2750	.7250	.0076	.7326	20′
50′	.2740	.9922	.2819	.7181	.0078	.7260	10′
11°00′	9.2806	9.9919	9.2887	10.7113	10.0081	10.7194	79°00′
10′	.2870	.9917	.2953	.7047	.0083	.7130	50′
20′	.2934	.9914	.3020	.6980	.0086	.7066	40′
30′	.2997	.9912	.3085	.6915	.0088	.7003	30′
40′	.3058	.9909	.3149	.6851	.0091	.6942	20′
50′	.3119	.9907	.3212	.6788	.0093	.6881	10′
12°00′	9.3179	9.9904	9.3275	10.6725	10.0096	10.6821	78°00′
10′	.3238	.9901	.3336	.6664	.0099	.6762	50′
20′	.3296	.9899	.3397	.6603	.0101	.6704	40′
30′	.3353	.9896	.3458	.6542	.0104	.6647	30′
40′	.3410	.9893	.3517	.6483	.0107	.6590	20′
50′	.3466	.9890	.3576	.6424	.0110	.6534	10′
13°00′	9.3521	9.9887	9.3634	10.6366	10.0113	10.6479	77°00′
10′	.3575	.9884	.3691	.6309	.0116	.6425	50′
20′	.3629	.9881	.3748	.6252	.0119	.6371	40′
30′	.3682	.9878	.3804	.6196	.0122	.6318	30′
40′	.3734	.9875	.3859	.6141	.0125	.6266	20′
50′	.3786	.9872	.3914	.6086	.0128	.6214	10′
14°00′	9.3837	9.9869	9.3968	10.6032	10.0131	10.6163	76°00′
	L cos *x*	L sin *x*	L cot *x*	L tan *x*	L csc *x*	L sec *x*	*x*

TABLE D   Four-Place Logarithms of Trigonometric Functions--Angle x in Degrees (continued)

Attach −10 to Logarithms Obtained from this Table

x	L sin x	L cos x	L tan x	L cot x	L sec x	L csc x	
14°00′	9.3837	9.9869	9.3968	10.6032	10.0131	10.6163	76°00′
10′	.3887	.9866	.4021	.5979	.0134	.6113	50′
20′	.3937	.9863	.4074	.5926	.0137	.6063	40′
30′	.3986	.9859	.4127	.5873	.0141	.6014	30′
40′	.4035	.9856	.4178	.5822	.0144	.5965	20′
50′	.4083	.9853	.4230	.5770	.0147	.5917	10′
15°00′	9.4130	9.9849	9.4281	10.5719	10.0151	10.5870	75°00′
10′	.4177	.9846	.4331	.5669	.0154	.5823	50′
20′	.4223	.9843	.4381	.5619	.0157	.5777	40′
30′	.4269	.9839	.4430	.5570	.0161	.5731	30′
40′	.4314	.9836	.4479	.5521	.0164	.5686	20′
50′	.4359	.9832	.4527	.5473	.0168	.5641	10′
16°00′	9.4403	9.9828	9.4575	10.5425	10.0172	10.5597	74°00′
10′	.4447	.9825	.4622	.5378	.0175	.5553	50′
20′	.4491	.9821	.4669	.5331	.0179	.5509	40′
30′	.4533	.9817	.4716	.5284	.0183	.5467	30′
40′	.4576	.9814	.4762	.5238	.0186	.5424	20′
50′	.4618	.9810	.4808	.5192	.0190	.5382	10′
17°00′	9.4659	9.9806	9.4853	10.5147	10.0194	10.5341	73°00′
10′	.4700	.9802	.4898	.5102	.0198	.5300	50′
20′	.4741	.9798	.4943	.5057	.0202	.5259	40′
30′	.4781	.9794	.4987	.5013	.0206	.5219	30′
40′	.4821	.9790	.5031	.4969	.0210	.5179	20′
50′	.4861	.9786	.5075	.4925	.0214	.5139	10′
18°00′	9.4900	9.9782	9.5118	10.4882	10.0218	10.5100	72°00′
10′	.4939	.9778	.5161	.4839	.0222	.5061	50′
20′	.4977	.9774	.5203	.4797	.0226	.5023	40′
30′	.5015	.9770	.5245	.4755	.0230	.4985	30′
40′	.5052	.9765	.5287	.4713	.0235	.4948	20′
50′	.5090	.9761	.5329	.4671	.0239	.4910	10′
19°00′	9.5126	9.9757	9.5370	10.4630	10.0243	10.4874	71°00′
10′	.5163	.9752	.5411	.4589	.0248	.4837	50′
20′	.5199	.9748	.5451	.4549	.0252	.4801	40′
30′	.5235	.9743	.5491	.4509	.0257	.4765	30′
40′	.5270	.9739	.5531	.4469	.0261	.4730	20′
50′	.5306	.9734	.5571	.4429	.0266	.4694	10′
20°00′	9.5341	9.9730	9.5611	10.4389	10.0270	10.4659	70°00′
10′	.5375	.9725	.5650	.4350	.0275	.4625	50′
20′	.5409	.9721	.5689	.4311	.0279	.4591	40′
30′	.5443	.9716	.5727	.4273	.0284	.4557	30′
40′	.5477	.9711	.5766	.4234	.0289	.4523	20′
50′	.5510	.9706	.5804	.4196	.0294	.4490	10′
21°00′	9.5543	9.9702	9.5842	10.4158	10.0298	10.4457	69°00′
	L cos x	L sin x	L cot x	L tan x	L csc x	L sec x	x

TABLE D   Four-Place Logarithms of Trigonometric Functions--Angle x in Degrees (continued)

Attach -10 to Logarithms Obtained from this Table

x	L sin x	L cos x	L tan x	L cot x	L sec x	L csc x	
21°00′	9.5543	9.9702	9.5842	10.4158	10.0298	10.4457	69°00′
10′	.5576	.9697	.5879	.4121	.0303	.4424	50′
20′	.5609	.9692	.5917	.4083	.0308	.4391	40′
30′	.5641	.9687	.5954	.4046	.0313	.4359	30′
40′	.5673	.9682	.5991	.4009	.0318	.4327	20′
50′	.5704	.9677	.6028	.3972	.0323	.4296	10′
22°00′	9.5736	9.9672	9.6064	10.3936	10.0328	10.4264	68°00′
10′	.5767	.9667	.6100	.3900	.0333	.4233	50′
20′	.5798	.9661	.6136	.3864	.0339	.4202	40′
30′	.5828	.9656	.6172	.3828	.0344	.4172	30′
40′	.5859	.9651	.6208	.3792	.0349	.4141	20′
50′	.5889	.9646	.6243	.3757	.0354	.4111	10′
23°00′	9.5919	9.9640	9.6279	10.3721	10.0360	10.4081	67°00′
10′	.5948	.9635	.6314	.3686	.0365	.4052	50′
20′	.5978	.9629	.6348	.3652	.0371	.4022	40′
30′	.6007	.9624	.6383	.3617	.0376	.3993	30′
40′	.6036	.9618	.6417	.3583	.0382	.3964	20′
50′	.6065	.9613	.6452	.3548	.0387	.3935	10′
24°00′	9.6093	9.9607	9.6486	10.3514	10.0393	10.3907	66°00′
10′	.6121	.9602	.6520	.3480	.0398	.3879	50′
20′	.6149	.9596	.6553	.3447	.0404	.3851	40′
30′	.6177	.9590	.6587	.3413	.0410	.3823	30′
40′	.6205	.9584	.6620	.3380	.0416	.3795	20′
50′	.6232	.9579	.6654	.3346	.0421	.3768	10′
25°00′	9.6259	9.9573	9.6687	10.3313	10.0427	10.3741	65°00′
10′	.6286	.9567	.6720	.3280	.0433	.3714	50′
20′	.6313	.9561	.6752	.3248	.0439	.3687	40′
30′	.6340	.9555	.6785	.3215	.0445	.3660	30′
40′	.6366	.9549	.6817	.3183	.0451	.3634	20′
50′	.6392	.9543	.6850	.3150	.0457	.3608	10′
26°00′	9.6418	9.9537	9.6882	10.3118	10.0463	10.3582	64°00′
10′	.6444	.9530	.6914	.3086	.0470	.3556	50′
20′	.6470	.9524	.6946	.3054	.0476	.3530	40′
30′	.6495	.9518	.6977	.3023	.0482	.3505	30′
40′	.6521	.9512	.7009	.2991	.0488	.3479	20′
50′	.6546	.9505	.7040	.2960	.0495	.3454	10′
27° 0′	9.6570	9.9499	9.7072	10.2928	10.0501	10.3430	63° 00′
10′	.6595	.9492	.7103	.2897	.0508	.3405	50′
20′	.6620	.9486	.7134	.2866	.0514	.3380	40′
30′	.6644	.9479	.7165	.2835	.0521	.3356	30′
40′	.6668	.9473	.7196	.2804	.0527	.3332	20′
50′	.6692	.9466	.7226	.2774	.0534	.3308	10′
28° 00′	9.6716	9.9459	9.7257	10.2743	10.0541	10.3284	62° 00′
	L cos x	L sin x	L cot x	L tan x	L csc x	L sec x	x

TABLE D   Four-Place Logarithms of Trigonometric Functions--Angle x in Degrees (continued)

Attach—10 to Logarithms Obtained from this Table

x	L sin x	L cos x	L tan x	L cot x	L sec x	L csc x	
28° 00′	9.6716	9.9459	9.7257	10.2743	10.0541	10.3284	62° 00′
10′	.6740	.9453	.7287	.2713	.0547	.3260	50′
20′	.6763	.9446	.7317	.2683	.0554	.3237	40′
30′	.6787	.9439	.7348	.2652	.0561	.3213	30′
40′	.6810	.9432	.7378	.2622	.0568	.3190	20′
50′	.6833	.9425	.7408	.2592	.0575	.3167	10′
29° 00′	9.6856	9.9418	9.7438	10.2562	10.0582	10.3144	61° 00′
10′	.6878	.9411	.7467	.2533	.0589	.3122	50′
20′	.6901	.9404	.7497	.2503	.0596	.3099	40′
30′	.6923	.9397	.7526	.2474	.0603	.3077	30′
40′	.6946	.9390	.7556	.2444	.0610	.3054	20′
50′	.6968	.9383	.7585	.2415	.0617	.3032	10′
30° 00′	9.6990	9.9375	9.7614	10.2386	10.0625	10.3010	60° 00′
10′	.7012	.9368	.7644	.2356	.0632	.2988	50′
20′	.7033	.9361	.7673	.2327	.0639	.2967	40′
30′	.7055	.9353	.7701	.2299	.0647	.2945	30′
40′	.7076	.9346	.7730	.2270	0654	.2924	20′
50′	.7097	.9338	.7759	.2241	.0662	.2903	10′
31° 00′	9.7118	9.9331	9.7788	10.2212	10.0669	10.2882	59° 00′
10′	.7139	.9323	.7816	.2184	.0677	.2861	50′
20′	.7160	.9315	.7845	.2155	.0685	.2840	40′
30′	.7181	.9308	.7873	.2127	.0692	.2819	30′
40′	.7201	.9300	.7902	.2098	.0700	.2799	20′
50′	.7222	.9292	.7930	.2070	.0708	.2778	10′
32° 00′	9.7242	9.9284	9.7958	10.2042	10.0716	10.2758	58° 00′
10′	.7262	.9276	.7986	.2014	.0724	.2738	50′
20′	.7282	.9268	.8014	.1986	.0732	.2718	40′
30′	.7302	.9260	.8042	.1958	0740	.2698	30′
40′	.7322	.9252	.8070	.1930	.0748	.2678	20′
50′	.7342	.9244	.8097	.1903	.0756	.2658	10′
33° 00′	9.7361	9.9236	9.8125	10.1875	10.0764	10.2639	57° 00′
10′	.7380	.9228	.8153	.1847	.0772	.2620	50′
20′	.7400	.9219	.8180	.1820	.0781	.2600	40′
30′	.7419	.9211	.8208	.1792	.0789	.2581	30′
40′	.7438	.9203	.8235	.1765	.0797	.2562	20′
50′	.7457	.9194	.8263	.1737	.0806	.2543	10′
34° 00′	9.7476	9.9186	9.8290	10.1710	10.0814	10.2524	56° 00′
10′	.7494	.9177	.8317	.1683	.0823	.2506	50′
20′	.7513	.9169	.8344	.1656	.0831	.2487	40′
30′	.7531	9160	.8371	.1629	.0840	.2469	30′
40′	.7550	.9151	.8398	.1602	.0849	.2450	20′
50′	.7568	.9142	.8425	.1575	.0858	.2432	10′
35° 00′	9.7586	9.9134	9.8452	10.1548	10.0866	10.2414	55° 00′
	L cos x	L sin x	L cot x	L tan x	L csc x	L sec x	x

TABLE D   Four-Place Logarithms of Trigonometric Functions—Angle x in Degrees (continued)

Attach—10 to Logarithms Obtained from this Table

x	L sin x	L cos x	L tan x	L cot x	L sec x	L csc x	
35° 00′	9.7586	9.9134	9.8452	10.1548	10.0866	10.2414	55° 00′
10′	.7604	.9125	.8479	.1521	.0875	.2396	50′
20′	.7622	.9116	.8506	.1494	.0884	.2378	40′
30′	.7640	.9107	.8533	.1467	.0893	.2360	30′
40′	.7657	.9098	.8559	.1441	.0902	.2343	20′
50′	7675	.9089	.8586	.1414	.0911	.2325	10′
36° 00′	9.7692	9.9080	9.8613	10.1387	10.0920	10.2308	54° 00′
10′	.7710	.9070	.8639	.1361	.0930	.2290	50′
20′	.7727	.9061	.8666	.1334	.0939	.2273	40′
30′	.7744	.9052	.8692	.1308	.0948	.2256	30′
40′	.7761	.9042	.8718	.1282	.0958	.2239	20′
50′	.7778	.9033	.8745	.1255	.0967	.2222	10′
37° 00′	9.7795	9.9023	9.8771	10.1229	10.0977	10.2205	53° 00′
10′	.7811	.9014	.8797	.1203	.0986	.2189	50′
20′	.7828	.9004	.8824	.1176	.0996	.2172	40′
30′	.7844	.8995	.8850	.1150	.1005	.2156	30′
40′	.7861	.8985	.8876	.1124	.1015	.2139	20′
50′	.7877	.8975	.8902	.1098	.1025	.2123	10′
38° 00′	9.7893	9.8965	9.8928	10.1072	10.1035	10.2107	52° 00′
10′	.7910	.8955	.8954	.1046	.1045	.2090	50′
20′	.7926	.8945	.8980	.1020	.1055	.2074	40′
30′	.7941	.8935	.9006	.0994	.1065	.2059	30′
40′	.7957	.8925	.9032	.0968	.1075	.2043	20′
50′	.7973	.8915	.9058	.0942	.1085	.2027	10′
39° 00′	9.7989	9.8905	9.9084	10.0916	10.1095	10.2011	51° 00′
10′	.8004	.8895	.9110	.0890	.1105	.1996	50′
20′	.8020	.8884	.9135	.0865	.1116	.1980	40′
30′	.8035	.8874	.9161	.0839	.1126	.1965	30′
40′	.8050	.8864	.9187	.0813	.1136	.1950	20′
50′	.8066	.8853	.9212	.0788	.1147	.1934	10′
40° 00′	9.8081	9.8843	9.9238	10.0762	10.1157	10.1919	50° 00′
10′	.8096	.8832	.9264	.0736	.1168	.1904	50′
20′	.8111	.8821	.9289	.0711	.1179	.1889	40′
30′	.8125	.8810	.9315	.0685	.1190	.1875	30′
40′	.8140	.8800	.9341	.0659	.1200	.1860	20′
50′	.8155	.8789	.9366	.0634	.1211	.1845	10′
41° 00′	9.8169	9.8778	9.9392	10.0608	10.1222	10.1831	49° 00′
10′	.8184	.8767	.9417	.0583	.1233	.1816	50′
20′	.8198	.8756	.9443	.0557	.1244	.1802	40′
30′	.8213	.8745	.9468	.0532	.1255	.1787	30′
40′	.8227	.8733	.9494	.0506	.1267	.1773	20′
50′	.8241	.8722	.9519	.0481	.1278	.1759	10′
42° 00′	9.8255	9.8711	9.9544	10.0456	10.1289	10.1745	48° 00′
	L cos x	L sin x	L cot x	L tan x	L csc x	L sec x	x

TABLE D   Four-Place Logarithms of Trigonometric Functions—Angle x in Degrees (continued)

Attach -10 to Logarithms Obtained from this Table

x	L sin x	L cos x	L tan x	L cot x	L sec x	L csc x	
42° 00′	9.8255	9.8711	9.9544	10.0456	10.1289	10.1745	48° 00′
10′	.8269	.8699	.9570	.0430	.1301	.1731	50′
20′	.8283	.8688	.9595	.0405	.1312	.1717	40′
30′	.8297	.8676	.9621	.0379	.1324	.1703	30′
40′	.8311	.8665	.9646	.0354	.1335	.1689	20′
50′	.8324	.8653	.9671	.0329	.1347	.1676	10′
43° 00′	9.8338	9.8641	9.9697	10.0303	10.1359	10.1662	47° 00′
10′	.8351	.8629	.9722	.0278	.1371	.1649	50′
20′	.8365	.8618	.9747	.0253	.1382	.1635	40′
30′	.8378	.8606	.9772	.0228	.1394	.1622	30′
40′	.8391	.8594	.9798	.0202	.1406	.1609	20′
50′	.8405	.8582	.9823	.0177	.1418	.1595	10′
44° 00′	9.8418	9.8569	9.9848	10.0152	10.1431	10.1582	46° 00′
10′	.8431	.8557	.9874	.0126	.1443	.1569	50′
20′	.8444	.8545	.9899	.0101	.1455	.1556	40′
30′	.8457	.8532	.9924	.0076	.1468	.1543	30′
40′	.8469	.8520	.9949	.0051	.1480	.1531	20′
50′	.8482	.8507	9.9975	.0025	.1493	.1518	10′
45° 00′	9.8495	9.8495	10.0000	10.0000	10.1505	10.1505	45° 00′
	L cos x	L sin x	L cot x	L tan x	L csc x	L sec x	x

APPENDIX B

ANSWERS

ANSWERS 1.1–1.4 (page 11)

1. A multiple of 2π

3. $75°15'$, $15°5'$

5. $109°10'$, $8°1'20''$

7. $130°55'15''$, $-10°34'45''$

9. $574°10'54''$, $-92°39'34''$

11. $-121°1'10''$, $39°35'16''$

13. $30°$, $\pi/6$

15. $45°$, $\pi/4$

17. $135°$, $-5\pi/4$

19. $-70°$, $29\pi/18$

21. $0°$, 4π

23. $120°$, $14\pi/3$

25. $45°$, $33\pi/4$

27. $-25°$, $5\pi/36$

29. 1, $57.3°$

31. π, $180°$

33. π, $-540°$

35. -0.48, $5729.58°$

37. 0, $18,000°$

39. $5.236 = (5\pi/3)$ feet.

ANSWERS 1.5, 1.6 (page 18)

1.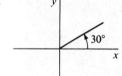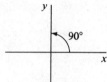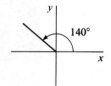

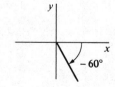 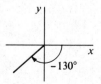

3. Perpendiculars intersect in common point.

5. The same, but the triangle is inverted

7. $74°$

9. 127.28 feet

11. 80 feet

13. 8.7 inches

17. Yes, because angles are all $60°$.
    No, angle size may vary.

19. $x = 4$, $y = 4$, $w = 3$, $z = 4\ 1/2$

ANSWERS 1.7 (page 24)

1, 3, 5

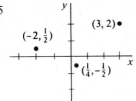

7. I, IV

9. III

11. 0

13. 1.414

15. 5/4

17. 8.2

19. 4.76

21. 5.1

25.

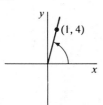

27.

ANSWERS 1.8 (page 29)

1. a. T   b. F   c. F   d. F   e. T

    f. T   g. F   h. F   i. T

3. a. $\{x \mid x$ is married to a person the same age$\}$

    b. $\{x \mid x$ is an air conditioned car in New York City$\}$

    c. $\{x \mid x$ is a United States citizen who owns a color t.v. set$\}$

5. a. $\{2, 4, 6, 8, 10\}$

    b. $\{6, 7, 8, 9, 10\}$

    c. $\{1, 5, 6, 7, 8, 9, 10\}$

7.

(a) 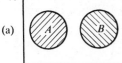   (b) 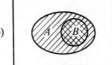   (c)

9. a. $\{1, 2, 3, 5, 6, 7, 8\}$ b. $\{1, 2, 3, 4, 5, 7, 8\}$

    c. $\{1, 3, 8\}$ d. $\{1, 2, 3, 4, 5, 6, 7, 8\}$

    e. $\{1, 2, 3, 5, 7, 8\}$ f. $\{1, 2, 3, 4, 5, 6, 7, 8\}$

    g. $\{1, 2, 3, 5, 8\}$ h. $\{1, 2, 3, 4, 5, 8\}$

ANSWERS 1.9 (page 33)

1. $-6, 6$

3. $6, -6$

5. $44, -4$

7. $A = f(r)$

9. $P = f(s)$

11. Domain: all reals
    Range: reals ≥ -4

13. Domain: all reals ≥ 25
    Range: all reals ≥ 0

15. Domain: all reals $\neq 0$
    Range: all reals $\neq 0$

17.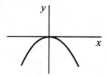

19.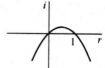

21.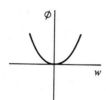

23.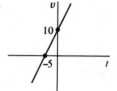

25. yes

27. yes

29. yes

31. yes

33. no

ANSWERS 2.1 (page 39)

(In 1, 3, 5, 7, 9, the trigonometric functions are listed in order: sine, cosine, tangent, cotangent, secant, cosecant.)

1. $4/5, 3/5, 4/3, 3/4, 5/3, 5/4$

3. $12/13, 5/13, 12/5, 5/12, 13/5, 13/12$

5. $2/\sqrt{5}, 1/\sqrt{5}, 2, 1/2, \sqrt{5}, \sqrt{5}/2$

7. $1/\sqrt{5}, 2/\sqrt{5}, 1/2, 2, \sqrt{5}/2, \sqrt{5}$

9. $\sqrt{2}/2, \sqrt{2}/2, 1, 1, \sqrt{2}, \sqrt{2}$

11. 1.5

13. 0.3536

15. 0.957

ANSWERS 2.2, 2.3 (page 43)

(The trigonometric functions are listed in order: sine, cosine, tangent, cotangent, secant, cosecant.)

1. $1/2, \sqrt{3}/2, \sqrt{3}/3, \sqrt{3}, 2/\sqrt{3}, 2$

3. $\sqrt{2}/2, \sqrt{2}/2, 1, 1, \sqrt{2}, \sqrt{2}$

5. $5/\sqrt{26}, 1/\sqrt{26}, 5, 1/5, \sqrt{26}, \sqrt{26}/5$

7. $t/\sqrt{1+t^2}, 1/\sqrt{1+t^2}, t, 1/t, \sqrt{1+t^2}, \sqrt{1+t^2}/t$

9. $\sqrt{t^2-1}/t, 1/t, \sqrt{t^2-1}, 1/\sqrt{t^2-1}, t, t/\sqrt{t^2-1}$

11. $4/5, 3/5, 4/3, 3/4, 5/3, 5/4$

13. $1/3, \sqrt{8}/3, 1/\sqrt{8}, \sqrt{8}, 3/\sqrt{8}, 3$

15. $\sqrt{3}/2, 1/2, \sqrt{3}, \sqrt{3}/3, 2, 2/\sqrt{3}$

17. $u/v, \sqrt{v^2-u^2}/v, u/\sqrt{v^2-u^2}, \sqrt{v^2-u^2}/u, v/\sqrt{v^2-u^2}, v/u$

19. $\sqrt{1-u^2}, u, \sqrt{1-u^2}/u, u/\sqrt{1-u^2}, 1/u, 1\sqrt{1-u^2}$

21. $\sin\theta = \sqrt{2/3}$

ANSWERS 2.4 (page 49)

1.	0.225	3.	0.306
5.	1.00	7.	3.27
9.	0.966	11.	0.174
13.	13°	15.	11°
17.	5°	19.	67°
21.	83°	23.	74°
25.	0.2476	27.	2.3515
29.	0.6412	31.	2.820
33.	0.6421	35.	1.011
37.	27°30′	39.	75°
41.	1.00	43.	1.33

ANSWERS 2.5 (page 53)

1.	0.6243	3.	0.8916
5.	1.2460	7.	0.9095
9.	1.2225	11.	0.3827
13.	0.6480	15.	0.8543
17.	0.9999	19.	50°54′
21.	54°28′	23.	59°17′

25.	26°34′	27.	56°15′
29.	14°29′	31.	0.137
33.	0.384	35.	1.167
37.	0.713	39.	0.105
41.	0.794		

ANSWERS 2.6 (page 58)

1. $A = 29°45′, B = 60°15′, c = 8.07$ 3. $A = 36°52′, B = 53°8′, b = 16$
5. $B = 80°35′, b = 30.15, c = 30.56$ 7. 1.36 miles
9. 8 A.M.   11. 55°, 35°
13. 67°40′, 22°20′   15. 38°56′

ANSWERS 2.7, 2.8 (page 64)

1. 948.68 mph, 288°26′   3. 28.4 mph, 61°21′
5. 36°52′   7. 8.65 mph, 259°8′

ANSWERS 2.9 (page 69)

1. 82°49′   3. 21,700 miles
5. 4,350 miles   7. 84°20′
9. 102.3 feet   11. 80°5′

ANSWERS 3.1 (page 74)

(The trigonometric functions are listed in order: sine, cosine, tangent, cotangent, secant, cosecant.)

1. $2/\sqrt{5}, 1/\sqrt{5}, 2, 1/2, \sqrt{5}, \sqrt{5}/2$
3. $16/\sqrt{337}, -9/\sqrt{337}, -16/9, -9/16, -\sqrt{337}/9, \sqrt{337}/16$
5. $-7/\sqrt{53}, 2/\sqrt{53}, -7/2, -2/7, \sqrt{53}/2, -\sqrt{53}/7$
7. $-1/\sqrt{10}, 3/\sqrt{10}, -1/3, -3, \sqrt{10}/3, -\sqrt{10}$
9. $-1/2, -\sqrt{3}/2, \sqrt{3}/3, \sqrt{3}, -2\sqrt{3}/3, -2$
11. a. I, II
    b. I, IV
    c. I, III
15. $-1, 0$, undefined, 0, undefined, -1
17. a. $\theta = (4n + 1)\pi/2$
    b. $\theta = 2n\pi$

ANSWERS 3.2, 3.3 (page 79)

1. 3/5, 4/5, 3/4, 4/3, 5/4, 5/3

3. −3/5, −4/5, 3/4, 4/3, −5/4, −5/3

5. 0, −1, 0, undefined, −1, undefined

7. 0, 1, 0, undefined, 1, undefined and 0, −1, 0, undefined, −1, undefined

9. $-1/2, -\sqrt{3}/2, \sqrt{3}/3, \sqrt{3}, -2/\sqrt{3}, -2$

11. $10/\sqrt{101}, 1/\sqrt{101}, 10, 1/10, \sqrt{101}, \sqrt{101}/10$

13. 0.94   15. 0.18

17. 0.42   19. −0.97

21. −0.57   23. −0.27

25. −2.92   27. −0.5

29. −0.71

ANSWERS 3.4 (page 84)

1. $-\cos 55°$ 3. $-\sin 45°$ 5. $-\tan 17°$

7. $-\sec 0.58$ 9. $\cos 1.04$ 11. 0.4384

13. −9.5144   15. −1.0439   17. 0.2728

19. −0.9245   21. −0.4618   23. −0.8820

25. 1.091   27. 0.2403   29. −0.9916

31. $\sqrt{3}/2$ 33. undefined   35. $\sqrt{3}$

37. 0   39. $-2/\sqrt{3}$ 41. 5.617

43. 3.978   45. 5.215   47. 334°50′

49. 198°15′   51. 98°20′

ANSWERS 4.1 (page 91)

1. $C = 80°, a = 7.62, b = 14.31$ 3. $B = 48°3', C = 81°57', a = 3.09$

5. $B = 65°, a = 78.0, c = 103.7$ 7. 90.3 feet

9. 123.2 feet

ANSWERS 4.2 (page 96)

1. $c = 39.7$ 3. $c = 45.8$

5. $a = 73.9$ 7. $C = 75°30'$

9. $A = 95°44'$ 11. $B = 118°4'$

13. $A = 141°11', B = 8°49', c = 3.19$

15. $A = 37°47'$, $B = 47°48'$, $c = 195.2$

17. $A = 28°57'$, $B = 46°34'$, $C = 104°29'$

19. $30°45'$

21. $A = 66°45'$, $C = 53°15'$, $\overline{AC} = 3,790$ feet

23.   346.4 feet

ANSWERS 4.3 (page 103)

1. $C = 100°$, $b = 14.02$, $c = 18.58$ 3. $B = 26°14'$, $C = 108°46'$, $c = 10.71$

5. $B = 90°$, $C = 60°$, $c = 8.66$ 7. $B = 46°12'$, $C = 13°48'$, $c = 1.65$

9. $h_1 = 500$, $h_2 = 1000$ 11. $\theta = 31°51'$

ANSWERS 4.4 (page 108)

1.   no solution

3.   two solutions

5.   one solution

7.   no solution

9. $B = 14°32'$, $C = 15°28'$, $b = 7.53$

11.   no solution

13. $A = 38°45'$, $B = 113°15'$, $b = 29.4$
   $A = 141°15'$, $B = 10°45'$, $b = 5.95$

15. $B = 41°48'$, $C = 108°12'$, $c = 570$
   $B = 138°12'$, $C = 11°48'$, $c = 1227$

ANSWERS 4.5 (page 109)

1. $C = 45°$, $b = 669.2$, $c = 489.8$ 3. $A = 60°$, $b = 1.19$, $c = 4.46$

5.   no solution   7. $A = 32°3'$, $B = 117°57'$, $c = 283$

9.   no solution   11.   no solution

13.   95.63 feet   15.   152 lbs, $25°17'$ from the 100 lb force

ANSWERS 4.6 (page 112)

1.   18.75

3.   39.43

5.   6

7.   Ratio of areas of similar triangles is the square of the ratio of corresponding sides.

9.   76.8 ounces

ANSWERS 5.1 (page 117)

1.   (a)   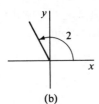 (b)   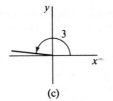 (c)   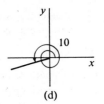 (d)

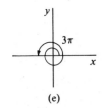 (e)   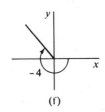 (f)   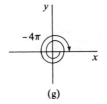 (g)   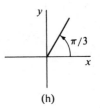 (h)

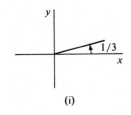 (i)   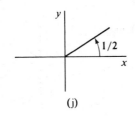 (j)   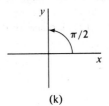 (k)

5. 0	7. 0.5480
9. 0.5	11. 1
13. −1	15. −0.8365
17. 0.2867	19. $(2n + 1)\pi/2$
21. $2n\pi$	23. $-\pi/2 < x < \pi/2, 3\pi/2 < x < 5\pi/2$ etc.
25. $x = (4n + 1)\pi/2$	27. $x = (2n + 1)\pi/2$

ANSWERS 5.2–5.6 (page 125)

1. a. sin x and cos x
Domain: all real numbers
Range: $-1 \leqq y \leqq 1$

b. tan x
Domain: $x \neq (2n + 1)\pi/2$
Range: all real numbers

c. cot x
Domain: $x \neq n\pi$
Range: all real numbers

d. sec x
Domain: $x \neq (2n + 1)\pi/2$
Range: $|y| \geqq 1$

e. csc x
Domain: $x \neq n\pi$
Range: $|y| \geqq 1$

3. Sine function: symmetric with respect to $x = \pi/2$.
   Cosine function: symmetric with respect to $x = \pi$.

5. Tangent: symmetric with respect to the origin.
   Cotangent: symmetric with respect to the origin.

9. *a, b, d, e*

11. a. with respect to origin
    b. with respect to *y* axis
    c. with respect to origin

15. *f(x)*

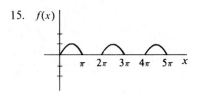

ANSWERS 5.7 (page 131)

1. $A = 3$, phase shift $= 0$, period $= 2\pi$

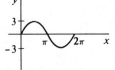

3. $A = 1$, phase shift $= -\pi/3$, period $= 2\pi$

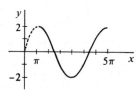

5. $A = 2$, phase shift $= \pi$, period $= 4\pi$

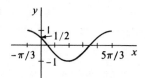

7. $A = 1$, phase shift $= -\pi/2$, period $= \pi$

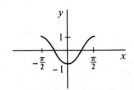

9. $\sin(2x - 3)$

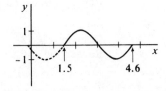

11.

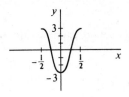

13. $2 \sin(x - \frac{1}{3}\pi)$

15. $3 \sin(\frac{1}{2}x + \frac{1}{4}\pi)$

17.

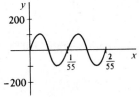

21. They are the same

ANSWERS 5.8 (page 134)

1. $x = 2 \cos 2\pi t$, $y = 2 \sin 2\pi t$, $(-2, 0)$, $(0, -2)$, $(2, 0)$

3. a. no effect
   b. increase in mass causes increase in period

5. $\sqrt{3/2}$

7.

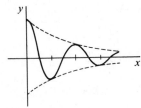

ANSWERS 5.9 (page 137)

1. 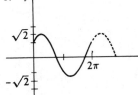 3. 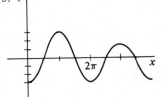 5.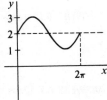

7. They are the same.

ANSWERS 5.10, 5.11 (page 141)

1. period $\pi/2$, phase shift 0

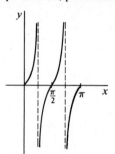

3. period π, phase shift $\pi/4$

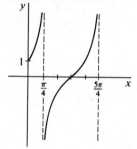

5. period $\pi/2$, phase shift $-\pi/6$

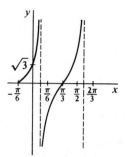

7. period π, phase shift $3\pi/2$

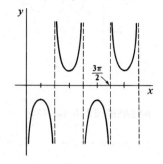

9. period π, phase shift $\pi/4$

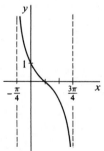

11. $\tan x = -\cot (x + \pi/2)$

13. they are the same

ANSWERS 5.12 (page 143)

3. 2

ANSWERS 6.1 (page 149)

1. $\sec \theta$

3. $\sec x \csc x$

5. $\cot x$

7. $\cot x$

9. $-\tan^2 x$

11. $\sin x$

13. 1

15. 1

17. $\sec x$

19. $\cos x$

21. $a \sec \theta, \; x/\sqrt{a^2 + x^2}$

23. $\sin \theta$

ANSWERS 6.2 (page 154)

1. $\pi/6, \; 5\pi/6$

3. $\pi/3$

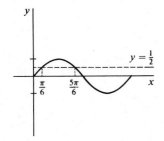

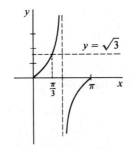

5. $\pi/3, \; 2\pi/3$

7. $7\pi/24, \; 11\pi/24$

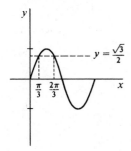

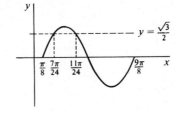

9. $15\pi/4, \; 23\pi/4$

11. $7\pi/6, \; 11\pi/6$

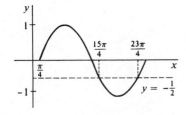

13. $0, \; 2\pi/3$

15. π

17. $0, \; \pi, \; \pi/6, \; 5\pi/6$

19. no solution

21. $\pi/4, \; 5\pi/4$

23. no solution

25. $\pi/6, \; 5\pi/6, \; 3\pi/2$

27. $\pi/2$

29. $0, \; \pi/4, \; \pi, \; 5\pi/4$

31. $0, \; \pi, \; \pi/4, \; 3\pi/4, \; 5\pi/4, \; 7\pi/4$

33. $0, \; 3\pi/2$

35. $\pi/2, \; \pi$

37. $\pi/4, \; 3\pi/4, \; 5\pi/4, \; 7\pi/4$

ANSWERS 6.3 (page 158)

1. Identity

3. $\pi/2, 3\pi/2$

5. Identity

7. Identity

9. Identity

ANSWERS 6.4 (page 162)

1. $x^2 + y^2 = 1$

3. $x^2 + y^2 = 1$

5. $x^2 + ay = a^2$

7. $y = x, -1 \leq x \leq 1$

9. $y = x, 0 \leq x \leq 1$

ANSWERS 6.5, 6.6 (page 164)

1. 0

3. 1.2, 3

5. 0.8

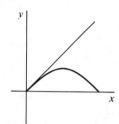

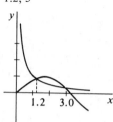

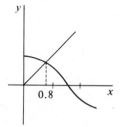

7. 0

9. 0.7, 2.3

11. $\pi/4 < x < \pi/2$
    $\pi < x < 5\pi/4$
    $3\pi/2 < x < 2\pi$

13. $x > 0.9$

15. $0 \leq x \leq \pi/4, 3\pi/4 \leq x \leq 5\pi/4, 7\pi/4 \leq x \leq 2\pi$

ANSWERS 7.1, 7.2 (page 172)

7. $\dfrac{\sqrt{2}}{4}(1 + \sqrt{3})$

9. $\dfrac{-\sqrt{2}}{4}(1 + \sqrt{3})$

21. $\cos 8x$

23. $(\sqrt{3} + \sqrt{8})/6$

25. $3/5$

27. $(5\sqrt{8} + \sqrt{11})/18$

29. Amplitude $= \sqrt{2}$, phase shift $= -\pi/4$

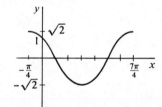

31. Amplitude = 2, phase shift = $\pi/6$

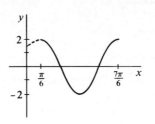

ANSWERS 7.3 (page 175)

1. $\dfrac{\sqrt{2}}{4}(1 + \sqrt{3})$

3. $\dfrac{\sqrt{2}}{4}(\sqrt{3} + 1)$

5. $\dfrac{\sqrt{3} - 1}{\sqrt{3} + 1}$

15. $\tan x$

17. $\tan(x + y + z)$

19. $36/325, \; 36/323$

21. $\sqrt{2}\sin(2x + \tfrac{1}{4}\pi)$

23. $2\sin(\pi x + \tfrac{1}{6}\pi)$

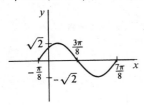

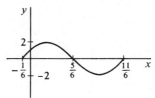

ANSWERS 7.4 (page 181)

1. $\sin 6x$

3. $-\cos 8x$

5. $\tan \tfrac{1}{3}x$

7. max = $1/2$ at $\pi/8$

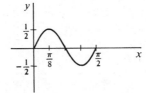

9. max = -2 at $3\pi/4$, undefined at $0, \pi/2, \pi$

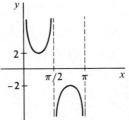

11. undefined at $x = 0, \pi/2, \pi$. Period = π

13. $24/25, \; 7/25, \; 24/7$

15. $336/625, \; 527/625, \; 336/527$

17. $\sqrt{2 - \sqrt{2}/2}$

19. $\sqrt{2}/(2 + \sqrt{2})$

21. $\sqrt{2 + \sqrt{3}/2}$

29. 1/5

31. $7/5\sqrt{2}$

33. $\pi/4, 5\pi/4$

35. $0, \pi, 2\pi$

37. $\pi/4, 5\pi/4$

39. $\pi/6, \pi/3, 2\pi/3, 5\pi/6, 4\pi/3, 7\pi/6, 5\pi/3, 11\pi/6$

41. 1

43. 1

45. 1

ANSWERS 7.5, 7.6 (page 185)

1. $2 \sin 2\theta \cos \theta$

3. $2 \sin 5x \cos 3x$

5. $-2 \sin 40° \sin 10°$

7. $2 \cos 1/2 \sin 1/4$

9. $1/2\left[\sin(\frac{3}{2}x) - \sin(\frac{1}{2}x)\right]$

11. $1/2(\cos 8x + \cos 4x)$

19. $\dfrac{-2 \sin \frac{1}{2}(2x + \Delta x) \cos \frac{1}{2}\Delta x}{\Delta x}$

21. $0, \pi/6, \pi/2, 5\pi/6, \pi$

23. $0, 2\pi/5, 4\pi/5$

25. Amplitude $= 2 \cos 1$
    Period $= 2\pi/3$

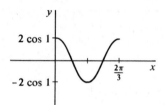

ANSWERS 8.1 (page 191)

1. All are relations
   All are functions except b and d

3.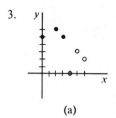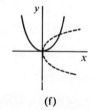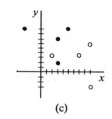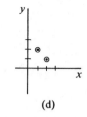

   (a)   (b)   (c)   (d)

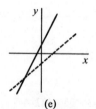 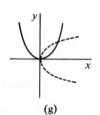 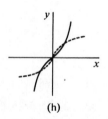

   (e)   (f)   (g)   (h)

5. The graph of f is symmetric about the line $y = x$

ANSWERS 8.2 (page 195)

1. $\pi/6$

3. $\pi/4$

5. $\pi/2$

7. $\pi/3$

9. 1

11. $2/\sqrt{5}$

13. $\sqrt{15}/4$

15. $\sqrt{1-x^4}$

17. $\pm\sqrt{1-(x-4)^2}$

21. $\sin x$

23. $\cos(x/3)$

25.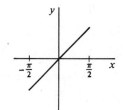

27. $\pm 2x\sqrt{1-x^2}$

29. $x\sqrt{1-y^2} + y\sqrt{1-x^2}$

ANSWERS 8.3 (page 198)

1.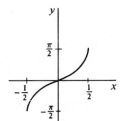

3.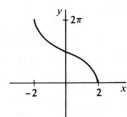

5.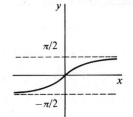

ANSWERS 8.4 (page 200)

1. 1

3. $\sqrt{2}/2$

5. $1/\sqrt{10}$

ANSWERS 9.1 (page 202)

1. $\log_2 x = 3$

3. $\log_5 M = -3$

5. $\log_7 L = 2$

7. $b = 2$

9. $b = 10$

11. $x = 10{,}000$

13. $x = 10$

15. $x = 4$

17. $x = 9$

19. $x = 2$

21. $x = a$

23. $x = 8$

25. $x = 36$

27. $x = 6$

29. a. 2
    b. -3
    c. 4

31. 2 days

ANSWERS 9.2 (page 204)

1.	0.1761	3.	1.0791
5.	1.9542	7.	0.1590
9.	3.3801	11.	$\log_2 x$
13.	0	17.	$x = -5/2$
19.	$x > 8$	21.	$x < 1001/2$

23. $4 < x < 8$

25. The same function for $x \geqq 0$ and $g(x)$ is undefined $x < 0$

27. $-2, -2$

29. a. For a given x, read y from graph and multiply by p.
 b. Add log p
 c. Translate log x, p units to the left
 d. Subtract log p

ANSWERS 9.3 (page 207)

1.	a. 0.7332	b. 3.7332	c. 7.7332 − 10	
3.	a. 0.9557	b. 6.9557 − 10	c. 5.9557	
5.	a. 1.2825	b. 0.1578		
7.	a. 1.3390	b. 7.4740 − 10		
9.	a. 5.9763	b. 8.8469 − 10		
11.	a. 1,820	b. 1.82	c. 0.0182	
13.	a. 15.2	b. 0.000000152	c. 1,520,000	
15.	a. 4.03	b. 0.00403	c. 0.403	

17. $x = 1.3979$

19. $x = 0.6505$

21. $x = 7.990$

ANSWERS 9.4 (page 209)

1.	0.3731	3.	7.9811 − 10
5.	0.4343	7.	5.8077
9.	3.0022	11.	129.1
13.	65,170,000	15.	0.005282
17.	1.778	19.	1,385
21.	$x = 0.4343$	23.	$x = 0.8686$

25. $x = 0.1681$

27. $N = 1,385$

29. $N = 3.162$

31. 0.5396

33. 2

ANSWERS 9.5 (page 212)

1. 0.2700

3. 13.68

5. 1.514

7. 33.37

9. 0.4034

11. -5740

13. 0.3709

15. 1.632

17. 1.652

19. -0.4062

21. 1.9 sec

ANSWERS 9.6 (page 214)

1. $9.6259 - 10$

3. $10.0000 - 10$

5. $9.7201 - 10$

7. $10.1170 - 10$

9. $11.2458 - 10$

11. $20°10'$

13. $50°$

15. $34°$

17. $0°10'$

19. $46°13'$

ANSWERS 9.7 (page 216)

1. $B = 51°50', b = 10.59, c = 13.48$

3. $A = 67°45', a = 130.9, c = 141.0$

5. $b = 60.32, A = 35°32', B = 54°28'$

7. $B = 29°30', b = 546.8, c = 1110$

9. $A = 61°42', b = 566.9, c = 1196$

ANSWERS 9.8 (page 219)

1. $C = 74°10', b = 419, c = 433$

3. $B = 34°1', a = 0.7928, b = 0.5514$

5. $b = 46.93, c = 28.98, A = 100°31'$

7. $A = 46°34', B = 104°29', C = 28°57'$

9. $A = 41°25', B = 97°10', C = 41°25'$

ANSWERS 10.1 (page 224)

1. $7 + 5i$

3. $-2 + 3i$

5. 4

7. $3 + i$

9. $-7 + 22i$

11. 26

13. $13 + 8\sqrt{3}i$

15. $18 + 24i$

17. $(5 - i)/2$

19. $(6 + 9i)/13$

21. $-i/5$

23. $\dfrac{(-4 + 3\sqrt{2}) - (12 + \sqrt{2})i}{18}$

ANSWERS 10.2 (page 226)

1. $7 + 6i$

3. $2 + 4i$

5. $-1 - 3i$

7. $-1 + 3i$

9. 10

11. $-1 + 8i$

13. $3 + (\sqrt{3} + 1)i$

15. $4i$

ANSWERS 10.3 (page 230)

1. $2 \operatorname{cis}(-60°)$

3. $3 \operatorname{cis} 41°49'$

5. $9 \operatorname{cis} 0°$

7. $5 \operatorname{cis}(-53°8')$

9. $\sqrt{61} \operatorname{cis}(-50°12')$

11. $\sqrt{3} + i$

13. $\dfrac{5\sqrt{2}}{2}(-1 + i)$

15. $\dfrac{-3 - \sqrt{3}i}{2}$

17. $\dfrac{3 - 3\sqrt{3}i}{2}$

19. $9.397 + 3.420i$

21. $12 \operatorname{cis} 90°$

23. $2 \operatorname{cis} 330°$

25. $20 \operatorname{cis} 135°$

27. $10 \operatorname{cis} 23°8'$

29. $5 \operatorname{cis}(-60°)$

31. $2 \operatorname{cis} 7°30'$

33. $\dfrac{\sqrt{2}}{2} \operatorname{cis}(-75°)$

35. $\dfrac{4}{\sqrt{2}} \operatorname{cis}(-45°)$

ANSWERS 10.4 (page 234)

1. $8 \operatorname{cis} 0°$

3. $9 \operatorname{cis} 240°$

5. $128\sqrt{2} \operatorname{cis} 315°$

7. $128 \operatorname{cis} 330°$

9. $841 \operatorname{cis} 272°48'$

11. $1 \operatorname{cis} 0° = 1$
    $1 \operatorname{cis} 72° = .3090 + .9511i$
    $1 \operatorname{cis} 144° = -.8090 + .5878i$
    $1 \operatorname{cis} 216° = -.8090 - .5878i$
    $1 \operatorname{cis} 288° = .3090 - .9511i$

13. 1 cis 22°30 = .9238 + .3827i
     1 cis 112°30 = −.3827 + .9239i
     1 cis 202°30 = −.9238 − .3827i
     1 cis 292°30 = .3827 − .9239i

15. $\sqrt[4]{2}$ cis 22°30′
     $\sqrt[4]{2}$ cis 202°30′

17. $\sqrt[6]{2}$ cis $(25° + M \cdot 60°)$ $M = 0, 1, 2, 3, 4, 5$

19. $\sqrt[4]{2}(\sqrt{3}/2 + i/2)$
     $\sqrt[4]{2}(-1/2 + i\sqrt{3}/2)$
     $\sqrt[4]{2}(-\sqrt{3}/2 - i/2)$
     $\sqrt[4]{2}(1/2 - i\sqrt{3}/2)$

23. 4 cis 60° = 2 + 2$\sqrt{3}i$
     4 cis 180° = −4
     4 cis 300° = 2 − 2$\sqrt{3}i$

INDEX